Assessment Source

W9-CGP-313

UC**S**MP
SCOTTFORESMAN

THE UNIVERSITY OF CHICAGO SCHOOL MATHEMATICS PROJECT

GEOMETRY

SCOTTFORESMAN INTEGRATED MATHEMATICS

About Assessment
Assessment Forms
Chapter Quizzes
Chapter Tests, Forms A, B, C, and D
Chapter Tests, Cumulative Form
Comprehensive Tests
Answers
Evaluation Guides

ScottForesman

ScottForesman
Editorial Offices: Glenview, Illinois
Regional Offices: San Jose, California • Tucker, Georgia
Glenview, Illinois • Oakland, New Jersey • Dallas, Texas

Contents

ISBN: 0-673-45792-3

Copyright © 1997
Scott, Foresman and Company, Glenview, Illinois
All Rights Reserved.
Printed in the United States of America.

1.800.554.4411
http://www.scottforesman.com

123456—MH—0099989796

Pages	*Contents*

Tests

Pages	*Contents*

Answers
Quizzes; Tests, Forms A and B, Cumulative Forms; Comprehensive Tests

Evaluation Guides
Tests, Forms C and D

Assessing Student Performance in Mathematics

The Changing Face of Mathematics Instruction and Assessment

In the past decade, the National Council of Teachers of Mathematics and other mathematics education organizations and professionals have examined the methods teachers use to instruct students in mathematics and have recommended ways to improve this instruction. Their recommendations stress the importance of providing more diverse methods of instruction including activities, open-ended investigations, and long-term projects, many of which utilize cooperative learning. They challenge us to make the goal of mathematics the acquisition of the dynamic processes of critical thinking and problem solving, rather than merely the mastery of a static body of facts and procedures.

Instruction and assessment are closely linked. As instructional methods change, the methods of evaluation need to change. New forms of assessment being proposed provide a more authentic way of evaluating the depth of our students' knowledge of mathematics rather than their ability to memorize facts and procedures. These alternative methods of assessment offer students the opportunity to display how they approach problem situations, collect and organize information, formulate and test conjectures, and communicate their mathematical insights.

An authentic assessment program contains tasks that are appropriate to the topics the students are learning and that provide outcomes that are valuable to the students. Such an assessment program allows for such highly individual factors as a school's curriculum objectives, a teacher's style of instruction, and a student's maturity level and preferred learning style. Each individual teacher determines the assessment program best suited to the needs of his or her students.

> In an instructional environment that demands a deeper understanding of mathematics, testing instruments that call for only identification of single correct responses no longer suffice. Instead, our instruments must reflect the scope and intent of our instructional program to have students solve problems, reason, and communicate.
>
> *NCTM Standards*

To help a teacher select the most appropriate evaluation tools for his or her classroom, this *Assessment Sourcebook* provides the following materials. (See pre-chapter pages in UCSMP **Geometry** Teacher's Edition for correlation of test items to chapter objectives.)

Assessment Forms

- student-completed forms
- teacher-completed forms for individual, group, and class activities

Assessment Instruments

- **Chapter Quizzes,** two per chapter, which cover three or four lessons and which contain mostly free-response items
- **Chapter Tests, Forms A and B,** which are alternate versions of each other and which test every chapter objective in primarily free-response format
- **Chapter Tests, Form C,** which consist of 4 to 6 performance-based, open-ended items, many of which assess several chapter objectives
- **Chapter Tests, Form D,** which are performance based and which often assess 5 or more chapter objectives as applied to a single larger task
- **Chapter Tests, Cumulative Form,** which contain mostly free-response items
- **Comprehensive Tests,** every three or four chapters, which are cumulative in nature and consist primarily of multiple-choice items

To assess development of a student's mathematical power, a teacher needs to use a mixture of means: essays, homework, projects, short answers, quizzes, blackboard work, journals, oral interviews, and group projects.

Everybody Counts:
A Report to the Nation on the Future
of Mathematics Education

Guidelines for Developing an Authentic Assessment Program

Developing an authentic program of assessment is an ongoing process. Some assessment instruments will seem perfectly suited to the teacher and his or her students from the start. Others may be effective only after the teacher has had a chance to experiment, and refine them. Still others may be inappropriate for a given class or instructional situation. The following are some guidelines that may be helpful when choosing the types of assessment for a particular program.

Assessment serves many purposes.

- For the teacher, assessment yields feedback on the appropriateness of instructional methods and offers some clues as to how the content or pace of instruction could be modified.

- For the students, assessment should not only identify areas for improvement, but it should also affirm their successes.

- Traditional forms of assessment yield a tangible score.

Make the assessment process a positive experience for students.

- Use a variety of assessment techniques.

- Provide opportunities for students to demonstrate their mathematical capabilities in an atmosphere that encourages maximum performance.

- Emphasize what students *do* know and *can* do, not what they do not know and cannot do.

- Motivate students to achieve by using tasks that reflect the value of their efforts.

Authentic assessment focuses on higher-order thinking skills.

- Provides a picture of the student as a critical thinker and problem solver

- Identifies *how* the student does mathematics, not just what answer he or she gets

Provide assessment activities that resemble day-to-day tasks.

- Use activities similar to instructional activities to assess.

- Use assessment activities to further instruction.

- Give students the immediate and detailed feedback they need to further the learning process.

- Encourage students to explore how the mathematics they are learning applies to real situations.

Include each student as a partner in the assessment process.

- Encourage students to reflect on what they have done.

- Encourage students to share their goals.

Portfolios and Notebooks

A portfolio is a collection of a student's work—projects, reports, drawings, reflections, representative assignments, assessment instruments—that displays the student's mathematical accomplishments over an extended period. The following suggestions for use should be adapted to the needs and organizational style of each situation.

A student notebook should reflect the student's day-to-day activities related to the mathematics class. It may include a section for journal entries as well as sections for homework, tests, and notes.

Getting Started

○ Provide file folders labeled *Portfolio.*

○ Provide guidelines for notebook format.

The Portfolio

○ The Portfolio can be used as the basis for assessing a student's achievements. The focus of the Portfolio should be on student thinking, growth in understanding over time, making mathematical connections, positive attitudes about mathematics, and the problem-solving process.

The Notebook

○ The notebook is for "work in progress." The student should keep in it all class and reading notes, group work, homework, reports and projects, and various student assessment forms, such as *Student Self-Assessment.*

○ Every two to six weeks students review their notebooks to determine the materials they would like to transfer to their Portfolios.

○ The teacher also selects student materials for the Portfolio and includes any appropriate assessment instruments.

○ The student completes the *About My Portfolio* form.

> **The opportunity to share mathematical ideas through portfolios can mark a real turning point in student attitudes.**
>
> *Mathematics Assessment (NCTM Publication)*

○ Portfolios may include:

  student selected items from the notebook; a letter from the student about the work; a math autobiography; other work selected by the teacher including math surveys; various assessment documents.

Evaluating a Portfolio

○ Keep in mind that portfolio evaluation is a matter of ongoing discussion.

○ Set aside time to discuss the Portfolio with the student.

○ Use the Portfolio when discussing the student's progress with his or her family.

○ Use it as a basis for identifying strengths and weaknesses and for setting goals for the next block of work.

○ Consider developing your own criteria for evaluating portfolios, for example, numeric scales.

Evaluating a Notebook

○ Notebooks should be evaluated based on agreed-upon guidelines.

○ Notebooks should be evaluated for organization and neatness, completeness, and timeliness.

○ Notebooks may be evaluated every week, every chapter, or any time you feel is appropriate.

○ You may choose to evaluate notebooks by checking items or by assigning numeric values to specific items.

Using Free-Response and Multiple-Choice Tests

Teachers use written tests for many purposes. Particularly when it is objective-referenced, a test can be a relatively quick and efficient method of diagnosing the scope of a student's mathematical knowledge. Tests can also provide valuable instructional feedback. And, of course, grades are a traditional instrument for reporting student achievement to parents, administrators, and the community. This *Sourcebook* provides a large number of both free-response and multiple-choice items.

Free-Response Tests

A free-response test, sometimes called a completion test, is a collection of items for which a student must supply requested information. While free-response tests are generally designed for written responses, they may also be used orally with individual students, especially those with limited English proficiency.

Multiple-choice Tests

A multiple-choice test consists of many well-defined problems or questions. The student is given a set of four or five possible answers for each item and is asked to select the correct or best answer. The other choices, often called distractors, usually reflect common misconceptions or errors.

This *Sourcebook* contains:

- Quizzes covering three or four lessons in each chapter. The quizzes are primarily free response in nature.

- Chapter Tests, Forms A and B, which are alternate forms of each other and which test every chapter objective. The tests contain primarily free-response items, but they may also include several multiple-choice items. These tests can be used as chapter pretests and posttests to help implement needed individualized instruction

- Chapter Tests, Cumulative Form, for Chapters 2-14, which are basically free-response assessment

- Comprehensive Tests for Chapters 1-3, 1-6, 1-9, and 1-14, which consist of mostly multiple-choice items and are cumulative in nature

Using Performance Assessment

In order to provide more authentic forms of assessment, this *Sourcebook* provides two forms of chapter tests that focus on students' ability to demonstrate their understanding of mathematical concepts.

Chapter Tests, Form C

The Form C Chapter Test items help you make a judgment of the students' understanding of mathematical concepts and their ability to interpret information, make generalizations, and communicate their ideas. Each assessment contains four to six open-ended questions, each of which is keyed to several chapter objectives.

Administering Form C Tests

The tests can be administered in a way that is best suited for the students. Provide manipulatives, extra paper, and other tools as needed. The use of calculators is assumed.

- Use all the assessment items.
- Use only one or two, along with a free-response or a multiple-choice test.
- Use the assessment items to interview each student.
- Have students give the explanations orally, and then write the answers.

Evaluating Form C Tests

Each test item is accompanied by a list of two or more evaluation criteria that can be used as a basis for judging student responses.

To rate how well students meet each criterion, a simple scale such as this may be used.

> + excellent
> ✓ satisfactory
> − inadequate

Evaluation Guides for these tests are found starting on page 251 of this *Sourcebook*.

Comparison of Form C Tests and Free-Response Tests

	Form C Tests	Free Response Tests
Number of items	4–6	15–35
Sample Format	o Draw 3 different rectangles that each have an area of 12 square centimeters.	o Find the area of a rectangle that is 4 centimeters long and 3 centimeters wide.
Mode of administration	o Interview o Written response o Combination of interview and written responses	o Written response
Answers	o May have more than one o May require an explanation by student	o Single, short
Scoring	o 2–4 evaluation criteria given o Use of simple rating scale	o One correct answer for each item
Benefits	o More accurate determination of instructional needs and strengths of students	o Easy to score

Chapter Tests, Form D

The Form D Chapter Tests in this *Sourcebook* are composed of large mathematical tasks which allow students to demonstrate a broad spectrum of their abilities:

○ how they reason through difficult problems;

○ how they make and test conjectures;

○ how their number sense helps them give reasonable answers;

○ how they utilize alternative strategies.

These performance tasks also give teachers a means of assessing qualities of imagination, creativity, and perseverance.

Administering Form D Tests

Some Classroom Management Tips

○ Whenever possible, use Form D Tests as cooperative group activities, listening as students interact in their groups.	○ Have any needed mathematical tools or manipulatives readily available. The use of calculators is assumed.
○ Ask students questions that will give you information about their thought processes.	○ Be sure all students understand the purpose of the task. Offer assistance as needed.

Evaluating Performance Assessments

For each assessment, a set of task-specific performance standards provides a means for judging the quality of the students' work. These standards identify five levels of performance related to the particular task. The specific standards were created using the following characteristics of student performance as general guidelines.

Level 5: Accomplishes and extends the task; displays in-depth understanding; communicates effectively and completely.

Level 4: Accomplishes the task competently; displays clear understanding of key concepts; communicates effectively.

Level 3: Substantially completes the task; displays minor flaws in understanding or technique; communicates successfully.

Level 2: Only partially completes the task; displays one or more major errors in understanding or technique; communicates unclear or incomplete information.

Level 1: Attempts the task, but fails to complete it in any substantive way; displays only fragmented understanding; attempts communication, but is not successful.

Each test is accompanied by a set of teacher notes that identifies the chapter objectives being assessed, as well as the mathematical concepts and skills involved in the performance task. The notes also list any materials that are needed and provide answers where appropriate. Questions to guide students as they seek solutions are provided, along with ideas for extending the activity. These notes, along with the performance standards as described at the left, are found in the Evaluation Guides starting on page 252 of this *Sourcebook*.

Since performance tasks are open-ended, student responses are as varied and individual as the students themselves. For this reason, it may be helpful to use these general guidelines as well as the task-specific standards when determining the level of each student's performance.

Using Assessment Forms

Using Student-Completed Forms

To do meaningful work in our fast-paced and ever-changing technological world, students must learn to assess their own progress. This *Sourcebook* provides four forms that can be used to help students with self-assessment. Use one or more depending on the needs of your students.

Using Teacher-Completed Forms

This *Sourcebook* also provides ten assessment forms that are designed to help you keep a record of authentic assessments. Some forms are for use with individual students, while others are for use with groups of students. Determine which would be best suited for use in your classroom.

	Form	Purpose	Suggested Uses
Student-Completed	Student Survey	Checklist of student attitudes toward various math activities	○ Periodically monitor the change in student attitudes toward math
	Student Self-Assessment	Checklist of student awareness of how well he or she works independently	○ Monitor student progress in working independently
	Cooperative Groups Self-Assessment	Form for students to describe their attitudes and interaction with other students in a cooperative-learning situation	○ Completed at the conclusion of group learning activities ○ Completed by individual students or groups of students
	About My Portfolio	Form for student to describe the contents of his or her portfolio	○ Completed when student transfers work from the notebook to the *Portfolio*
Teacher-Completed	Portfolio Assessment	Form to assess student's mathematical accomplishments over time	○ Use to discuss student's progress in discussions with family
	Notebooks, Individual Assessment	Form to record student's organizational skills and completeness of assignments	○ Describe student's attention to specified daily tasks
	Notebooks, Class Checklist	Checklist to record students' notebook maintenance	○ Use when setting goals for improving study skills
	Problem Solving, Individual Assessment	Form to assess each student in a problem-solving situation	○ Describe level of student performance ○ Modify the level to meet individual needs
	Problem Solving, Class Checklist	Checklist to assess groups of students in problem-solving situations	○ Assess the entire class ○ Assess small groups over time
	Observation, Individual Assessment	Form to determine the student's thought processes, performances, and attitudes	○ Record observation of student in classroom
	Observation, Class Checklist	Checklist for observing several students at one time	○ Provide a mathematical profile of the entire class ○ Identify common strengths and weaknesses ○ Help in modifying content or pace and in determining appropriate groupings
	Cooperative Groups, Class Checklist	Checklist to assess students' abilities to work constructively in groups	○ Assess one or more cooperative groups
	Project Assessment	Form for evaluating extended projects or oral presentations	○ Evaluate an individual or group project or presentation ○ Prepare students for presentations or projects
	Overall Student Assessment, Class Checklist	Checklist summary of students' overall performance	○ Evaluate student performance over an entire instructional period

Student Survey

Answer the following questions using the rating scale provided.

5 Always
4 Usually
3 Sometimes
2 Rarely
1 Never

_____ **1.** I read material more than once if I don't understand it.

_____ **2.** I use the reading heads and bold terms to help me preview the material.

_____ **3.** I review for a test more than one day before it is given.

_____ **4.** I concentrate when I study.

_____ **5.** I try all the examples.

_____ **6.** I do all of my assigned homework.

_____ **7.** I pay attention in class.

_____ **8.** I take notes and keep my notebook up-to-date and neat.

_____ **9.** I bring the required materials to class.

_____ **10.** I really try to get good grades.

_____ **11.** I ask questions and try to get help when I need it.

_____ **12.** I use the Progress Self-Test and Chapter Review to prepare for tests.

_____ **13.** I make up work when I have been absent.

_____ **14.** I look for uses of math in real life.

_____ **15.** I can solve most problems.

_____ **16.** I like to try new strategies.

_____ **17.** I give up too easily.

_____ **18.** I work cooperatively.

My favorite kind of math is _____

because _____

List some activities in which you have used math.

_____

_____

_____

Student Self-Assessment

Assignment _____

Complete the following sentences to describe your learning experience.

I was supposed to learn _____

_____

I started the work by _____

_____

_____

As a group member, I contributed _____

_____

_____

I learned _____

_____

_____

I am still confused by _____

_____

_____

I enjoyed the assignment because _____

_____

_____

I think the assignment was worthwhile because _____

_____

_____

Check the sentences that describe your work on this assignment.

☐ I was able to do the work.
☐ I did not understand the directions.
☐ I followed the directions but got wrong answers.
☐ I can explain how to do this assignment to someone else.
☐ The assignment was easier than I thought it would be.
☐ The assignment was harder than I thought it would be.

Cooperative Groups Self-Assessment

Assignment _____

Reader: _____   Writer: _____

Materials handler: _____   Checker: _____

Others in group: _____

Materials: _____

Check the sentences that describe your work.

☐ We had a new idea or made a suggestion.
☐ We asked for more information.
☐ We shared the information we found.
☐ We tried different ways to solve the problem.
☐ We helped others explain their ideas better.
☐ We pulled our ideas together.
☐ We were reminded to work together.
☐ We demonstrated a knowledge of the mathematical concept.
☐ We encouraged those who did not understand.

Complete each sentence.

We learned

_____

_____

We found an answer by

_____

_____

After we found an answer, we

_____

_____

By working together, we

_____

_____

About My Portfolio

Complete the following sentences about the work you are putting into your portfolio.

Describe the assignment.

_____

_____

_____

I chose this work as part of my portfolio because

_____

_____

_____

I began my work by

_____

_____

_____

Doing this work helped me

_____

_____

_____

The work was   ☐ too easy   ☐ easy   ☐ just right   ☐ hard   ☐ too hard

because _____

_____

_____

Portfolio Assessment

The work in this portfolio:

shows growth in the student's mathematical understanding.

exhibits the student's ability to reason mathematically.

makes connections within mathematics.

makes connections to other disciplines.

shows that the student is able to work on mathematical tasks in cooperative groups.

illustrates the appropriate use of a variety of tools.

Notebooks

Rate items, based upon your requirements, as follows:

+   if excellent
✓   if satisfactory
-    if needs improvement
NA   if not applicable

Written Assignments   **Comments**

_____ **1.** Assignment sheet

_____ **2.** Daily homework

_____ **3.** Lesson Warm-ups

_____ **4.** Lesson Masters

_____ **5.** Activities

_____ **6.** Projects

Reading and Class Notes   **Comments**

_____ **7.** Definitions

_____ **8.** Properties

_____ **9.** Examples

_____ **10.** Class notes, handouts

Assessment   **Comments**

_____ **11.** Chapter Quizzes

_____ **12.** Chapter Progress Self-Test

_____ **13.** Chapter Review

_____ **14.** Chapter Tests

_____ **15.** Cumulative Chapter Test

_____ **16.** Comprehensive Test

Other   **Comments**

_____ **17.**

_____ **18.**

_____ **19.**

_____ **20.**

Overall Rating/Comments

_____

_____

Notebooks

Class _____

Rate each item as follows:

+   if excellent
✓   if satisfactory
-     if needs improvement
NA   if not applicable

Students	Date	Written Assignments		Reading/Class Notes		Assessment				
1.										
2.										
3.										
4.										
5.										
6.										
7.										
8.										
9.										
10.										
11.										
12.										
13.										
14.										
15.										
16.										
17.										
18.										
19.										
20.										
21.										
22.										
23.										
24.										
25.										
26.										
27.										
28.										
29.										
30.										

Name _____ Date _____

Problem Solving   **Individual Assessment**

**Check each statement below that accurately describes
the student's work. This list includes suggested student
behaviors to consider. Feel free to modify it to suit your needs.**

Reads carefully   **Comments**

☐ Looks up unfamiliar words
☐ Understands lesson concepts and can apply
   them
☐ Rereads
☐ Finds/uses information appropriately
☐
☐

Creates a plan   **Comments**

☐ Chooses an appropriate strategy
☐ Estimates the answer
☐
☐
☐

Carries out the plan   **Comments**

☐ Works systematically and with care
☐ Shows work in an organized fashion
☐ Computes correctly
☐ Rereads the problem if the first attempt is
   unsuccessful
☐ Rereads the problem and interprets the solution
☐ States the answer in required format
☐
☐
☐

Checks the work   **Comments**

☐ Checks by estimating
☐ Tries alternate approaches
☐
☐
☐

Problem Solving

Class

Rate each item as follows:
+   if excellent
✓   if satisfactory
-     if needs improvement
NA   if not applicable

Students	Date	Looks up unfamiliar words	Understands the question/task	Uses information appropriately	Chooses an appropriate strategy	Estimates the answer	Is systematic and careful	Computes correctly	Rereads the problem if necessary	States answer in required format	Tries alternate approaches
1.											
2.											
3.											
4.											
5.											
6.											
7.											
8.											
9.											
10.											
11.											
12.											
13.											
14.											
15.											
16.											
17.											
18.											
19.											
20.											
21.											
22.											
23.											
24.											
25.											
26.											
27.											
28.											
29.											
30.											

Name _____ *Date* _____

Observation

	Usually	Sometimes	Rarely
Understanding			
Demonstrates knowledge of skills	☐	☐	☐
Understands concepts	☐	☐	☐
Selects appropriate solution strategies	☐	☐	☐
Solves problems accurately	☐	☐	☐
Work Habits			
Works in an organized manner	☐	☐	☐
Works neatly	☐	☐	☐
Submits work on time	☐	☐	☐
Works well with others	☐	☐	☐
Uses time productively	☐	☐	☐
Asks for help when needed	☐	☐	☐
Confidence			
Initiates questions	☐	☐	☐
Displays positive attitude	☐	☐	☐
Helps others	☐	☐	☐
Flexibility			
Tries alternative approaches	☐	☐	☐
Considers and uses ideas of others	☐	☐	☐
Likes to try alternative methods	☐	☐	☐
Perseverance			
Shows patience and perseverance	☐	☐	☐
Works systematically	☐	☐	☐
Is willing to try	☐	☐	☐
Checks work regularly	☐	☐	☐
Other			
_____	☐	☐	☐
_____	☐	☐	☐
_____	☐	☐	☐

Observation

Class

Rate each item as follows:
+   if excellent
✓   if satisfactory
-      if needs improvement
NA   if not applicable

Students	Date	Demonstrates knowledge of skills	Understands concepts	Works neatly and systematically	Works well with others	Asks for help when needed	Uses time productively	Displays positive attitude	Tries alternative approaches	Considers and uses ideas of others	Shows patience and perseverance
1.											
2.											
3.											
4.											
5.											
6.											
7.											
8.											
9.											
10.											
11.											
12.											
13.											
14.											
15.											
16.											
17.											
18.											
19.											
20.											
21.											
22.											
23.											
24.											
25.											
26.											
27.											
28.											
29.											
30.											

Cooperative Groups

Class

Rate each item as follows:

+	if excellent
✓	if satisfactory
-	if needs improvement
NA	if not applicable

Students	Date	Works with others in the group	Considers and uses ideas of others	Tutors and helps others	Has a positive attitude	Disagrees but is not disagreeable	Shows patience and perseverance	Works systematically	Initiates questions		
1.											
2.											
3.											
4.											
5.											
6.											
7.											
8.											
9.											
10.											
11.											
12.											
13.											
14.											
15.											
16.											
17.											
18.											
19.											
20.											
21.											
22.											
23.											
24.											
25.											
26.											
27.											
28.											
29.											
30.											

Project Assessment

Project _____

Rate each item as follows:
+   if excellent
✓   if satisfactory
-     if needs improvement
NA   if not applicable

The Project

_____ Demonstrates mathematical concepts properly

_____ Communicates ideas clearly

_____ Shows connection to another subject

_____ Shows evidence of time spent in planning and preparation

_____ Is original and creative

_____ Includes charts, tables, and/or graphs where appropriate

_____ Uses available technology effectively

_____ Stimulates further investigation of the topic

_____ Includes a short written report if the project is a model or demonstration

_____ Lists resources used

The Oral Presentation

_____ Is organized (includes an introduction, main section, and conclusion)

_____ Uses audio-visual materials where appropriate

_____ Speaks clearly and paces presentation properly

_____ Answers questions and stimulates further interest among classmates

_____ Holds audience's attention

Overall Project Rating/Comments

_____

_____

_____

_____

Overall Student Assessment

Class

Rate each item as follows:

+   if excellent
✓   if satisfactory
-     if needs improvement
NA   if not applicable

Students	Date	Class Work	Discussion	Cooperative Groups	Problem Solving	Homework	Notebooks	Projects	Tests		
1.											
2.											
3.											
4.											
5.											
6.											
7.											
8.											
9.											
10.											
11.											
12.											
13.											
14.											
15.											
16.											
17.											
18.											
19.											
20.											
21.											
22.											
23.											
24.											
25.											
26.											
27.											
28.											
29.											
30.											

1. *Multiple choice.* Choose the correct pair of adjectives to describe the line shown at the right.

   (a) discrete, vertical   (b) dense, vertical

   (c) dense, horizontal   (d) discrete, oblique

   1. _____

2. Using the number line below, find *ST*.

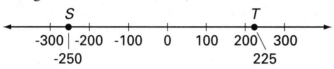

   2. _____

In 3 and 4, from its equation classify the line as *vertical*, *horizontal*, or *oblique*.

3. $y = -7x + 3$

   3. _____

4. $x = -2.8$

   4. _____

5. Graph the line with equation $-3x + y = 5$ on the coordinate axes at the right.

   5.

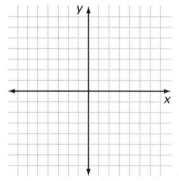

6. On Interstate I-35 in Texas, as you leave San Antonio, you pass a road marker that reads Waco, 178 miles. Along the same road you later pass a marker that reads Waco, 69 miles. How far have you traveled between markers?

   6. _____

7. The diagram at the right shows the front of a shirt.

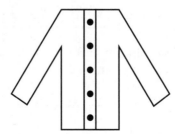

   a. What might the discrete line represent?

   7. a. _____

   b. What might the dense lines represent?

   b. _____

QUIZ

You will need a ruler for this quiz.

1. Identify the four descriptions of a point that are discussed in your textbook.

   _____

   _____

In 2–5, refer to the network at the right below.

2. How many nodes are there?

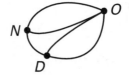

   2. _____

3. How many arcs are there?

   3. _____

4. How many *even* nodes are there?

   4. _____

5. Is the network traversable? Is so, give a path. If not, explain why not.

   _____

   _____

6. In the space at the right, draw this cube in perspective.

   6. _____

7. Consider the following definition:

   A figure is a set of points.

   What undefined geometric term(s) is/are used in this definition?

   7. _____

8. **a.** The diagram shows the floor plan of a school. In the space at the right, represent the floor plan with a network of nodes and arcs.

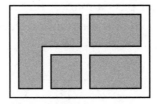

   8. **a.** _____

   b. Could a security guard patrol all the hallways without retracing steps? Explain your answer.

   _____

   _____

CHAPTER 1 TEST, Form A

You will need a ruler for this test.

1. Using the number line below, find *GK*.

1. _____

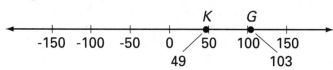

2. In 1992, the highest recorded temperature in Caribou, Maine, was 93°F. The lowest recorded temperature was -21°F. What is the range of temperatures?

2. _____

3. Locate the vanishing point in the perspective drawing of a trunk that is shown at the right.

3. _____

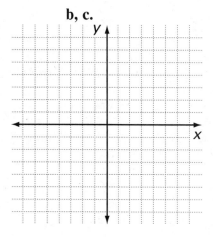

4. In the space at the right, draw this school desk in perspective.

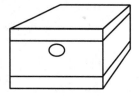

4.

5. a. Name two points that lie on the line with equation -4x + y = -1.

5. **a.** _____

   b. Graph the line on the coordinate axes at the right.

b, c.

   c. Graph the line with equation y = 4 on the same set of axes.

6. Is the network shown at the right traversable? If so, give a path. If not, explain why not.

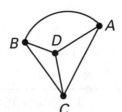

6. _____

_____

_____

_____

7. **a.** The diagram shows the paths through a garden. In the space at the right, represent the paths with a network of nodes and arcs.

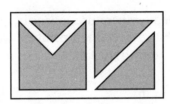

7. **a.**

b. A groundskeeper wants to sweep leaves from the paths in this garden without retracing steps. Describe a path that the groundskeeper could traverse.

b. _____

8. How many dimensions does your classroom have?

8. _____

9. *True or false.* In Euclidean geometry, through any two points, there is exactly one line.

9. _____

10. The graph on a number line of the set of points with coordinate t satisfying $-30 \le t \le -10$ is the geometric figure called a(n) ___?___.

10. _____

In 11 and 12, from its equation classify the line as *vertical, horizontal,* **or** *oblique.*

11. $x = -11$

11. _____

12. $y = \frac{1}{4}x - 15$

12. _____

In 13 and 14, use $\overleftrightarrow{PT}$ at the right below.

13. Give another name for $\overrightarrow{OI}$.

13. _____

14. If $PI = 29$, $IT = 32$, and $NT = 6.3$, find PN.

14. _____

15. Are $\overline{NT}$ and $\overline{TN}$ the same set of points? Explain why or why not.

_____

_____

16. Two points are 40 units apart on a number line. The coordinate of one point is -18. What are the possible coordinates of the other point?

16. _____

17. Use the road mileage chart for three cities in Louisiana shown at the right. If you drive from Shreveport to Monroe through Alexandria, how much farther is it than driving directly from Shreveport to Monroe?

	Alexandria	Monroe	Shreveport
Alexandria		96	125
Monroe	96		102
Shreveport	125	102	

17. _____

18. Consider this definition: *Space is the set of all points.* What undefined geometric term(s) is/are used in this definition?

18. _____

19. In the space at the right, draw a vertical discrete line that crosses a horizontal discrete line without having any points in common.

19.

20. The statement, *Between any two points there is another point*, is not true in graph theory. Explain why by drawing a diagram in the space at the right and then describing your diagram in a sentence.

20.

_____

_____

21. Consider the diagram of a wristwatch at the right.

   a. What does the discrete line represent?

   21. a. _____

   b. What do the dense circles represent?

   b. _____

Check all your work carefully.

CHAPTER 1 TEST, Form B

You will need a ruler for this test.

1. Using the number line below, find *PS*.

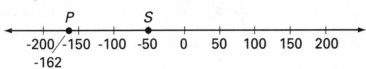

1. _____

2. The lowest temperature ever recorded in Norfolk, Virginia, is -3°F. The highest temperature recorded is 104°F. What is the range of temperatures?

2. _____

3. Locate the vanishing point of the perspective drawing of a lunch box that is shown at the right.

3.

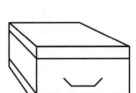

4. Draw this dictionary in perspective in the space at the right.

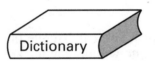

4.

5. **a.** Name two points that lie on the line with equation $-\frac{1}{5}x + y = -3$.

5. **a.** _____

   b. Graph the line on the coordinate axes at the right.

   b, c.

   c. Graph the line with equation $x = -4$ on the same set of axes.

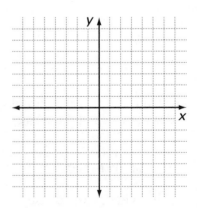

6. Is the network shown at the right traversable? If so, give a path. If not, explain why not.

6. _____

_____

_____

_____

7. **a.** The diagram shows the plan of one floor of a hospital. In the space at the right, represent the floor plan with a network of nodes and arcs.

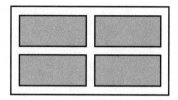

7. **a.**

b. The head nurse wants to walk down every hallway on this floor without retracing steps. Use your network to explain why this is not possible.

_____

_____

8. How many dimensions does a pencil have?

8. _____

9. *True or false.* In Euclidean geometry, two different lines intersect in at most one point.

9. _____

10. The graph on a number line of the set of points with coordinate t satisfying $15 \le t$ is the geometric figure called a(n) ___?___.

10. _____

In 11 and 12, from its equation classify the line as
vertical, horizontal, or **oblique.**

11. $y = -1.5$

11. _____

12. $y = -\frac{1}{3}x + 7$

12. _____

In 13 and 14, use $\overleftrightarrow{LS}$ at the right below.

13. Give another name for $\overrightarrow{EL}$.

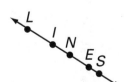

13. _____

14. If $LS = 48$, $IS = 34$, and $IE = 29.8$, find LE.

14. _____

15. Are $\overrightarrow{MT}$ and $\overrightarrow{TM}$ the same set of points? Explain why or why not.

_____

_____

16. Two points are 61 units apart on a number line. The coordinate of one point is -23. What are the possible coordinates of the other point?

16. _____

17. Use the road mileage chart for three cities in Michigan shown at the right. If you drive from Grand Rapids to Kalamazoo through Lansing, how much farther is it than driving directly from Grand Rapids to Kalamazoo?

17. _____

	Grand Rapids	Kalamazoo	Lansing
Grand Rapids		51	68
Kalamazoo	51		76
Lansing	68	76	

18. Consider this definition: *A circle is the set of all points in a plane at a certain distance from a certain point.* What undefined geometric term(s) is/are used in this definition?

18. _____

19. In the space at the right, draw a horizontal discrete line that intersects an oblique discrete line at exactly one point.

19.

20. The statement, *Through two points there is exactly one line*, is not true in discrete geometry. Explain why by drawing a diagram in the space at the right and then describing your diagram in a sentence.

20.

_____

_____

21. Consider the diagram of a notebook at the right.

a. What does the discrete line represent?

21. a. _____

b. What do the dense lines represent?

b. _____

Check all your work carefully.

CHAPTER 1 TEST, Form C

1. In terms of the types of geometry studied in this chapter, how are figure *A* and figure *B* alike? How are they different?

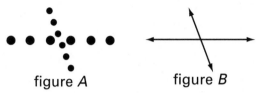

   figure *A*   figure *B*

2. Points *A*, *B*, and *C* lie on $\overleftrightarrow{AB}$, *AB* = 5.7, and *BC* = 9.2. Janelle says this means that *AC* = 14.9. Roger says that *AC* = 3.5. Considering the given information, explain how both Janelle and Roger could be correct.

3. **a.** Draw a network that is traversable. Identify a path through this network.

   b. Draw a network that is *not* traversable. Explain how you know there is no path through this network.

4. Describe an equation of the line that might be the one graphed on the axes at the right.

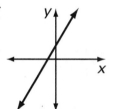

5. Explain how the following calculation is related to distance on a number line.

$$|18 - 42| = |-24| = 24$$

Write a real-world problem about distance that can be solved using this calculation. Then give the solution of your problem.

6. Make a perspective drawing of a three-dimensional object or scene of your choice. Identify the vanishing point(s) in your drawing.

CHAPTER 1 TEST, Form D

Suppose you have a part-time job at a design studio. The owner of the studio is creating a new style of type, and the employees are trying to devise a way to draw the letters and numbers by giving coded instructions to a computer. Three suggested methods are shown below. Each shows a simple capital letter A and a code that can be used to draw it.

I.

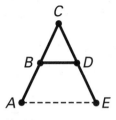

Code:

(pen down)

B-C-D-B-A

(pen up)

-E

(pen down)

-D

II.

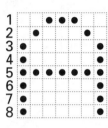

Code:

row 1: 0-0-1-1-1-0-0
row 2: 0-1-0-0-0-1-0
row 3: 1-0-0-0-0-0-1
row 4: 1-0-0-0-0-0-1
row 5: 1-1-1-1-1-1-1
row 6: 1-0-0-0-0-0-1
row 7: 1-0-0-0-0-0-1
row 8: 1-0-0-0-0-0-1

III.

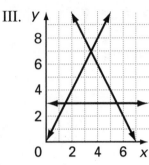

Code:

$y = 3$

$y = 2x$

$y = -2x + 14$

a. In this chapter, you studied four different types of geometry: discrete geometry, synthetic geometry, coordinate geometry, and graph theory. To which of these types is each drawing above most closely related? Explain your reasoning.

b. The capital letter E is shown at the right. Make three drawings of this letter, using each of the three methods shown above. For each drawing, write the coded instructions for the computer.

c. Choose at least two capital letters other than A and E. Make three drawings of each letter, using each of the three methods. For each drawing, write the coded instructions for the computer.

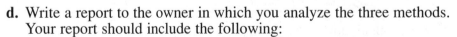

d. Write a report to the owner in which you analyze the three methods. Your report should include the following:

• a list of the advantages and disadvantages of using each method;

• your judgment as to which method you think is least effective, and the reason(s) for your judgment;

• your recommendation for the method you think is most effective, and the reason(s) for your recommendation;

• any other observations that you think are important.

QUIZ

**In 1 and 2, consider the shaded set of points. Is the
set *convex* or *nonconvex*?**

1.   2.

1. _____

2. _____

**In 3 and 4, refer to the statement, *If a figure is a line,
then it is a convex set.***

3. **a.** Write the antecedent.   _____

   b. Write the consequent.   _____

4. **a.** Write the converse of the statement.

   _____

   b. Is the converse true or false?   **b.** _____

5. Rewrite the statement, *All ostriches have long necks*, as a conditional.

   _____

6. Let p be the statement $x \geq 25$. Let q be the statement $x > 30$.

   a. Write $p \Rightarrow q$ in words. Is this statement true?

   _____

   b. Write $q \Rightarrow p$ in words. Is this statement true?

   _____

7. Bettina's mother always keeps her promises. She said to Bettina,
   "If you make the honor roll, then you can have your own phone."
   Bettina made the honor roll. What will happen?

   _____

8. A radio announcer said, "Everyone who attends the game on Friday
   will receive a team poster." On Saturday, Ari had a team poster.
   Does this mean he attended the game on Friday? Explain.

   _____

   _____

Name

QUIZ

1. Classify the polygon at the right by the number of its sides and by whether or not it is convex.

1. _____

2. In the space at the right, draw a convex quadrilateral region.

2.

3. *True or false.* All isosceles triangles are scalene.

3. _____

In 4–6, refer to the figure at the right below.

4. List the segments or points of $\triangle NET \cap \overline{ES}$.

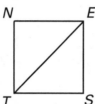

4. _____

5. List the segments or points of $\triangle NET \cup \triangle TES$.

5. _____

6. Describe $\overline{NT} \cap \overline{ES}$.

6. _____

7. *True or false.* All definitions may be written as two true conditionals.

7. _____

8. Name one characteristic of a good definition.

8.

_____

_____

9. At the right, M is the midpoint of $\overline{GS}$, $MS = 2x + 5$, and $GM = 4x - 9$. Write and solve an equation to find the value of x. Then find GS.

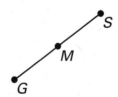

9. _____

_____

CHAPTER 2 TEST, Form A

In 1 and 2, refer to the figures below.

I. II. III.

1. Which figure is a nonconvex octagon?   1. _____

2. Which figure is a convex octagonal region?   2. _____

3. Let *r = The temperature is above 100°F*. Let *s = My car overheats*. Write *r ⇔ s* in words.

_____

_____

4. Name a property of a good definition that is violated by this "bad" definition: *An isosceles triangle is a triangle with two sides of equal length and two angles of equal measure that are called base angles.*

_____

_____

5. Write this definition of straight angle as two conditionals: *A straight angle is an angle whose measure is 180.*

_____

_____

6. Consider this conditional: *Flowers wilt if you don't water them.*

   a. Write the antecedent.   _____

   b. Write the consequent.   _____

7. Given the conditional *If x ≤ 14, then x < 13*,

   a. give an instance of the conditional.   7. a. _____

   b. give a counterexample to the conditional.   b. _____

8. *True or false.* If the converse of a statement is true, then the statement itself must also be true.   8. _____

In 9 and 10, refer to the statement, *Every isosceles triangle is a polygon with two sides of equal length.*

9. a. Write the statement as a conditional.

_____

   b. Is the conditional true or false?   **b.** _____

10. a. Write the converse of the conditional.

_____

   b. Is the converse true or false?   **b.** _____

In 11–13, refer to the figure at the right below.

11. List the segments
  of $\triangle KLN \cap \triangle MLN$.   **11.** _____

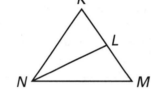

12. List the segments
  of $\triangle KLN \cup \triangle MLN$.   **12.** _____

13. Describe $\overline{KN} \cap \overline{LN}$.   **13.** _____

14. Can the numbers 18.3, 29.1, and 49 be lengths of three
  sides of a triangle?   **14.** _____

15. In Oregon, the distance from Eugene to Corvallis is 45 miles
  and the distance from Corvallis to Portland is 81 miles.
  From these facts alone, what conclusion can you draw about
  the distance from Eugene to Portland?

_____

_____

16. On the number line at the right,
  point *I* has coordinate 212 and
  point *R* has coordinate 225.
  If point *R* is the midpoint of $\overline{IT}$,
  what is the coordinate of point *T*?   **16.** _____

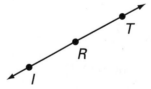

Name _____

17. At the right, P is the midpoint of $\overline{XY}$, $XP = 4a + 5$, and $XY = 18a - 30$. Find PY.

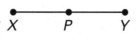

17. _____

18. At the right, draw the hierarchy relating the following: polygon, equilateral triangle, isosceles triangle, quadrilateral, and triangle.

19. Use the polygon *BOTHER* at the right below.

   a. Name a pair of consecutive sides.

   b. *True or false.* R and T are consecutive vertices.

   c. Name the diagonals from vertex B.

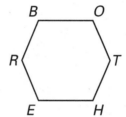

19. a. _____

   b. _____

   c. _____

20. Pictured at the right is an old schoolhouse clock. What is the name given to the polygon that is the outline of the clock?

20. _____

21. Lupita's brother told her, "If you do my chores, then you'll get a dollar." Later that day, Lupita had a dollar to spend on ice cream. Did she do her brother's chores? Explain your reasoning.

_____

_____

22. Two sides of a triangle have lengths 45 inches and 50 inches. How long can the third side be?

22. _____

Check all your work carefully.

CHAPTER 2 TEST, Form B

In 1 and 2, refer to the figures below.

I.   II.   III.

1. Which figure is a nonconvex pentagonal region? 1. _____

2. Which figure is a convex pentagon? 2. _____

3. Let *m* = *The power fails.* Let *n* = *The lights go off.*
   Write *m* ⇔ *n* in words.

   _____

   _____

4. Name a property of a good definition that is violated by this "bad"
   definition: *A scalene triangle is a normal triangle without any
   special features.*

   _____

   _____

5. Write this definition of acute angle as two conditionals: *An acute
   angle is an angle whose measure is greater than 0 and less than 90.*

   _____

   _____

6. Consider this conditional: *The food will spoil if you don't refrigerate it.*

   a. Write the antecedent. _____

   b. Write the consequent. _____

7. Given the conditional *If* $t \leq 21$, *then* $t < 20$,

   a. give an instance of the conditional. **7. a.** _____

   b. give a counterexample to the conditional. **b.** _____

8. *True or false.* The converse of $h \Rightarrow j$ is $j \Rightarrow h$. **8.** _____

Name _____

In 9 and 10, refer to the statement, *every equilateral triangle is a polygon with three sides of equal length.*

9. **a.** Write the statement as a conditional.

_____

   b. Is the conditional true or false?   **b.** _____

10. **a.** Write the converse of the conditional.

_____

   b. Is the converse true or false?   **b.** _____

In 11–13, refer to the figure at the right below. *NORS* and *PORQ* are parallelograms.

11. List the segments of *NORS* ∩ *PORQ*.   11. _____

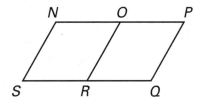

12. List the segments of *NORS* ∪ *PORQ*.   12. _____

13. Describe $\overline{NS} \cap \overline{PQ}$.   13. _____

14. Can the numbers 12.5, 4.6, and 16.9 be lengths of three sides of a triangle?   14. _____

15. In Utah, the distance from Ogden to Provo is 78 miles and the distance from Provo to Salt Lake City is 43 miles. From these facts alone, what conclusion can you draw about the distance from Ogden to Salt Lake City?

_____

_____

16. On the number line at the right, point *E* has coordinate 40 and point *R* has coordinate 112. If point *R* is the midpoint of $\overline{TE}$, what is the coordinate of point *T*?   16. _____

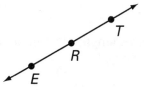

17. At the right, X is the midpoint of $\overline{MB}$, $MX = 10 - 2c$, and $MB = 14c - 16$. Find XB.

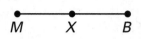

17. _____

18. At the right, draw the hierarchy relating the following: triangle, octagon, scalene triangle, figure, quadrilateral.

19. Use the polygon *MONTH* at the right below.

   a. Name a pair of consecutive vertices.

   b. *True or false.* $\overline{MO}$ and $\overline{HM}$ are consecutive sides.

   c. Name the diagonals from vertex M.

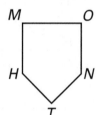

19. a. _____

   b. _____

   c. _____

20. Pictured at the right is a block letter N. What is the name given to the polygon that is the outline of the letter?

20. _____

21. Karl's father told him, "If you stay up late, then you will be tired tomorrow morning." Karl was tired the next morning. Did he stay up late? Explain your reasoning.

   _____

   _____

22. Two sides of a triangle have lengths 15 mm and 17 mm. How long can the third side be?

22. _____

Check all your work carefully.

CHAPTER 2 TEST, Form C

1. Write a conditional about a real-world situation. Is your conditional true or false? Write the converse of your conditional. Is the converse true or false?

2. Draw a figure that illustrates this statement:

$$\triangle BET \cap \triangle TEN = \overline{ET}$$

Now, using the figure that you drew, list the segments $\triangle BET \cup \triangle TEN$.

3. When asked to give a definition of a diagonal, a student wrote the following:

$\overline{AZ}$ is a diagonal of a polygon. $\Rightarrow$ *A* and *Z* are vertices of a polygon.

Do you think this response is correct? Explain your reasoning. If you think it is not correct, show how to correct it.

4. Mia, Tran, and Jennifer used an odometer to calculate the distances between their houses. Their results were as follows.

Mia's house to Jennifer's house: 1.9 miles

Mia's house to Tran's house: 4.8 miles

Jennifer's house to Tran's house: 2.7 miles

Explain how you know that at least one of these distances is incorrect.

5. Separate the figures at the right into two sets. List the figures that are in each set and describe what geometric property you used to decide in which set you would place each figure. Then separate the figures into two sets using a different geometric property. Again, list the figures in each set and name the property.

figure A

figure B

figure C

figure E

figure D

figure F

figure G

CHAPTER 2 TEST, Form D

In the following activity, you will have a chance to demonstrate your understanding of what constitutes a good definition.

a. Explain why the following is *not* a good definition of the word *house: A house is a place where human beings live.*

b. Choose one term from the list at the right. Consider the word as a noun and write what is, in your judgment, a good definition of it. **Do not refer to a dictionary.**

c. Write your definition from Part **b** as two conditionals. Identify which is the *"term ⇒ characteristics"* conditional and which is the *"characteristics ⇒ term"* conditional.

d. Are both your conditionals in Part **c** true? If they are, write your definition as a biconditional. If either is false, adjust your definition so that you have two true conditionals. Then write the definition as a biconditional.

e. Repeat Parts **b**, **c**, and **d** for one other term in the list at the right.

airplane
blue
carpet
chair
clock
cousin
ice
mile
shoe
spaghetti
spoon
winter

f. Suppose you work on the staff of your school newspaper. Write an original feature article about the reasons that good definitions are important. Your article may take the form of an essay or a short story. (An *essay* is a straightforward statement of facts and/or opinions. A *short story* relates a point of view through fiction.) Your article could address the importance of good definitions in one or more of the following areas.

The Clarion

- the study of mathematics

- the study of another school subject, such as history or science

- real-world situations outside of school, such as buying consumer products, working at a job, doing a craft project, organizing a sporting event or a concert, and so on

CHAPTER 2 TEST, Cumulative Form

You will need a ruler for this test.

1. Graph the line with equation $16x + 4y = 20$ on the coordinate axes at the right.

1.

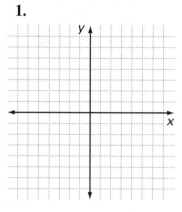

2. *True or false.* The line with equation $y = 100$ is a vertical line.

2. _____

In 3 and 4, refer to the statement, *If a figure is a triangle, then it is a convex polygon.*

3. Write the converse of the statement.

_____

4. Is the converse true or false? Explain your answer.

_____

_____

5. Rewrite the statement, *All spiders have eight legs*, as a conditional.

_____

6. *True or false.* In synthetic geometry, a point has size and shape.

6. _____

7. Refer to the network at the right below.

   a. How many arcs are there?

   b. How many odd nodes are there?

   c. Is the network traversable?

7. a. _____

   b. _____

   c. _____

8. Consider the diagram of a rose garden at the right.

   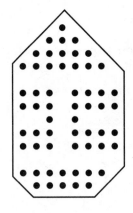

   a. What is the name given to the polygon that is the outline of the garden?

   b. What might the dense lines represent?

   c. What might the discrete lines represent?

   8. a. _____

   b. _____

   c. _____

9. Consider this definition of midpoint: *The midpoint of segment $\overline{AB}$ is the point M on $\overline{AB}$ with AM = MB.*

   a. What undefined geometric term is used in this definition?

   b. Name a previously defined geometric term used in this definition.

   9. a. _____

   b. _____

10. Consider the following conjecture: *If T is on $\overline{RS}$, then T is the midpoint of $\overline{RS}$.*

    Multiple choice. For each example, tell whether it is

    (i) an instance of the conjecture.

    (ii) a counterexample to the conjecture.

    (iii) neither an instance of nor a counterexample to the conjecture.

    a.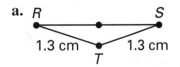

    b. R   T   S
        1.3 cm   1.3 cm

    c. R   T   S
        1.4 cm   1.2 cm

    10. a. _____

    b. _____

    c. _____

In 11–13, refer to the figure at the right below.

11. List the segments of quadrilateral *PENT* ∩ △*PAT*.

12. List the segments of pentagon *PENTA* ∪ △*PAT*.

13. Describe $\overline{EN} \cap \overline{AP}$.

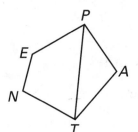

11. _____

12. _____

13. _____

14. On the number line at the right, point T has coordinate -15 and point M has coordinate -27. If point T is the midpoint of $\overline{MA}$, what is the coordinate of point A?

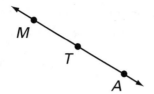

14. _____

For 15–17, let p be the statement $x \geq 2$. Let q be the statement $x \geq 3$.

15. Write $p \Rightarrow q$.

_____

16. Give an instance of $p \Rightarrow q$.

16. _____

17. Give a counterexample to $p \Rightarrow q$.

17. _____

18. Clare told her mother, "If I stay out past my curfew, then I understand I will be grounded for a week." Clare was grounded for a week. Did she stay out past her curfew? Explain your reasoning.

_____

_____

19. Write this definition of obtuse angle as two conditionals: *An obtuse angle is an angle whose measure is greater than 90 and less than 180.*

_____

_____

20. At the right, I is the midpoint of $\overline{NB}$, $NB = 11x + 3$, and $NI = 3x + 9$. Find NB.

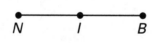

20. _____

21. Can the numbers 10.5, 11, and 30 be lengths of three sides of a triangle?

21. _____

22. Tell which property of a good definition is violated by this "bad" definition: *A quadrilateral is a convex or nonconvex polygon with four sides and four angles the sum of whose measures is 360.*

_____

23. At the right, draw the hierarchy relating the following:
triangle, figure, polygon, pentagon.

24. Point X is between point Z and point W. If $XZ = 7$
and $XW = 19$, find WZ.

24. _____

25. In Wisconsin, the distance from Sheboygan to Green Bay is
64 miles and the distance from Green Bay to Milwaukee is
117 miles. From these facts alone, what conclusion can you
draw about the distance from Sheboygan to Milwaukee?

_____

_____

26. Consider this conditional: *A coat is handsome if it has brass buttons.*

   a. Write the antecedent.   _____

   b. Write the consequent.   _____

27. In the space at the right, draw a nonconvex
hexagonal region.

27.

28. Find the vanishing point of the
perspective drawing of a dresser
that is shown at the right.

28.

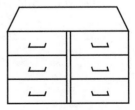

Check all your work carefully.

QUIZ

You will need a ruler and protractor for this quiz.

1. In the space at the right, draw an angle with measure 108.   1.

2. In the figure at the right,
   m∠ARO = 78 and $\overrightarrow{RH}$
   is the bisector of ∠ORC.
   Find m∠HRC.

   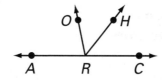

   2. _____

In 3–5, use the figure at the right below.

3. **a.** Name a linear pair.

   b. Name a pair of vertical angles.

   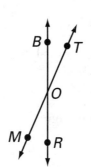

   3. a. _____

   b. _____

4. Suppose that m∠BOT = 24.

   a. Find m∠ROM.

   b. Find m∠TOR.

   4. a. _____

   b. _____

5. Suppose that m∠BOT = 20y + 9 and
   m∠ROM = 2y + 45. Find m∠MOB.

   5. _____

6. If the measure of an angle is 2a, what is the measure of its
   complement?

   6. _____

7. In the figure at the right, $\overline{BD}$
   is a diameter of ⊙A.
   Find m$\overset{\frown}{BDC}$.

   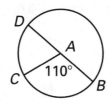

   7. _____

8. In the figure at the
   right, △F′Y′I′ is the
   image of △FYI
   under a rotation
   about point O. What
   is the magnitude of
   this rotation?

   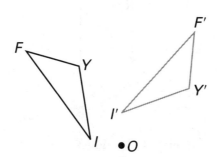

   8. _____

Name _____

1. State the Transitive Property of Equality.

_____

_____

2. If $m\angle T < m\angle P$ and $m\angle R < m\angle T$, make a conclusion   **2.** _____
   using the Transitive Property of Inequality.

In 3–5, *multiple choice*. Use the figure at the right. Which statement justifies the conclusion?

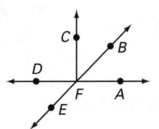

   (a) **Vertical Angles Theorem**

   (b) **definition of acute angle**

   (c) **definition of vertical angles**

   (d) **definition of angle bisector**

3. Given: $\angle DFE$ and $\angle AFB$ are vertical angles.   **3.** _____
   Conclusion: $m\angle DFE = m\angle AFB$.

4. Given: $m\angle CFB = 45$.   **4.** _____
   Conclusion: $\angle CFB$ is an acute angle.

5. Given: $m\angle CFB = m\angle AFB$.   **5.** _____
   Conclusion: $\overrightarrow{FB}$ bisects $\angle CFA$.

6. Refer to the figure at the right.   **6.** _____
   If $PO + OS = 4.75$ and
   $PO = ST$, what property
   allows you to conclude that
   $ST + OS = 4.75$?

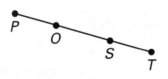

In 7–9, use the figure at the right below, in which $m \parallel n$.

7. $\angle 4$ and ___?___ are   **7.** _____
   corresponding angles.

8. Suppose that $m\angle 8 = 129$.

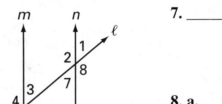

   a. Find $m\angle 6$.   **8. a.** _____

   b. Find $m\angle 5$.   **b.** _____

9. If $m\angle 5 = 2a + 1$ and   **9.** _____
   $m\angle 7 = 45$, find a.

10. Give the slope of the line through $(-4, 2)$ and $(5, -1)$.   **10.** _____

CHAPTER 3 TEST, Form A

You will need a protractor, a compass, and a straightedge for this test.

1. $\angle PAQ$ is an acute angle, and $\overrightarrow{AR}$ is its bisector. Draw a picture of this situation in the space at the right.

1. _____

2. In the space at the right, draw two complementary angles, $\angle 1$ and $\angle 2$, that are not adjacent.

2.

In 3 and 4, refer to the figure at the right.

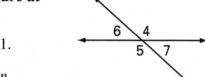

3. Find m$\angle 7$ if m$\angle 6 = 41$.

3. _____

4. Find m$\angle 7$ if m$\angle 5 = 6n$.

4. _____

5. Suppose $\angle 1$ and $\angle 2$ form a linear pair, with m$\angle 1 = 9j + 1$ and m$\angle 2 = 8j + 9$.

   a. Find j.

   5. a. _____

   b. Find m$\angle 2$.

   b. _____

6. Rotate $\triangle ABC$ -140° about point P.

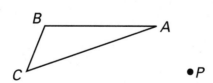

Name _____

► **CHAPTER 3 TEST, Form A** *page 2*

7. The gabled roof of a house meets the gutter at an angle of 126°, as pictured at the right. What is the measure *d* of the angle formed by the gable and the down spout side of the gutter?

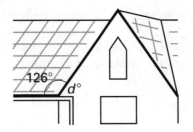

7. _____

8. ∠1 and ∠2 are vertical angles. If m∠1 = 10*s* and m∠2 = 95, find *s*.

8. _____

In 9 and 10, use the figure at the right below. In the figure, *RO* + *OA* = 10 cm.

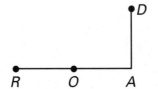

9. If *RO* = *AD*, make a conclusion about *OA* and *AD* using the Substitution Property.

9. _____

10. Make a conclusion about *RO* using the Equation to Inequality Property.

10. _____

11. Pictured at the right is the dial of an egg timer. What is the magnitude of the rotation needed to turn the dial from 3 to 0?

11. _____

12. The figure at the right shows how a house is positioned relative to the street. The homeowner wants to lay a gravel pathway from the front door of the house to the street. Draw the position of the shortest possible pathway.

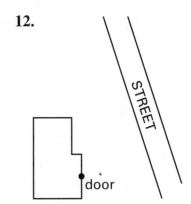

12.

13. In the figure at the right, $\overline{AC}$ is a diameter of $\odot P$ and $m\widehat{BC} = 117$.

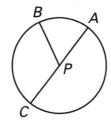

   a. Find $m\angle BPC$.

   b. Find $m\widehat{AB}$.

   c. Find $m\widehat{BAC}$.

13. a. _____

   b. _____

   c. _____

In 14 and 15, use the figure at the right below, in which $s \parallel t$.

14. Suppose that $m\angle 7 = 130$.

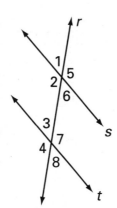

   a. Find $m\angle 3$.

   b. Find $m\angle 1$.

   c. Find $m\angle 2$.

14. a. _____

   b. _____

   c. _____

15. Suppose that $m\angle 6 = 3u + 4$ and $m\angle 8 = 7u - 44$.

   a. Find u.

   b. Find $m\angle 3$.

15. a. _____

   b. _____

16. *Multiple choice.* Use the figure at the right. Which statement justifies the conclusion?

Given: $\overline{AE} \perp \overline{ED}$, $\overline{BD} \parallel \overline{AE}$.

Conclusion: $\overline{ED} \perp \overline{BD}$.

   (a) definition of perpendicular

   (b) If $\ell \parallel m$ and $m \parallel n$, then $\ell \parallel n$.

   (c) If $\ell \parallel m$ and $m \perp n$, then $\ell \perp n$.

   (d) If $\ell \perp m$ and $m \perp n$, then $\ell \parallel n$.

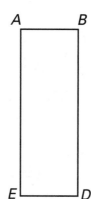

16. _____

17. Given $m\angle PTR = m\angle STR$ in the figure at the right, what can you conclude using the Angle Addition Property and the Substitution Property?

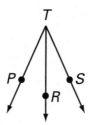

17. _____

18. Give the slope of the line through (-2, -4) and (-1, 6).

18. _____

19. If a line has slope $-\frac{9}{10}$, then each line perpendicular to it has slope ___?___ and each line parallel to it has slope ___?___.

19. _____

_____

20. Line *r* has equation $-3x + 4y = 16$. If line *s* is parallel to *r*, what is the slope of *s*?

20. _____

21. *Multiple choice.* Use the figure at the right. Which statement justifies the conclusion that ∠*GHK* is supplementary to ∠*KHI?*

    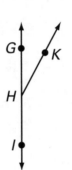

    (a) definition of supplementary angles

    (b) Angle Addition Postulate

    (c) Linear Pair Theorem

    (d) definition of angle bisector

21. _____

22. Use a compass and a straightedge to construct the perpendicular bisector of $\overline{MN}$.

Check all your work carefully.

CHAPTER 3 TEST, Form B

You will need a protractor, a compass, and a straightedge for this test.

1. $\angle AOB$ is an obtuse angle, and $\overrightarrow{OC}$ is its bisector. Draw   **1.**
a picture of this situation in the space at the right.

2. In the space at the right, draw two supplementary angles,   **2.**
$\angle 1$ and $\angle 2$, that are not adjacent.

In 3 and 4, refer to the figure at the right.

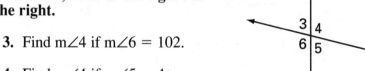

3. Find $m\angle 4$ if $m\angle 6 = 102$.   **3.** _____

4. Find $m\angle 4$ if $m\angle 5 = 4t$.   **4.** _____

5. Suppose $\angle 6$ and $\angle 7$ are complementary, with
$m\angle 6 = 5r - 4$ and $m\angle 7 = 6r - 5$.

   a. Find r.   **5. a.** _____

   b. Find $m\angle 6$.   **b.** _____

6. Rotate $\triangle PQR$ 75° about point L.

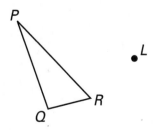

7. Pictured at the right is the throttle of a speedboat. If the measure of the larger angle formed is 137, what is the measure x of the smaller angle?

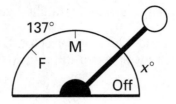

7. _____

8. $\angle 1$ and $\angle 2$ are vertical angles. If $m\angle 1 = 18s$ and $m\angle 2 = 99$, find s.

8. _____

In 9 and 10, use the figure at the right below.

9. If $m\angle 1 = m\angle 2$, make a conclusion about $\angle NEL$ and $\angle AEG$ using the Addition Property of Equality.

9. _____

10. If $m\angle NEL = 78$, make a conclusion about $m\angle 2$ using the Equation to Inequality Property.

10. _____

11. Pictured at the right is the dial of a sixty-minute timer. What is the magnitude of the rotation needed to turn the dial from 35 to 0?

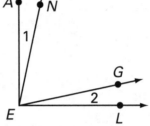

11. _____

12. The figure at the right shows how a buoy is positioned relative to a beach. Draw the shortest route that a person can take to row from the buoy to the beach.

12.

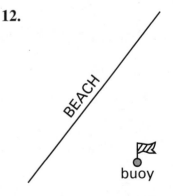

Name _____

13. In the figure at the right, $\overline{PR}$ is a
    diameter of $\odot S$ and $m\overset{\frown}{QR} = 146°$.

    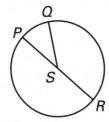

    a. Find $m\angle PSQ$.

    b. Find $m\overset{\frown}{PQ}$.

    c. Find $m\overset{\frown}{QPR}$.

13. a. _____

    b. _____

    c. _____

In 14 and 15, use the figure at the right below, in which *m* // *n*.

14. Suppose that $m\angle 8 = 73$.

    a. Find $m\angle 1$.

    b. Find $m\angle 3$.

    c. Find $m\angle 5$.

14. a. _____

    b. _____

    c. _____

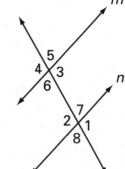

15. Suppose that $m\angle 8 = 9d + 2$
    and $m\angle 4 = 12d - 11$.

    a. Find d.

    b. Find $m\angle 7$.

15. a. _____

    b. _____

16. *Multiple choice.* Use the figure at
    the right. Which statement justifies
    the conclusion?

    Given: $\overline{AF} \perp \overline{DE}$, $\overline{AC} \perp \overline{AF}$.
    Conclusion: $\overline{DE}$ // $\overline{AC}$.

    (a) If ℓ // m and m // n, then ℓ // n.

    (b) definition of parallel lines

    (c) If ℓ // m and $m \perp n$, then $\ell \perp n$.

    (d) If $\ell \perp m$ and $m \perp n$, then ℓ // n.

16. _____

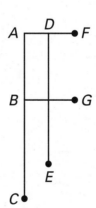

17. Given $VX = XW$ in the figure at
    the right, what can you conclude
    using the Additive Property of
    the Distance Postulate and the
    Substitution Property?

17. _____

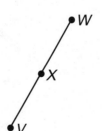

18. Give the slope of the line through (-9, 5) and (6, 8).   18. _____

19. If a line has slope $\frac{5}{8}$, then each line parallel to it   19. _____

    has slope ___?___ and each line perpendicular to it   _____

    has slope ___?___ .

20. Line *j* has equation $-2x + 5y = 20$. If line *k* is   20. _____
    perpendicular to *j*, what is the slope of *k*?

21. *Multiple choice.* Use the figure   21. _____
    at the right. If m∠1 = 90,
    which statement justifies the
    conclusion that ∠1 is a right angle?

    (a) definition of supplementary angles

    (b) definition of right angle

    (c) Linear Pair Theorem

    (d) definition of perpendicular lines

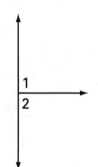

22. Use a compass and a straightedge
    to construct the perpendicular
    bisector of $\overline{EF}$.

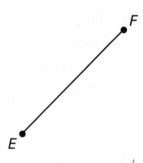

Check all your work carefully.

CHAPTER 3 TEST, Form C

1. State as many facts as you can about the lines and angles in the figure at the right.

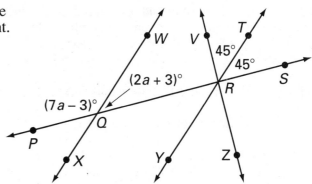

2. Write a brief paragraph to describe the situation that is represented by this picture. In your paragraph, make an estimate of the value of x.

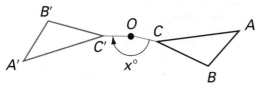

3. The figure at the right shows a circular track for running. The small circle is the inner lane of the track; the large circle is the outer lane. How is the trip from A to B on the track similar to the trip from X to Y? How is it different?

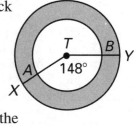

4. State one property of equality or inequality that was reviewed in this chapter. Then draw a picture of a geometric situation in which you can use this property to make a conclusion. State the given information and the conclusion.

5. a. Give equations of two lines that are parallel. Explain how you know that these lines are parallel.

b. Give equations of two lines that are perpendicular. Explain how you know that these lines are perpendicular.

CHAPTER 3 TEST, Form D

The historic district of an old town has been neglected for a very long
time. Four historic sites are on a large plot of land at the edge of town, but
no one has ever laid out streets to connect them. Shown below is a street
plan that was proposed many years ago, but was only partially completed.

a. Name all the streets that are parallel to the north/south direction.

b. Name all the streets that are perpendicular to the north/south direction.

c. Suppose you walk clockwise around Forest Circle from Elm Road to
Linden Road. What is the degree measure of the arc that you walk?

d. Find the measure of the smaller angle formed at the intersection of State
Street and Jefferson Road. Explain how you obtained your answer.

e. The town council is holding a contest to find an efficient and attractive
street plan for the historic district. To enter the contest, you may
complete the plan below, or you may present an entirely new plan. The
only requirement is that each of the four historic sites—the old town
hall, the old court house, the fort, and the war monument—must be
surrounded by a traffic circle similar to those in the plan below. Draw
an original street plan that you could enter in this contest. Make your
drawing as neat and as accurate as possible.

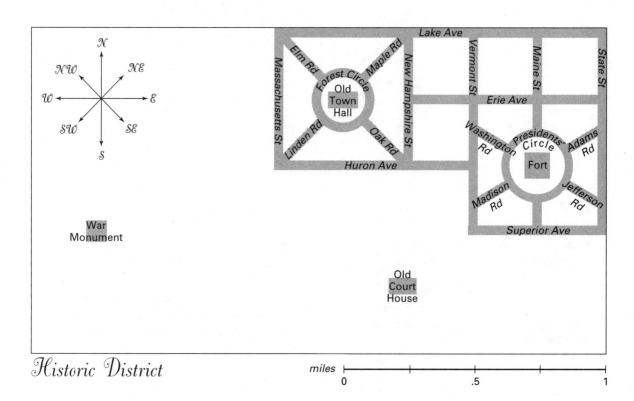

Historic District   miles

CHAPTER 3 TEST, Cumulative Form

You will need a protractor, a compass, and a straightedge for this test.

1. In the space at the right, draw a pair of adjacent
   supplementary angles, $\angle 1$ and $\angle 2$, such that the
   measure of the larger angle is 120.

   1. _____

In 2–4, use the figure at the right below.

2. Suppose that $m\angle POT = 149$.
   Find $m\angle SOR$.

   2. _____

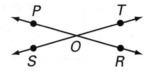

3. Suppose that $m\angle POT = 8b$.
   Find $m\angle POS$.

   3. _____

4. Suppose that $m\angle TOR = 11k + 1$ and
   $m\angle POS = k + 26$. Find $m\angle POT$.

   4. _____

5. Two sides of a triangle have lengths 91 cm and
   205 cm. How long can a third side be?

   5. _____

6. **a.** Write the converse of this statement: *If the measure of an angle is
   180, then the angle is a straight angle.*

   _____

   b. Is the converse true or false?

   b. _____

7. Rotate quadrilateral *PQRS*
   -120° about point *L*.

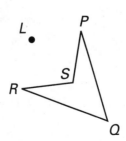

8. a. Write the definition of *right angle* as a biconditional.

_____

b. Write the definition of *right angle* as two conditionals.

_____

_____

9. The distance from Hector's house to the Johnson School is
1.2 miles. The distance from Li's house to the Johnson School is
2.7 miles. From this information alone, what can you conclude
about the distance between Hector's house and Li's house?

_____

_____

10. In the space at the right, draw a convex
heptagonal region.

10.

11. In the figure at the right, $\overline{RM}$ is a
diameter of $\odot T$ and m∠NTR = 106.

a. Find m$\overparen{NR}$.

b. Find m∠NTM.

c. Find m$\overparen{NRM}$.

11. a. _____

b. _____

c. _____

12. At the right is pictured part of
a trellis that is used to support
morning glories. It consists of
two sets of parallel slats of
wood. If $x = 78$, find y.

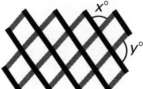

12. _____

13. In the space at the right, draw a horizontal discrete line.

13.

In 14 and 15, use the figure at the right, in which *r // s*.

14. Suppose that m∠5 = 33.

    a. Find m∠1.

    b. Find m∠2.

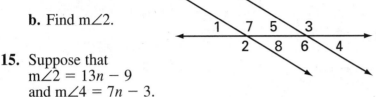

14. a. _____

    b. _____

15. Suppose that
m∠2 = 13n − 9
and m∠4 = 7n − 3.
Find m∠3.

15. _____

16. Ignoring its thickness, how many dimensions does
a tabletop have?

16. _____

17. *Multiple choice.* Use the figure at
the right. Which statement justifies
the conclusion that $\overline{EF}$ // $\overline{CD}$?

    (a) definition of parallel lines

    (b) If ℓ // m and m // n, then ℓ // n.

    (c) If ℓ ⊥ m and m ⊥ n, then ℓ // n.

    (d) If ℓ // m and m ⊥ n, then ℓ ⊥ n.

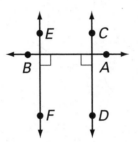

17. _____

In 18 and 19, use the figure at the right below.

18. Make a conclusion about
∠1 and ∠MAN using the
Equation to Inequality Property.

19. If m∠MAN = 90, make a
conclusion about ∠1 and ∠2.

18. _____

19. _____

20. *True or false.* If r ⇒ s is true, then s ⇒ r also is true.

20. _____

21. Draw this carton in
perspective in the space
at the right. Identify
the vanishing point of
your drawing.

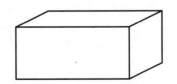

21.

22. In the figure at the right, $\overrightarrow{ML}$ bisects ∠*AMB*, m∠*AML* = 6*s*, and m∠*BML* = *s* + 20.

    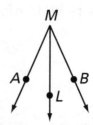

    a. Find *s*.

    b. Find m∠*AMB*.

    22. a. _____

    b. _____

In 23 and 24, refer to the line with equation $y = -3x + 7$.

23. Classify the line as *horizontal, vertical,* or *oblique.*

    23. _____

24. What is the slope of a line perpendicular to this line?

    24. _____

25. Refer to the figure at the right.

    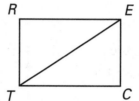

    a. List the set of points of ∠*RTC* ∩ $\overline{ET}$.

    b. List the set of segments of △*RET* ∩ △*ETC*.

    25. a. _____

    b. _____

26. *True or false.* In Euclidean geometry, only one line can contain two different points.

    26. _____

27. The figure at the right shows how a well is positioned relative to a road. Draw the position of the shortest possible path from the well to the road.

    27.

    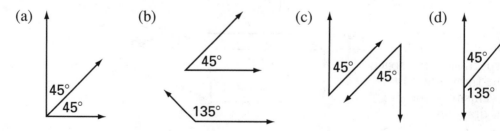

28. *Multiple choice.* Identify the figure that shows a counterexample to the following statement: *If two angles are complementary, then they are adjacent.*

    28. _____

(a)
45°
45°

(b)
45°
135°

(c)
45°
45°

(d)
45°
135°

Check all your work carefully.

COMPREHENSIVE TEST, CHAPTERS 1–3 ▶

Multiple choice. **Give the letter of the correct answer.**

1. A counterexample to $r \Rightarrow s$ is a situation for which ___?___ .

   (a) r is false and s is false   (b) r is true and s is true

   (c) r is false and s is true   (d) r is true and s is false

   1. _____

2. In which geometry is it true that lines are dense?

   (a) graph theory   (b) discrete geometry

   (c) coordinate geometry   (d) none of these

   2. _____

3. In the network at the right, there are ___?___ odd nodes.

   (a) 5   (b) 4

   (c) 2   (d) 0

   3. _____

4. Which statement is true in Euclidean geometry?

   (a) A point has no size or shape.

   (b) Through any two points, there can be many lines.

   (c) Two different lines can intersect in two or more points.

   (d) none of these

   4. _____

5. To what geometry(ies) does the Point-Line-Plane Postulate apply?

   (a) discrete geometry and synthetic geometry

   (b) coordinate geometry and synthetic geometry

   (c) graph theory and coordinate geometry

   (d) synthetic geometry only

   5. _____

6. In coordinate geometry, the graph of the line with equation $y = -400$ is a(n) ___?___ line.

   (a) horizontal   (b) vertical   (c) oblique   (d) discrete

   6. _____

7. The graph of the inequality $x \leq 100$ on a number line is the geometric figure called a ___?___ .

   (a) ray   (b) segment   (c) line   (d) none of these

   7. _____

8. On a number line, $AT = 40$ and the coordinate of A is -5. What are the possible coordinates of T?

   (a) -45 only   (b) 35 only   (c) -45 or 35   (d) -35 or 45

   8. _____

▶ **COMPREHENSIVE TEST, Chapters 1–3** *page 2*

9. Consider the conditional: *I'll take my umbrella if it looks like rain.*   9. _____
   Which statement is the converse of this conditional?

   (a) If it looks like rain, I'll take my umbrella.

   (b) If I take my umbrella, then it looks like rain.

   (c) If it doesn't look like rain, then I'll take my umbrella.

   (d) If I take my umbrella, then it doesn't look like rain.

10. Which property of a good definition is violated by this "bad"   10. _____
    definition?

       *An obtuse angle is an angle whose measure is greater than 90
       and less than 180 and is in a triangle or other polygon.*

    (a) It is unclear.

    (b) It uses terms that are not defined.

    (c) It contains unnecessary information.

    (d) none of these

11. Suppose that the lengths of two sides of a triangle are 100 cm and   11. _____
    102 cm, and that the length of the third side is q cm. Which are
    the restrictions on the value of q?

    (a) There are no restrictions on the value of q.

    (b) $q > 2$ only

    (c) $q < 202$

    (d) $2 < q < 202$

12. Consider the conditional: *If a bouquet is made of red roses,*   12. _____
    then it is beautiful. An ugly bouquet of red roses is ___?___.

    (a) an instance of the conditional

    (b) a counterexample to the conditional

    (c) neither an instance of nor a counterexample to the conditional

13. The figure at the right is a ___?___.   13. _____

    (a) hexagon   (b) heptagon

    (c) hexagonal region   (d) heptagonal region

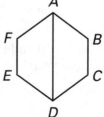

14. In the figure at the right, quadrilateral   14. _____
    $ADEF$ ∪ hexagon $ABCDEF$ contains

    (a) $\overline{AF}, \overline{FE}, \overline{ED}, \overline{AD}, \overline{AB}, \overline{BC}$, and $\overline{CD}$.

    (b) $\overline{AF}, \overline{FE}, \overline{ED}, \overline{CD}, \overline{BC}$, and $\overline{AB}$.

    (c) $\overline{AD}$ only.

    (d) no segments.

▶ **COMPREHENSIVE TEST, Chapters 1–3** *page 3*

15. *True or false.* Every definition can be written as a biconditional. 15. _____

16. How many counterexamples are needed to show that a conditional 16. _____
is false?

(a) none   (b) at least 5 (c) 2   (d) 1

17. Two angles are supplementary. The measure of the larger angle is 17. _____
$6j$, and the measure of the smaller is $2j$. What are the measures
of the two angles?

(a) 22.5 and 135   (b) 45 and 135

(c) 22.5 and 67.5   (d) cannot be determined

18. Let $P = (-3, -5)$ and $R = (2, -7)$. What is the slope of $\overleftrightarrow{PR}$ 18. _____

(a) $-\frac{5}{2}$ (b) $\frac{5}{2}$ (c) $-\frac{2}{5}$ (d) $\frac{12}{1}$

19. The slope of any line perpendicular to the line with equation 19. _____
$-2x + 3y = 9$ is ___?___ .

(a) $\frac{2}{3}$ (b) $-\frac{2}{3}$ (c) $\frac{3}{2}$ (d) $-\frac{3}{2}$

20. Use the figure at the right, in which $m \parallel n$. 20. _____
If m∠4 = 33, then m∠7 = ___?___ .

(a) 57

(b) 157

(c) 147

(d) none of these

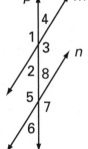

21. In the figure at the right, $\overrightarrow{MR}$ is the bisector 21. _____
of ∠AMT and $\overrightarrow{MT}$ is the bisector of ∠RMB.
If m∠AMT = 88, then m∠RMB = ___?___ .

(a) 44   (b) 132

(c) 90   (d) 88

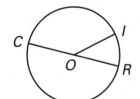

22. In the figure at the right, $\overline{CR}$ is a 22. _____
diameter of ⊙O. If m$\widehat{ICR}$ = 319°,
then m∠COI = ___?___ .

(a) 139   (b) 41

(c) 159.5   (d) none of these

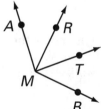

23. *True or false.* When an obtuse angle is bisected, two acute angles are formed.

23. _____

24. In the figure at the right, you *cannot* assume that ___?___.

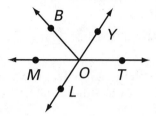

24. _____

    (a) $\overleftrightarrow{YL}$ and $\overleftrightarrow{MT}$ intersect at point O

    (b) ∠*BOY* is a right angle

    (c) points *M, O,* and *T* are collinear

    (d) ∠*YOT* and ∠*LOM* are vertical angles

25. Consider the figure at the right. Given that m∠1 = m∠2, which statement justifies the conclusion that $\overrightarrow{BC}$ bisects ∠*ABD*?

25. _____

    (a) Linear Pair Theorem

    (b) Angle Addition Property

    (c) definition of angle bisector

    (d) Addition Property of Equality

26. Consider the figure at the right. Given that *s // r* and *p ⊥ r*, what conclusion can be drawn?

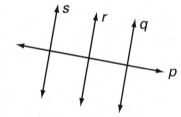

26. _____

    (a) *q // s*   (b) *p ⊥ s*

    (c) *p ⊥ q*   (d) none of these

27. Frank's father told him, "If you drive too fast, you'll get a ticket." The next week, Frank got a ticket. Did he drive too fast? Explain your reasoning.

_____

_____

28. The figure at the right shows the layout of part of a park. A row of lights is to run parallel to Elm Street through the intersection of walkway *A* and walkway *B*. Draw the line of lights.

28.

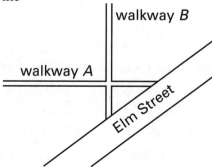

Check all your work carefully.

Name _____

QUIZ

You will need a ruler and a protractor for this quiz.

In 1–3, use the figure at the right below, where *m* is a line of reflection.

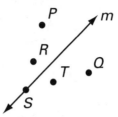

1. What is $r_m(P)$?

1. _____

2. What is $r_m(S)$?

2. _____

3. If $r_m(T) = R$, then *m* is the
   ___?___ of $\overline{RT}$.

3. _____

4. Use the figure at the right. Draw $r_\ell(\triangle ABC)$.

4.

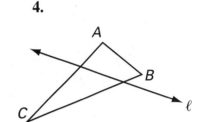

5. *True or false.* Reflections preserve distance.

5. _____

6. *Multiple choice.* $M'N'O'P'$ is the image of *MNOP* under a reflection. If the orientation of *MNOP* is clockwise, then the orientation of $M'N'O'P'$:

6. _____

   (a) is clockwise.   (b) is counterclockwise.

   (c) cannot be determined from the given information.

7. What are the coordinates of $r_{x\text{-axis}}(a, b)$?

7. _____

8. At the right is a diagram of a miniature golf hole. Draw a path to get the ball *G* into the hole *H*.

8.

9. Suppose *A*, *B*, and *C* are distinct points such that T(*A*) = *B* and T(*A*) = *C*. Is T a transformation? Explain why or why not.

_____

_____

Name _____

QUIZ   **Lessons 4-4 Through 4-6**

You will need a ruler and a protractor for this quiz.

1. In the figure at the right, $p \,/\!/\, q$ and $r_p \circ r_q(\triangle JKL) = \triangle J''K''L''$.

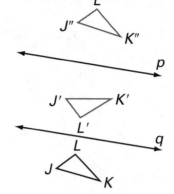

a. Name the transformation that maps $\triangle JKL$ onto $\triangle J''K''L''$.

1. a. _____

b. If lines p and q are 2.5 cm apart, what is the length of $\overline{JJ''}$?

b. _____

2. a. Use the figure at the right. Draw $r_b \circ r_a(PATH)$.

2. a.

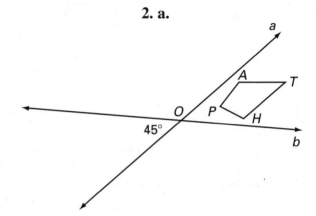

b. Name the transformation performed in Part **a** and describe its direction and magnitude.

b. _____

3. In the figure at the right, draw the translation image of $UVWXYZ$ determined by $\overrightarrow{RS}$

3.

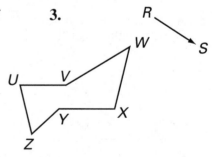

4. Name two properties that are preserved by rotations.

4. _____

_____

5. Give the image of (3, 2) when translated by the vector (-6, 6).

5. _____

Name _____

CHAPTER 4 TEST, Form A

You will need a ruler and a protractor for this test.

1. In the space at the right, draw and label a figure so that
   $r_m(\overline{TL}) = \overline{TL'}$.

   1.

2. In the figure at the right, draw the reflection image of
   GHOST over line ℓ.

   2.

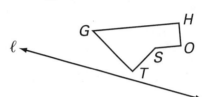

In 3 and 4, use the figure below. Suppose
$r_m(\triangle PQT) = \triangle RST$. **Justify the conclusion.**

3. $m \perp \overline{QS}$

4. $m\angle PQT = m\angle RST$

3. _____

4. _____

5. Give the image of (p, q) when translated by the
   vector (-5, 2).

   5. _____

6. $\triangle PRQ$ at the right has
   vertices $P = (0, 5)$,
   $R = (3, 0)$, and
   $Q = (-1, -4)$. Give the
   coordinates of the
   vertices of its reflection
   image over the *y*-axis.

   6. _____

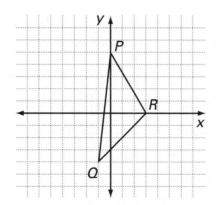

7. List four properties preserved under a glide reflection.

   _____

   _____

8. Name the isometries that preserve orientation.

_____

9. In the figure at the right, $A'B'C'D'$ is the image
of $ABCD$ under a glide reflection $r \circ T$. Draw the
translation vector for T.

9.

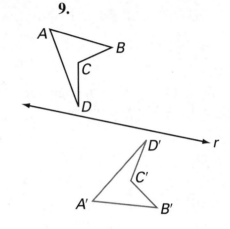

10. **a.** Use the figure at the right.
Draw $r_m \circ r_\ell(\triangle XYZ)$.

10. a.

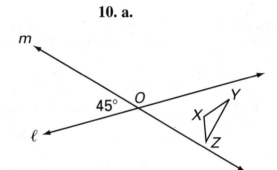

   b. Name the transformation performed in Part **a** and
   describe its direction and magnitude.

b. _____

_____

11. To translate $\overline{PQ}$ by 5.8 cm, you can reflect it successively
across two ___?___ lines where the distance between
them is ___?___.

11. _____

_____

12. In the figure at the right,
$s \parallel t$ and $t \perp r$. Name and
describe the transformation
performed if figure G is
reflected first over t and
then that image is reflected
over r.

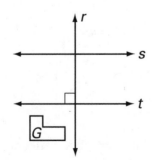

12. _____

_____

13. In the figure at the right,
$r_{\overleftrightarrow{PQ}}(A) = B$. If m$\angle APB = 97$,
find m$\angle APQ$.

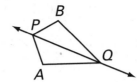
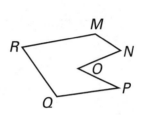

13. _____

14. In the figure at the right, draw the translation
image of *MNOPQR* determined by $\vec{RO}$.

14.

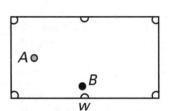

15. Use the billiard table shown at the right. Draw a path
so that ball *A* bounces off wall *w* and hits ball *B*.

15.

**In 16 and 17, name the type of isometry that maps
Figure I onto Figure II.**

16.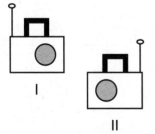

17.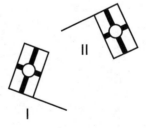

16. _____

17. _____

18. *Multiple choice.* Which is a pair of congruent letters?

18. _____

(a) **A** A   (b) **B ꓭ**   (c) **M M**   (d) **P ꟼ**

Check all your work carefully.

CHAPTER 4 TEST, Form B

You will need a ruler and a protractor for this test.

1. In the space at the right, draw and label a figure so that
   $r_s(\triangle ABC) = (\triangle ADE)$.

   1.

2. In the figure at the right, draw the reflection image of
   STORY over line *p*.

   2.

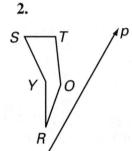

In 3 and 4, use the figure below. Suppose
$r_\ell(\triangle ABC) = \triangle XYZ$. **Justify the conclusion.**

3. $AB = XY$

4. ℓ is the bisector of $\overline{AX}$.

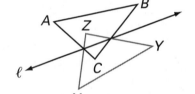

3. _____

4. _____

5. Give the image of (r, s) when translated by the
   vector (3, -7).

   5. _____

6. $\triangle XYZ$ at the right has
   vertices $X = (-3, 0)$,
   $Y = (-4, -5)$, and
   $Z = (0, 1)$. Give the
   coordinates of the
   vertices of its reflection
   image over the *y*-axis.

   6. _____

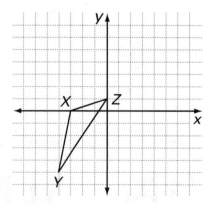

7. List five properties preserved under a translation.

   _____

   _____

8. Name the isometries that do *not* preserve orientation.

_____

9. In the figure at the right, *P'Q'R'S'* is the image
of *PQRS* under a glide reflection T ∘ n. Draw
the translation vector for T.

9.

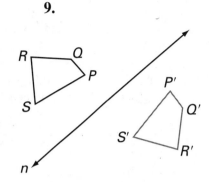

10. a. Use the figure at the right.
Draw $r_t \circ r_s(\triangle ABC)$.

10. a.

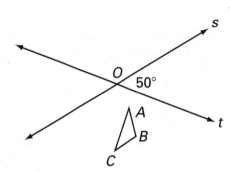

b. Name the transformation performed in Part **a** and describe
its direction and magnitude.

b. _____

_____

11. To rotate $\overline{MR}$ 160° about point *N*, you can reflect
it successively over two lines that form an angle
of ___?___ and whose vertex is ___?___.

11. _____

_____

12. In the figure at the right,
m // p and *p ⊥ n*. Name and
describe the transformation
performed if figure *H* is
reflected first over *p* and
then the image is reflected
over *m*.

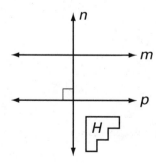

12. _____

_____

13. In the figure at the right,
    $r_{\overleftrightarrow{AB}}(X) = Z$. If m∠XAB = 28,
    find m∠XAZ.

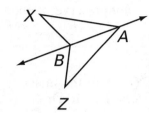

13. _____

14. In the figure at the right, draw the translation
    image of *MNOPQR* determined by $\overrightarrow{NP}$.

14.

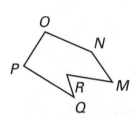

15. Use the billiard table shown at the right. Draw a path
    so that ball *C* bounces off wall *w* and hits ball *D*.

15.

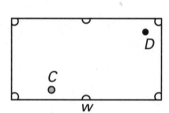

**In 16 and 17, name the type of isometry that maps
Figure I onto Figure II.**

16.

17.

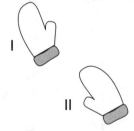

16. _____

17. _____

18. *Multiple choice.* Which is a pair of congruent letters?

18. _____

    (a) **F Ⅎ**   (b) **Q ɒ**   (c) **Z Z**   (d) **A ➢**

Check all your work carefully.

CHAPTER 4 TEST, Form C

1. In the figure at the right, is △*XYZ* the reflection image of △*ABC* over line *m*? If you think it is, write a convincing argument to support your answer. If you think it is not, first justify your answer; then locate the correct reflection image.

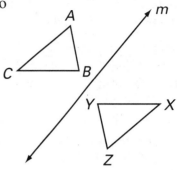

2. Suppose you are asked to make the following a true statement by filling in the blank with the name of one transformation.

   A ___?___ is a composite of reflections over lines.

   Explain why you cannot complete the statement without being given more information. Make a drawing to illustrate your answer.

3. On the coordinate axes below, draw a translation image of △*RST*. Then give the ordered-pair description of the vector that represents your translation.

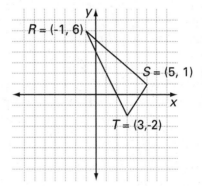

4. The figure at the right shows a game table and one student's planned path for getting ball *B* into hole *H*. Is this path possible? Explain why or why not?

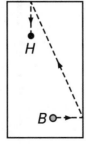

5. Identify a real-world situation that illustrates congruence. Give a brief explanation of how the situation you chose shows congruence.

Midville Manufacturing Company is moving to a new building. The floor plan of the manufacturing area of the new building is shown at the bottom of this page.

Midville Manufacturing is a small company. The owner has only enough money to hire one security guard to monitor the entire manufacturing area at any one time. So, the owner made the following plan.

- The security guard will remain at a guard station centrally located in the manufacturing area. The location of the proposed guard station is shown in the floor plan below.

- Mirrors will be placed along the entire length of the back wall.

From the guard station, the security guard can see all the mirrors. Every part of the manufacturing area is reflected in the mirrors. So, the owner reasoned, the guard will be able to remain at the station and monitor activities in all parts of the manufacturing area.

a. Assume that the owner's plan is put into effect. Explain why the security guard will *not* be able to see activities in all parts of the manufacturing area from the guard station.

b. Suppose that you work as an assistant to the owner. Plan a different way to place the mirrors so that one security guard *will* be able to see activities in all parts of the manufacturing area. In creating your plan, use mirrors efficiently. You may place mirrors at whatever angle you think is necessary, and you may change where the guard is located. Then write a short report in which you present your plan to the owner and justify why it will work.

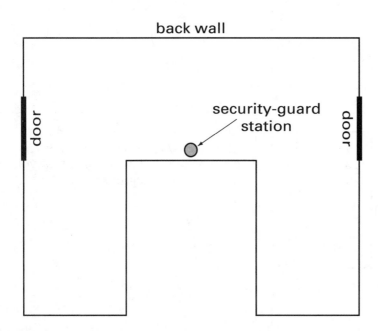

Name _____

You will need a ruler and a protractor for this test.

1. Use the figure at the right. Draw $r_\ell(MNOP)$.

1.

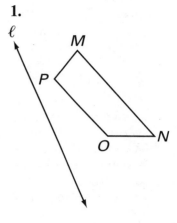

2. If $r_p(A) = A$, what conclusion can you draw?

_____

3. Suppose $SR = 119.58$, $ST = 55.66$, and $TR = 63.95$. Is T between S and R? Explain. In the space at the right, make a drawing to illustrate your answer.

_____

_____

4. Give the slope of the line through (-4, -7) and (-1, 5).

4. _____

5. *True or false.* Any line perpendicular to the line with equation $3x + y = 7$ must have slope $-\frac{1}{3}$.

5. _____

In 6 and 7, suppose $r_\ell(T) = S$ and $r_\ell(P) = P$. Justify the conclusion.

6. $SP = TP$

6. _____

7. $\overleftrightarrow{TS} \perp \ell$

7. _____

8. In the space at the right, draw and label $\angle PAQ$ with measure 74. Then draw and label its bisector, $\overrightarrow{AN}$.

8.

9. In the figure at the right, suppose that m∠*RSZ* = 5*n* + 6 and m∠*TSZ* = 8*n* − 9.6.

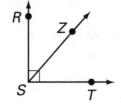

  a. Find *n*.

  b. Find m∠*ZST*.

9. a. _____

   b. _____

10. △*JKL* at the right has vertices *J* = (0, 4), *K* = (1, -4), and *L* = (-5, -2). Give the coordinates of the vertices of its reflection image over the *x*-axis.

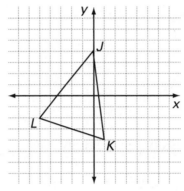

10. _____

In 11 and 12, give the coordinates of *P*.

11. *P* = r$_{y\text{-axis}}$(-19, 44)

11. _____

12. *P* is the image of (-11, -10) when translated by the vector (20, 10).

12. _____

13. Name a property of a good definition that is violated by this "bad" definition: *An obtuse angle is larger than an acute angle.*

_____

_____

14. Consider the following conjecture: *If an isometry is the composite of three reflections, then it is a glide reflection.*

Multiple choice. For each example, tell whether it is

  i. an instance of the conjecture.

  ii. a counterexample to the conjecture.

  iii. neither an instance of nor a counterexample to the conjecture.

14. a. _____

   b. _____

   c. _____

  a.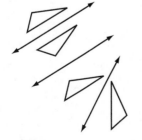

  b.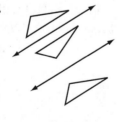

  c.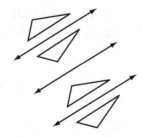

In 15 and 16, *true or false*.

15. In graph theory, there can be more than one line through any two points.

15. _____

16. In coordinate geometry, there can be more than one line through any two points.

16. _____

17. a. Write the converse of this statement: *If $r_m(P) = P'$, then m is the perpendicular bisector of $\overline{PP'}$.*

_____

b. Is the converse true or false?

b. _____

18. a. Use the figure at the right. Draw $r_p \circ r_q(ABCD)$.

18. a.

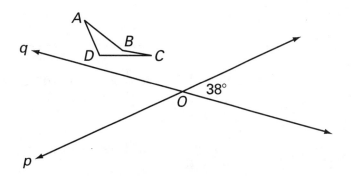

b. Name the transformation performed in Part **a** and describe its direction and magnitude.

b. _____

_____

19. In the figure at the right, $r \parallel s$ and $s \perp t$. Name and describe the transformation performed if figure H is reflected first over t and then its image is reflected over r.

19. _____

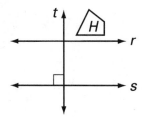

20. In the figure at the right, draw the translation image of *MNOPQ* determined by $\overrightarrow{MP}$.

20.

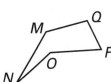

21. Use the billiard table shown at the right. Draw a path so that ball *R* bounces off wall *w* and hits ball *J*.

21.

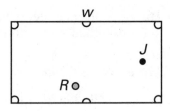

22. The distance from Albuquerque, New Mexico, to Seattle, Washington, is 1453 miles. The distance from Albuquerque to Boise, Idaho, is 940 miles. From these facts alone, what conclusion can you draw about the distance from Boise to Seattle?

_____

_____

23. Can the numbers $\frac{1}{2}$, $\frac{1}{8}$, and $\frac{3}{4}$ be lengths of three sides of a triangle?

23. _____

In 24 and 25, name the type of isometry that maps Figure I onto Figure II.

24.

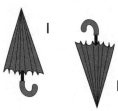

25.

24. _____

25. _____

In 26 and 27, use the figure below, in which *j // k*.

26. If m∠6 = 84, find m∠4.

26. _____

27. Suppose that m∠8 = 8*w* + 12 and m∠6 = 10*w* − 6.

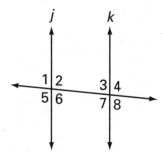

a. Find *w*.

27. a. _____

b. Find m∠4.

b. _____

Check all your work carefully.

QUIZ

1. Suppose $\triangle WET \cong \triangle DRY$. List the six pairs of congruent parts.

   _____

   _____

2. State the Segment Congruence Theorem.

   _____

   _____

In 3 and 4, $r_\ell(\angle DOG) = \angle CAT$.

3. *True or false.* By the definition of congruence, $\angle DOG \cong \angle CAT$.

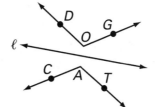

3. _____

4. If $m\angle DOG = 108$, then $m\angle CAT = $ ____?____ .

4. _____

5. In the figure at the right, $\overline{PT} \cong \overline{RS}$, M is the midpoint of $\overline{PT}$, and N is the midpoint of $\overline{RS}$. If $PT = 22$, what is NS?

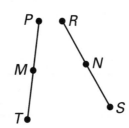

5. _____

6. *Multiple choice.* Choose the appropriate justification for the following statement: *If MENA $\cong$ SPRK and SPRK $\cong$ XYLO, then MENA $\cong$ XYLO.*

   (a) CPCF Theorem

   (b) Transitive Property of Congruence

   (c) Figure Reflection Theorem

   (d) none of the above

6. _____

7. In the figure at the right, points F and R lie on $\odot T$. What can you deduce about the figure by using the definition of circle?

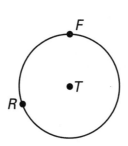

7. _____

QUIZ

You will need a ruler and a compass for this quiz.

In 1 and 2, use the figure at the right below.

1. Supply justifications in the argument.
   Given: $\overleftrightarrow{PQ}$ is the $\perp$ bisector of $\overline{TS}$.
   To prove: $\overline{PT} \cong \overline{PS}$.

   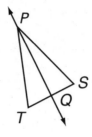

   a. 0. $\overleftrightarrow{PQ}$ is the $\perp$ bisector of $\overline{TS}$.   1. a. _____

   b. 1. $r_{\overleftrightarrow{PQ}}(T) = S$; $r_{\overleftrightarrow{PQ}}(P) = P$ b. _____

   c. 2. $r_{\overleftrightarrow{PQ}}(\overline{PT}) = \overline{PS}$ c. _____

   d. 3. $\overline{PT} \cong \overline{PS}$ d. _____

2. *Multiple choice.* The proof in Question 1 is written in   2. _____

   (a) paragraph form.

   (b) argument form.

   (c) two-column form.

3. In the figure at the right,   3. _____
   $s \,/\!/\, t$. If m$\angle 4 = 38$
   and m$\angle 3 = 65$,   _____
   find m$\angle 1$ and m$\angle 2$.

   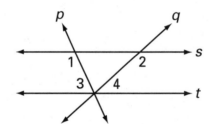

4. Justify this conclusion.   4. _____
   Given: $\overline{AB} \cong \overline{BC}$ and $\overline{BC} \cong \overline{CD}$.
   Conclusion: $\overline{AB} \cong \overline{CD}$.

5. In the space at the right, construct an equilateral   5.
   triangle with side length equal to $\overline{XC}$.

CHAPTER 5 TEST, Form A

You will need a compass and a ruler for this test.

In 1–3, *BLUNT* ≅ *SCANT*.

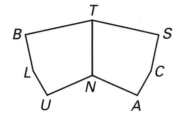

1. Name a segment
   congruent to $\overline{LU}$.

2. If m∠U = 99,
   then ___?___ = 99.

3. BT = ___?___

1. _____

2. _____

3. _____

4. In the figure at the right,
   p // q and m∠8 = 7k.
   Give an expression for

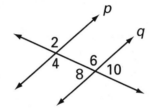

   a. m∠6.

   b. m∠4.

4. a. _____

   b. _____

5. In the figure at the right,
   t is the perpendicular bisector
   of $\overline{MN}$. If NO = 7.5 and
   NL = 19, find

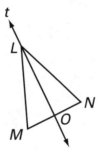

   a. ML.

   b. MN.

5. a. _____

   b. _____

6. Use the figure at the right. Supply
   justifications in the argument.

   Given: $\overrightarrow{QN}$ bisects ∠MQO;
   $\overrightarrow{QO}$ bisects ∠NQP.
   To prove: ∠MQN ≅ ∠OQP

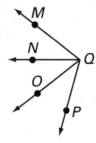

   a. 0. $\overrightarrow{QN}$ bisects ∠MQO;
      $\overrightarrow{QO}$ bisects ∠NQP.

   b. 1. ∠NQO ≅ ∠MQN;
      ∠PQO ≅ ∠NQO

   c. 2. ∠MQN ≅ ∠PQO

6. a. _____

   b. _____

   c. _____

Name _____

7. The measures of the angles of a triangle are in the extended ratio 2 : 4 : 9. Find the measure of the largest angle.

7. _____

8. Write an argument for this proof.

Given: ⊙O and ⊙P;
R is the midpoint of
$\overline{OP}$; R and Q are
on ⊙P.

To prove: $\overline{OR} \cong \overline{PQ}$.

Conclusions	Justifications
_____	_____
_____	_____
_____	_____
_____	_____

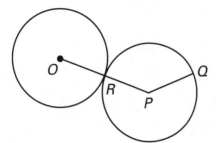

9. In *PENTA* at the right find *d* and m∠T.

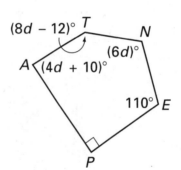

9. _____

_____

10. In the figure at the right, $\overline{SL} \cong \overline{RG}$; P and Q are midpoints of $\overline{SL}$ and $\overline{RG}$, respectively; and PL = 19y. Find RQ and RG.

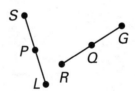

10. _____

_____

11. Write an argument for this proof.

Given: $r_\ell(M) = K$; $r_\ell(A) = O$.
To prove: △BAM ≅ △BOK.

Conclusions	Justifications
_____	_____
_____	_____
_____	_____
_____	_____

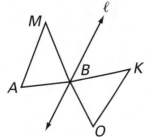

12. In the space below, construct the circle that contains the vertices of △*TIL*.

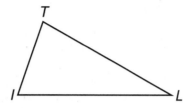

13. At the right is pictured a bookcase. $\overline{AB}$ and $\overline{CD}$ are metal rods used for support at the back. The measure of ∠*DAB* is 50, and the measure of ∠*CBA* is also 50. Are the sides of the bookcase parallel? Justify your answer.

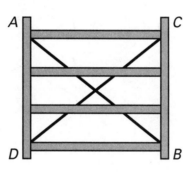

13. _____

_____

_____

_____

_____

_____

14. *True or false.* In non-Euclidean geometries, there may be two lines parallel to a given line through a point not on the given line.

14. _____

In 15 and 16, use △*RST* below. Is each figure uniquely determined?

15. perpendicular bisector of $\overline{RS}$

16. bisector of ∠*T*

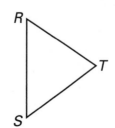

15. _____

16. _____

Check all your work carefully.

CHAPTER 5 TEST, Form B

You will need a compass and a ruler for this test.

In 1–3, *HOUSE* ≅ *HARTE*.

1. Name an angle congruent to ∠S.

2. If *UO* = 16, then ___?___ = 16.

3. *RE* = ___?___

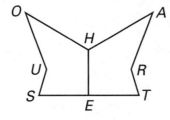

1. _____

2. _____

3. _____

4. In the figure at the right, ℓ // *m* and m∠9 = 4*h*. Give an expression for

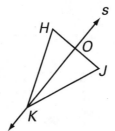

a. m∠3.

b. m∠1.

4. a. _____

b. _____

5. In the figure at the right, *s* is the perpendicular bisector of $\overline{HJ}$. If *HK* = 8.2 and *HJ* = 7, find

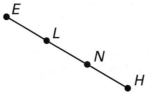

a. *JK*.

b. *OH*.

5. a. _____

b. _____

6. Use the figure at the right. Supply justifications in the argument.

Given: *L* is the midpoint of $\overline{EN}$; *N* is the midpoint of $\overline{LH}$.

To prove: $\overline{EL} \cong \overline{NH}$.

a. 0. *L* is the midpoint of $\overline{EN}$; *N* is the midpoint of $\overline{LH}$.

b. 1. $\overline{EL} \cong \overline{LN}$; $\overline{NH} \cong \overline{LN}$

c. 2. $\overline{EL} \cong \overline{NH}$

6. a. _____

b. _____

c. _____

7. The measures of the angles of a triangle are in the extended ratio 3 : 4 : 8. Find the measure of the largest angle.

7. _____

8. Write an argument for this proof.

   Given: △WHY ≅ △TOC;
           △TOC ≅ △PAL.
   To prove: $\overline{WH} \cong \overline{PA}$.

   Conclusions   Justifications

   _____   _____

   _____   _____

   _____   _____

   _____   _____

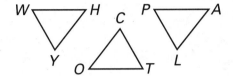

9. In *HEXAGO* at the right, find c and m∠G.

   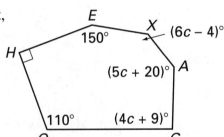

9. _____

   _____

10. In the figure at the right, $\overline{LC} \cong \overline{JT}$; M and N are midpoints of $\overline{LC}$ and $\overline{JT}$, respectively; and MC = 14z. Find *NT* and *JT*.

    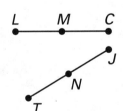

10. _____

    _____

11. Write an argument for this proof.

    Given: ℓ is the ⊥ bisector of $\overline{MN}$.
    To prove: △AMB ≅ △ANB.

    Conclusions   Justifications

    _____   _____

    _____   _____

    _____   _____

    _____   _____

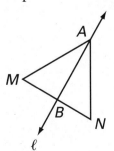

12. In the space below, construct the circle that contains the vertices of △*WAH*.

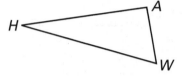

13. At the right is pictured a wooden frame that supports a wall. The top of the frame, $\overline{AB}$, is parallel to the bottom, $\overline{DC}$. What is the relationship between ∠*BAE* and ∠*AED*? Justify your answer.

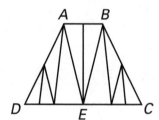

13. _____

_____

_____

_____

_____

14. *True or false.* Playfair's Parallel Postulate is a true statement in Euclidean geometry.

14. _____

In 15 and 16, use *PQRS* below. Is each figure uniquely determined?

15. perpendicular bisector of $\overline{PQ}$

16. bisector of $\overline{PQ}$

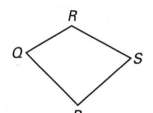

15. _____

16. _____

Check all your work carefully.

Name _____

CHAPTER 5 TEST, Form C

1. Draw and label two triangles that are congruent. Use symbols to state the congruence between the figures. Then list all pairs of congruent corresponding parts of the two figures.

2. Explain the Perpendicular Bisector Theorem in your own words. Then give an example of a real-world situation that illustrates this theorem.

3. Explain how you can tell that the figure at the right is labeled incorrectly. Suppose you were asked to correct the error by making just one change. What would you suggest? Justify your answer.

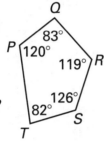

4. In the figure at the right, $m \parallel n$. State one fact about the figure that you can prove by using the Transitive Property of Congruence. Then write an argument to prove that fact.

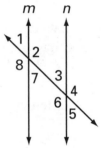

5. At the end of the school year, Sari found the construction at the right in her geometry notebook. However, she had not identified it, and she could not remember what she had constructed. Identify the construction for Sari. Then write a description of the steps that were taken to perform the construction.

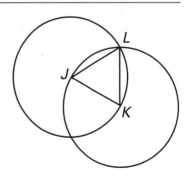

CHAPTER 5 TEST, Form D

The student council of Springfield High School wants to design a new banner for the school. They hope that the basic design of the banner can consist of four congruent regions that represent the four classes of the school–Grades 9, 10, 11, and 12.

a. One member of the student council proposed a banner in the shape of a parallelogram. The basic plan for the design is shown in Design I at the right. In this design, $\overline{AB} \parallel \overline{DC}$, $\overline{AD} \parallel \overline{BC}$, and $\overline{AC}$ and $\overline{DB}$ are transversals. This student recalled that, when parallel lines are cut by a transversal, several pairs of congruent angles are formed. So, this student reasoned, the four small triangles formed must be congruent. Show that the four small triangles are *not* all congruent. Are any of the triangles congruent to each other?

Design I

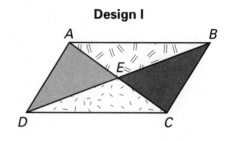

b. What conclusion or conclusions *can* you make about Design I as a result of the given information that $\overline{AB} \parallel \overline{DC}$ and $\overline{AD} \parallel \overline{BC}$?

c. A different member of the student council proposed a triangular banner. The basic plan for this design is shown in Design II at the right. In this design, $\triangle XYZ$ is an equilateral triangle and points R, S, and T are the midpoints of the sides. Show that the four small triangles *are* all congruent.

Design II

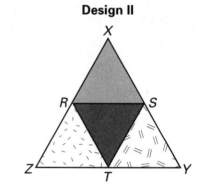

d. Using a compass and straightedge, make a new drawing of Design II in which the large triangle has side length equal to that of $\overline{MN}$ below.

e. The student council has decided to hold a contest in which all students are invited to submit a basic design for the banner. Create an original design that can be entered into the contest. Then write a brief report to accompany your contest entry. In your report, you should

   i. give a general description of your design;

   ii. identify the four congruent regions of the banner;

   iii. provide a justification for your statement that the four regions are congruent; and

   iv. provide step-by-step instructions for constructing your design.

CHAPTER 5 TEST, Cumulative Form

You will need a ruler and a compass for this test.

In 1 and 2, _PLOID_ ≅ _BRAID_.

1. Name an angle
   congruent to ∠L.

1. _____

2. _True or false._ $\overline{PI} \cong \overline{BI}$

2. _____

In 3–5, use the figure at the right below, in which _p // q_.

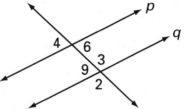

3. **a.** Identify a pair of
      corresponding angles.

3. **a.** _____

   b. Identify a pair of alternate
      interior angles.

   b. _____

4. Suppose m∠6 = 2t.

   a. Find m∠9.

4. **a.** _____

   b. Find m∠3.

   b. _____

5. Suppose m∠6 = 5a + 1 and m∠3 = 13a − 10.
   Find _a_ and m∠9.

5. _____

6. Give the image of (-7, 12) under each transformation.

   a. reflection over the _x_-axis

6. **a.** _____

   b. reflection over the _y_-axis

   b. _____

7. In the figure at the right,
   A and Z are pennants and
   $r_m \circ r_\ell(A) = Z$. Describe the
   transformation $r_m \circ r_\ell$.

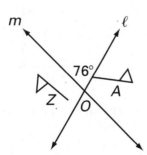

7. _____

   _____

   _____

8. From its equation, classify each line as _vertical, horizontal,_
   or _oblique._

   a. $y = 7x - 10$

8. **a.** _____

   b. $x = -4$

   b. _____

In 9 and 10, refer to this statement: *A hamburger is tasty if it is cooked on a grill.*

9. a. Write the antecedent. _____

b. Write the consequent. _____

10. Write the converse of the statement.

_____

In 11–13, consider the following conjecture: *If ℓ and m are lines, then* $r_m \circ r_\ell$ *is a translation.*

Multiple choice. **For each example, tell whether it is**

i. an instance of the conjecture.

ii. a counterexample to the conjecture.

iii. neither an instance of nor a counterexample to the conjecture.

11. 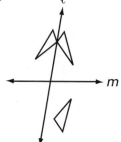 **12.** **13.**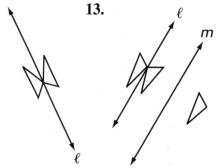

11. _____

12. _____

13. _____

14. Use the portion of the map of Chicago shown at the right. In the map, Belmont and North Avenues are perpendicular to Western Avenue. Chicago Avenue is parallel to North Avenue.

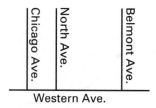

Multiple choice. Choose a justification for each conclusion from the following.

i. Two Perpendiculars Theorem

ii. Perpendicular to Parallels Theorem

iii. Transitivity of Parallelism Theorem

a. Belmont Avenue is parallel to North Avenue.

b. Chicago Avenue is perpendicular to Western Avenue.

14. a. _____

b. _____

Name _____

15. Find the sum of the measures of the angles of a convex nonagon.

15. _____

16. The measures of the angles of a triangle are in the extended ratio 14 : 8 : 2. Find the measure of the largest angle.

16. _____

17. Draw this television cabinet in perspective in the space at the right.

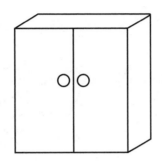

17.

18. Use the figure at the right. Supply justifications in the argument.

Given: $\overline{WA} \cong \overline{RA}$; $\overline{DR} \cong \overline{WA}$.

To prove: R is the midpoint of $\overline{DA}$.

a. 0. $\overline{WA} \cong \overline{RA}$; $\overline{DR} \cong \overline{WA}$.

18. a. _____

b. 1. $\overline{RA} \cong \overline{DR}$

b. _____

c. 2. R is the midpoint of $\overline{DA}$.

c. _____

19. Write an argument for this proof.

Given: $r_m(A) = E$; $r_m(B) = T$.

To prove: $\triangle GAB \cong \triangle GET$.

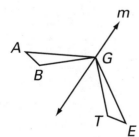

<u>Conclusions</u>   <u>Justifications</u>

_____   _____

_____   _____

_____   _____

_____   _____

20. *True or false.* In Euclidean geometry, the sum of the measures of the angles of a triangle is 180.

20. _____

21. In the space below, construct the circle that contains the vertices of △*CIR*.

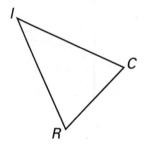

In 22–24, use the figure below. Each answer is one of the named points.

22. $r_q(L) =$ ___?___

23. *M* is the reflection of ___?___ across line *q*.

24. $r_p(N) =$ ___?___

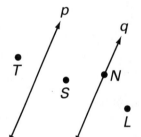

22. _____

23. _____

24. _____

Check all your work carefully.

QUIZ

You will need a ruler for this quiz.

1. In the figure at the right, draw all lines that seem to be symmetry lines.

1.

2. *True or false.* A circle has infinitely many symmetry lines.

2. _____

In 3 and 4, use △*TOP* at the right below.

3. *True or false.* The symmetry line of the triangle bisects $\overline{TP}$.

3. _____

4. If m∠*P* = 37, find m∠*T* and m∠*O*.

4. _____

_____

5. Use the figure at the right. Supply justifications in the argument.

Given: *SI* = *SO*; *TR* = *TO*.
To prove: m∠*I* = m∠*R*.

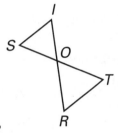

  a. 0. *SI* = *SO*; *TR* = *TO*

5. **a.** _____

  b. 1. m∠*I* = m∠*SOI*; m∠*R* = m∠*TOR*

  b. _____

  c. 2. m∠*SOI* = m∠*TOR*

  c. _____

  d. 3. m∠*I* = m∠*R*

  d. _____

6. From the information given in the drawing at the right, what quadrilateral is pictured? Be as specific as possible.

6. _____

7. In the space at the right, draw a rhombus that is *not* a square.

7.

QUIZ

You will need a ruler for this quiz.

1. Given kite *PQRS* at the right, with ends *Q* and *S*. If m∠*PSQ* = 19, m∠*PQS* = 47, and *PQ* = 10, find

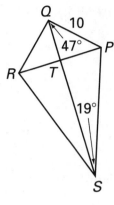

   a. *RQ*.

   b. m∠*PTS*.

   c. m∠*TPS*.

   d. m∠*PQR*.

   1. a. _____

   b. _____

   c. _____

   d. _____

2. Name all of the seven special types of quadrilaterals you studied in this chapter that have 2-fold rotation symmetry.

   _____

   _____

3. Use the figure at the right. Supply justifications in the argument.

   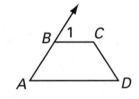

   Given: *ABCD* is a trapezoid with bases $\overline{BC}$ and $\overline{AD}$; m∠*D* = m∠1.

   To prove: *ABCD* is an isosceles trapezoid.

   a. 1. $\overline{BC} \,/\!/ \, \overline{AD}$

   b. 2. m∠1 = m∠*A*

   c. 3. m∠*D* = m∠*A*

   d. 4. *ABCD* is an isosceles trapezoid.

   3. a. _____

   b. _____

   c. _____

   d. _____

4. **a.** Locate the center of symmetry of the figure at the right. Label it as point *O*.

   4. a.

   b. The figure in Part **a** has ___?___-fold rotation symmetry.

   b. _____

CHAPTER 6 TEST, Form A

You will need a ruler for this test.

1. Draw all symmetry lines in regular pentagon *HASTE* at the right.

1.

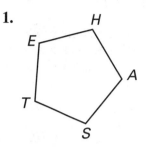

2. a. Locate the center of symmetry of regular hexagon *PLANET* at the right. Label it as point *X*.

2. a.

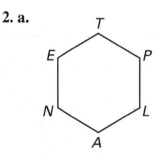

   b. Regular hexagon *PLANET* has ___?___-fold rotation symmetry.

   b. _____

3. *True or false.* Each symmetry line of a regular heptagon is the perpendicular bisector of a side of the heptagon.

3. _____

4. In the figure at the right, *TRIP* is a rhombus. If m∠1 = 73, find

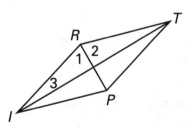

   a. m∠2.

   4. a. _____

   b. m∠3.

   b. _____

5. From the information given in the drawing at the right, what quadrilateral is pictured? Be as specific as possible.

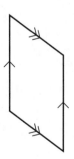

5. _____

In 6 and 7, quadrilateral *LONG* below is a kite with ends *L* and *N*.

6. If the length of $\overline{NO}$ is 19, which other segment has length 19?

6. _____

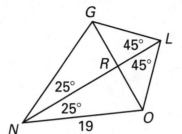

7. **a.** Find m∠*LOR*.

   b. Find m∠*NGL*.

7. **a.** _____

   b. _____

In 8 and 9, △*PQR* below is isosceles with base $\overline{QR}$.

8. If m∠*P* = 34, find m∠*Q*.

8. _____

9. If m∠*Q* = 10*t* and m∠*R* = 40 + 2*t*, find *t* and m∠*P*.

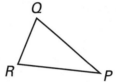

9. _____

   _____

10. **a.** In the space at the right, draw a quadrilateral that is equiangular but not regular.

10. **a.**

   b. What is the name of the quadrilateral that you drew in Part **a**? Be as specific as possible.

   b. _____

11. **a.** In the space at the right, draw the hierarchy relating the following: kite, parallelogram, quadrilateral, square, rhombus.

11. **a.**

   b. *True or false.* Every rhombus is a kite.

   b. _____

12. Use the figure at the right. Supply justifications in the argument.

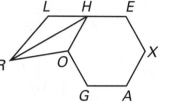

Given: *HEXAGO* is a regular hexagon; *HORL* is a kite with ends *H* and *R*.

To prove: $\overline{AG} \cong \overline{LH}$.

a. 0. *HEXAGO* is a regular hexagon; *HORL* is a kite with ends *H* and *R*.

b. 1. $\overline{AG} \cong \overline{HO}$

c. 2. $\overline{HO} \cong \overline{LH}$

d. 3. $\overline{AG} \cong \overline{LH}$

12. a. _____

b. _____

c. _____

d. _____

In 13–15, use the figure below. *k* **and** *ℓ* **are symmetry lines of regular nonagon** *MNOPQRSTU.*

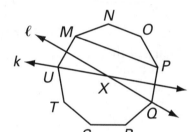

13. Name two segments that are congruent to $\overline{MP}$.

14. Find m∠*MUX*.

15. Find m∠*QXT*.

13. _____

14. _____

15. _____

16. Write an argument for this proof.

Given: ∠1 ≅ ∠*B*.
To prove: *ABCD* is a trapezoid.

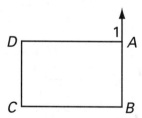

Conclusions   Justifications

_____   _____

_____   _____

_____   _____

_____   _____

17. In the figure at the right, *p* and *t* are symmetry lines for rectangle *ABCD*.

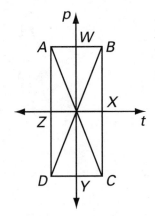

   a. If the length of $\overline{BD}$ is 39, which other segment has length 39?

   b. If *AD* = 35, then *AZ* = ___?___.

   c. *ABCD* has ___?___-fold rotation symmetry.

17. a. _____

    b. _____

    c. _____

18. *PARL* at the right is a parallelogram. If *PA* = 9 and *PL* = 15, find *AR* and *LR*.

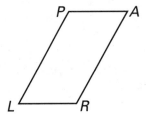

18. _____

    _____

19. a. Locate the center of symmetry of the design at the right. Label it as point *A*.

19. a.

   b. The design in Part **a** has ___?___-fold rotation symmetry.

   b. _____

20. *Multiple choice.* A regular polygon has *n*-fold rotation symmetry. How many lines of symmetry must it have?

   (a) $\dfrac{n}{2}$ (b) *n*   (c) *n* + 1

20. _____

21. Make a schedule for a round-robin tournament for six teams, A–F.

21. _____

    _____

    _____

    _____

    _____

Check all your work carefully.

CHAPTER 6 TEST, Form B

You will need a ruler for this test.

1. Draw all symmetry lines in regular heptagon *MASTERY* at the right.

1.

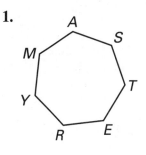

2. **a.** Locate the center of symmetry of regular pentagon *VENUS* at the right. Label it as point *Y*.

2. a.

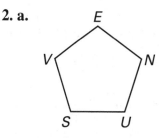

   b. Regular hexagon *VENUS* has ___?___-fold rotation symmetry.

   b. _____

3. *True or false.* Each symmetry line of a regular hexagon is the perpendicular bisector of a side of the hexagon.

3. _____

4. In the figure at the right, *HOME* is a rhombus. If m∠1 = 70, find

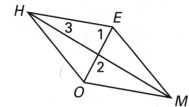

   a. m∠3.

4. a. _____

   b. m∠2.

   b. _____

5. From the information given in the drawing at the right, what quadrilateral is pictured? Be as specific as possible.

5. _____

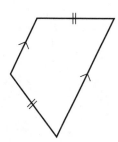

In 6 and 7, quadrilateral *MICE* below is a kite with ends *I* and *E*.

6. If the length of $\overline{EM}$ is 19, which other segment has length 19?

7. a. Find m∠*EMI*.

  b. Find m∠*EIC*.

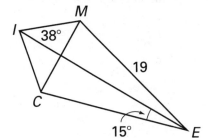

6. _____

7. a. _____

  b. _____

In 8 and 9, △*PQR* below is isosceles with base $\overline{PR}$.

8. If m∠*Q* = 108, find m∠*P*.

9. If m∠*P* = 9*n* and m∠*R* = 33 + 3*n*, find *n* and m∠*Q*.

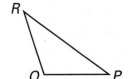

8. _____

9. _____

  _____

10. a. In the space at the right, draw a regular quadrilateral.

10. a.

  b. What is the name of the quadrilateral that you drew in Part **a**? Be as specific as possible.

  b. _____

11. a. In the space at the right, draw the hierarchy relating the following: quadrilateral, trapezoid, square, kite, parallelogram.

11. a.

  b. *True or false.* All kites are squares.

  b. _____

12. Use the figure at the right. Supply justifications in the argument.

   Given: *MARYB* is a regular pentagon; *LMBE* is a rhombus.

   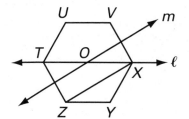

   To prove: $\overline{LE} \cong \overline{AR}$.

   a. 0. *MARYB* is a regular pentagon; *LMBE* is a rhombus.

   b. 1. $\overline{LE} \cong \overline{MB}$

   c. 2. $\overline{MB} \cong \overline{AR}$

   d. 3. $\overline{LE} \cong \overline{AR}$

   12. a. _____

   b. _____

   c. _____

   d. _____

In 13–15, use the figure below. ℓ and *m* are symmetry lines of regular hexagon *TUVXYZ*.

13. Name two segments that are congruent to $\overline{XZ}$.

14. Find m∠*VXO*.

15. Find m∠*TOV*.

13. _____

14. _____

15. _____

16. Write an argument for this proof.

   Given: $\overline{LM} \parallel \overline{KJ}$; ∠1 ≅ ∠*K*.
   To prove: *JKLM* is a parallelogram.

   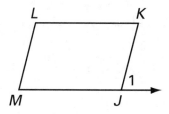

Conclusions	Justifications
_____	_____
_____	_____
_____	_____
_____	_____

17. In the figure at the right,
ℓ and m are symmetry lines
for rectangle *WXYZ*.

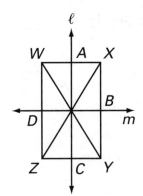

    a. If the length of $\overline{XZ}$ is 29,
which other segment has
length 29?

    b. If *WA* = 9, then *YZ* = ___?___.

    c. *WXYZ* has ___?___-fold
rotation symmetry.

17. a. _____

    b. _____

    c. _____

18. *ISMO* at the right is an
isosceles trapezoid with
bases $\overline{IS}$ and $\overline{OM}$.
If m∠*S* = 108, find
m∠*O* and m∠*I*.

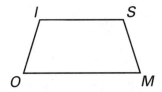

18. _____

_____

19. a. Locate the center of symmetry of the
design at the right. Label it as point *Z*.

19. a.

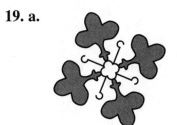

    b. The design in Part **a** has ___?___-fold rotation symmetry.

    b. _____

20. *Multiple choice.* A regular *n*-gon has symmetry lines
that pass through opposite vertices. Then *n* is ___?___.

    (a) even   (b) odd   (c) either even or odd

20. _____

21. Make a schedule for a round-robin tournament for five
teams, A–E.

21. _____

_____

_____

_____

_____

Check all your work carefully.

1. When asked to illustrate a trapezoid, Hoa and Jen drew these figures.

   Hoa's drawing   Jen's drawing

   Is either drawing appropriate? Is it possible that both are appropriate? Justify your answer. If you think that neither drawing is appropriate, make an appropriate drawing.

2. In the figure at the right, *MNOPQR* is a regular hexagon. State as many additional facts as you can about the figure.

3. The word *asymmetric* means "not symmetric." Draw a quadrilateral that you think is asymmetric. Then explain why you believe it is asymmetric.

4. Taneesha was sick and missed a day of math class. On the day before she was absent, the class was studying regular polygons. When she returned, she wondered why the class was discussing round-robin tournaments. How would you explain this to Taneesha?

5. Luis's little sister spilled grape juice on his homework. He was supposed to do the proof at the right, but now he doesn't know what the given information was. What do you think it might have been? Show how Luis can use your "given" to prove that *JKLM* is a kite.

   Given:

   Prove: *JKLM* is a kite.

CHAPTER 6 TEST, Form D

The design below is made from a set of *pattern blocks*. (If the blocks look familiar, it may be that you used them to study patterns, fractions, or other topics in elementary school.)

a. There are six basic shapes in the set of pattern blocks in the design above. Identify each shape. Be as specific as possible.

b. For each shape you identified in Part **a**, determine the measure of each interior angle *without using a protractor*.

c. Describe the symmetries of the design shown above.

d. Suppose you want to place this design of pattern blocks in a square frame, as shown in the sketch at the right. What additional types of blocks would you need to fill in the empty white spaces at the sides of the frame? Describe each type of block as completely as possible.

e. Design your own original set of pattern blocks, different from the traditional set used in the design above. Your set of blocks should include at least six shapes. You may use *some* of the shapes in the traditional set of pattern blocks, but not all.

Prepare a report in which you describe each shape in your set as completely as possible. Also include in your report at least one sample design that has been made from your blocks. Describe the symmetries of each design.

CHAPTER 6 TEST, Cumulative Form

You will need a ruler, a protractor, and a compass for this test.

In 1 and 2, use the regular hexagon at the right.

1. **a.** Draw the symmetry line(s) for the figure.

   b. Locate the center of symmetry of the figure.
   Label is as point *O*.

1.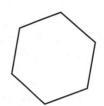

2. The figure has ___?___-fold rotation symmetry.

2. _____

In 3–5, △*MNO* at the right below is isosceles with base $\overline{NO}$.

3. Draw the symmetry line(s) for the figure.

3.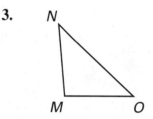

4. If m∠*M* = 96, find m∠*N*.

4. _____

5. If m∠*N* = 7*k* and m∠*O* = 20 + 2*k*, find *k* and m∠*M*.

5. _____

   _____

6. From the information given
   in the drawing at the right,
   what quadrilateral is pictured?
   Be as specific as possible.

6. _____

7. In the figure at the right,
   $\overrightarrow{OL}$ bisects ∠*BOW*,
   m∠*BOL* = 21 + *x*, and
   m∠*BOW* = 4*x* − 4.
   Find *x* and m∠*BOW*.

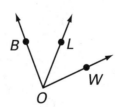

7. _____

   _____

8. Can the numbers 5, 9.1, and 5.6 be lengths of three
   sides of a triangle?

8. _____

9. Quadrilateral *TRAP* at the right
is an isosceles trapezoid with bases
$\overline{TR}$ and $\overline{PA}$. If m∠*T* = 117,
find the measures of all the other
angles of the trapezoid.

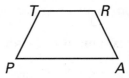

9. _____

_____

_____

10. Supply justifications in the argument.

Given: $\overleftrightarrow{AB}$ is the ⊥ bisector of $\overline{DC}$.
To prove: *ACBD* is a kite.

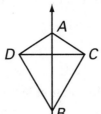

a. 0. $\overleftrightarrow{AB}$ is the ⊥ bisector of $\overline{DC}$.

b. 1. $\overline{AD} \cong \overline{AC}$; $\overline{BD} \cong \overline{BC}$

c. 2. *ACBD* is a kite.

10. a. _____

b. _____

c. _____

11. In the figure at the right, *p* // *q*.
If m∠1 = 2*y* + 25 and
m∠2 = 3*y* − 20, find
y and m∠3.

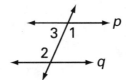

11. _____

_____

12. If *AB* = 15.55, *BC* = 14.25, and *AC* = 29.9, can you conclude
that *B* is between *A* and *C*? Explain why or why not.

_____

_____

13. Quadrilateral *WXYZ* below is a rhombus.

a. If *WX* = 7,
what is *ZY*?

b. If m∠*XWY* = 73,
find m∠*WXZ*
and m∠*WYX*.

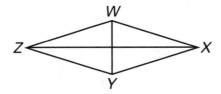

13. a. _____

b. _____

14. In the figure at the right, ℓ and *m*
are symmetry lines of regular
octagon *FGHIJKLM*.
Find m∠*HIM*.

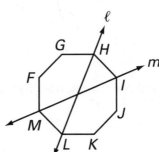

14. _____

Name _____

15. Write an argument for this proof.

Given: $\angle 1 \cong \angle 2$.
To prove: *NAME* is a trapezoid.

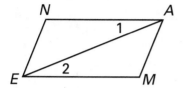

Conclusions

Justifications

_____   _____

_____   _____

_____   _____

_____   _____

16. Suppose $\triangle HOP \cong \triangle TOP$.

    a. In the space at the right, draw a figure to illustrate this situation.

    16. a.

    b. If the length of $\overline{HO}$ is 36, which other segment has length 36?

    b. _____

17. In the space at the right, construct an equilateral triangle with side length equal to *PT*.

    17.

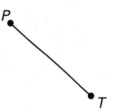

18. *True or false.* The converse of $p \Rightarrow q$ is $q \Rightarrow p$.

    18. _____

19. In the figure at the right, draw $r_m(PQRS)$.

19.

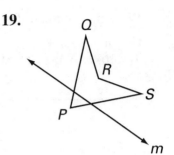

20. In the figure at the right, $r_\ell(\overline{BC}) = \overline{DC}$, and M and N are the midpoints of $\overline{BC}$ and $\overline{DC}$, respectively. If $MB = 3.5t$, what is CD?

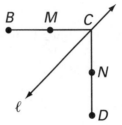

20. _____

21. The design at the right has ___?___-fold rotation symmetry.

21. _____

22. In the situation shown at the right, name the type of isometry that maps Figure I onto Figure II.

22. _____

23. In the figure at the right, find z and $m\angle E$.

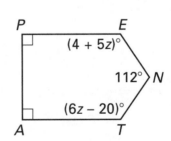

23. _____

_____

Check all your work carefully.

You will need a ruler, a protractor, and a compass for this test.

In 1–20, *multiple choice*. Give the letter of the correct answer.

1. In coordinate geometry, the graph of the line with equation
   $y = -7$ is a(n) ___?___ line.
   (a) horizontal   (b) vertical   (c) oblique   (d) discrete

   1. _____

2. Which is a heptagonal region?

   2. _____

   (a)   (b)   (c)   (d)

3. In the figure at the right, N is the
   midpoint of $\overline{RT}$. If $RN = 20 - 3x$
   and $NT = x + 4$, then $RT =$ ___?___.

   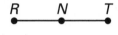

   (a) 16   (b) 12   (c) 8   (d) 4

   3. _____

4. Consider the figure at the right. Which
   statement justifies the conclusion that
   $\angle 1$ is supplementary to $\angle 2$?
   (a) definition of supplementary angles
   (b) Linear Pair Theorem
   (c) definition of a straight angle
   (d) definition of adjacent angles

   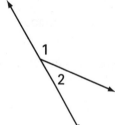

   4. _____

5. Orientation is preserved by both
   (a) reflections and rotations.
   (b) rotations and translations.
   (c) translations and glide reflections.
   (d) reflections and glide reflections.

   5. _____

6. The figure at the right shows a dial on a
   stove. The dial is marked in equal sections.
   A setting is chosen by rotating the arrow
   about the center. What is the magnitude of
   the rotation required to move the arrow
   from OFF to 5 in a clockwise direction?

   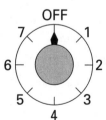

   (a) 225°   (b) -225°
   (c) 135°   (d) -135°

   6. _____

7. In the figure at the right, △*ADC* ∩ △*ABC* = ___?___.   **7.** _____

    (a) { }   (b) { $\overline{AD}$, $\overline{AC}$, $\overline{BD}$, $\overline{AB}$}

    (c) {*C*}   (d) {$\overline{AC}$}

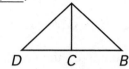

8. In △*TOP* at the right, m∠*O* = ___?___. $(2x + 2)°$ $(4x - 9)°$ **8.** _____

    (a) 85   (b) 59

    (c) 36   (d) 17

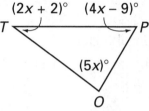

9. Consider the figure at the right. Given that   **9.** _____
$\overline{MP} \perp \overline{MO}$ and $\overline{OR} \perp \overline{MO}$, what
conclusion can be made.

    (a) ∠*M* is a right angle.

    (b) $\overline{MP}$ // $\overline{OR}$

    (c) m∠*O* = 90

    (d) All of the above can be made.

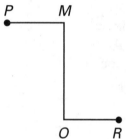

10. Each figure below pictures a figure and its image under an   **10.** _____
isometry. Which is a rotation?

    (a)   (b)   (c)   (d)

11. In the figure at the right,   **11.** _____
if m∠*TON* = 10*x*, then
m∠*COW* = ___?___.

    (a) 18   (b) 180 − 10*x*

    (c) 10*x*   (d) 360 − 10*x*

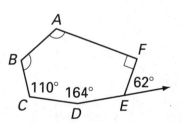

12. In the figure at the right,   **12.** _____
find m∠*A*.

    (a) 148   (b) 138

    (c) 119   (d) 28

13. The reflection image over the *y*-axis of the point with   **13.** _____
coordinates (*c*, *d*) is

    (a) (-*c*, *d*).   (b) (*c*, -*d*).   (c) (-*c*, -*d*).   (d) (*d*, *c*).

14. Which is the most specific name possible
for the figure shown at the right?

(a) trapezoid   (b) parallelogram

(c) rectangle   (d) isosceles trapezoid

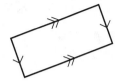

14. _____

15. What is the sum of the measures of the interior angles of a
convex 15-gon?

(a) 5400   (b) 2700   (c) 2520   (d) 2340

15. _____

16. In the figure at the right,
$r_n \circ r_m(ABCD) = A'B'C'D'$.
If $m\angle 1 = 43$, what is the
magnitude of this rotation?

(a) 43°

(b) -43°

(c) 86°

(d) -86°

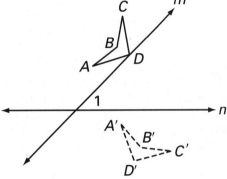

16. _____

17. Quadrilateral *RSTU* at the right is a
trapezoid with bases $\overline{UR}$ and $\overline{TS}$.
If $m\angle R = 117$ and $m\angle T = 86$,
then $m\angle S = \underline{\quad ? \quad}$.

(a) 63   (b) 86

(c) 94   (d) 117

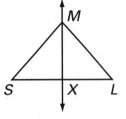

17. _____

18. In the figure at the right, $\overleftrightarrow{MX}$ is
the ⊥ bisector of $\overline{SL}$, $SL = 20g$,
and $ML = 15g$. What is MS?

(a) 7.5*g*   (b) 10*g*

(c) 15*g*   (d) 20*g*

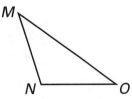

18. _____

19. △*MNO* at the right is isosceles with
base $\overline{MO}$. The measure of ∠*N* is
three times the measure of ∠*O*.
What is the measure of ∠*N*?

(a) 36   (b) 72

(c) 108   (d) 135

19. _____

20. Which is a pair of congruent letters?   20. _____

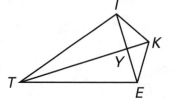

(a) **Zz** (b) **ZZ** (c) **ZƧ** (d) **NZ**

21. *True or false.* In Euclidean geometry, lines are dense.   21. _____

22. Quadrilateral *KITE* at the right is a kite with ends *K* and *T*. Name three distinct pairs of congruent segments in the figure.   22. _____

_____

_____

23. The distance from Tom's house to Rosa's house is 3.2 miles. The distance from Tom's house to Abdul's house is 1.4 miles. The distance from Rosa's house to Abdul's house is 4.5 miles. Is it accurate to say that Tom's house is between Rosa's house and Abdul's house? Explain and make a drawing at the right to illustrate your answer.

_____

_____

24. Give the slope of the line through (-7, 15) and (2, 10).   24. _____

25. Construct the circle that passes through points *F, G,* and *H.*

F
•

H•

•
G

26. a. Locate the center of symmetry of the regular 11-gon at the right. Label it as point *C*.

26. a.

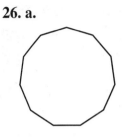

b. The regular 11-gon in Part **a** has ___?___-fold rotation symmetry.

b. _____

27. a. In the figure at the right, draw $r_n \circ r_m (\triangle ABC)$.

27. a.

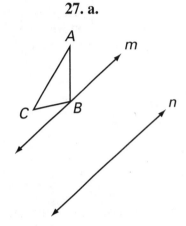

b. What transformation is $r_n \circ r_m$?

b. _____

28. Use the figure at the right. Supply justifications in the argument.

Given: $r_s(P) = M$.

To prove: *RMLP* is a kite.

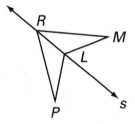

a. 0. $r_s(P) = M$

28. a. _____

b. 1. $r_s(R) = R$; $r_s(L) = L$

b. _____

c. 2. $RP = RM$; $PL = ML$

c. _____

d. 3. *RMLP* is a kite.

d. _____

29. Write an argument for this proof.

Given: ∠B ≅ ∠1.
To prove: ∠B ≅ ∠BCA.

Conclusions	Justifications
_____	_____
_____	_____
_____	_____
_____	_____

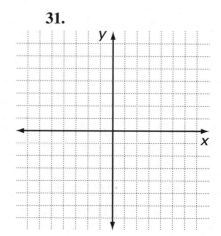

30. Laura told her sister, "If you take my turn doing dishes on Sunday, I'll take your turn on Monday." Laura did the dishes on Monday. Did Laura's sister do the dishes on Sunday? Explain your reasoning.

_____

_____

31. On the coordinate axes at the right, draw $\overline{PQ}$ with endpoints $P = (-3, -2)$ and $Q = (4, 1)$. Then draw the translation image of $\overline{PQ}$ determined by the vector (-1, 2).

31.

32. Draw the symmetry line(s) of the design at the right.

32.

Check all your work carefully.

QUIZ

In 1 and 2, a triangle is drawn with certain measures indicated.
a. Are all triangles with these measures congruent?
b. Why or why not?

1.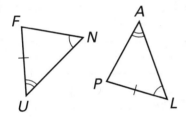

2.

1. a. _____

   b. _____

   _____

2. a. _____

   b. _____

   _____

In 3 and 4, if the triangles are congruent, justify with a triangle congruence theorem and indicate corresponding vertices. Otherwise, write *not enough information to know*.

3. 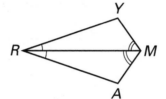 4.

3. _____

   _____

4. _____

   _____

5. **a.** Which sides of $\triangle XYZ$ at the right are congruent?

   b. What theorem justifies your answer to Part **a**?

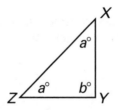

5. a. _____

   b. _____

6. Write an argument for this proof.

   Given: $\overline{MN} \cong \overline{MP}$;
   $\overrightarrow{MO}$ bisects $\angle NMP$.
   To prove: $\angle MON \cong \angle MOP$.

   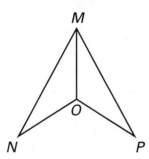

Conclusions	Justifications
_____	_____
_____	_____
_____	_____
_____	_____

QUIZ

You will need a ruler for this quiz.

1. A floor is to be pieced together using tiles shaped like the triangle at the right. In the space at the right, draw a section of the floor.

1.

2. Name *two pairs* of overlapping triangles in the figure at the right.

2. _____

_____

3. Write an argument for this proof.

Given: *MNOP* is a kite with ends *P* and *N*; $\overline{PT} \cong \overline{PS}$.

To prove: $\triangle SMP \cong \triangle TOP$.

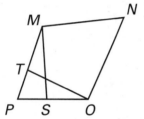

Conclusions	Justifications
_____	_____
_____	_____
_____	_____
_____	_____

In 4 and 5, what triangle congruence theorem tells you that the triangles in each pair are congruent?

4.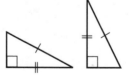

5.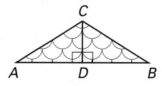

4. _____

5. _____

6. In the figure at the right, $\overline{AC}$ and $\overline{BC}$ are beams of the same length at the end of a roof. $\overline{CD}$ is a support beam that is perpendicular to base beam $\overline{AB}$. Explain why $\angle A \cong \angle B$.

_____

_____

CHAPTER 7 TEST, Form A

In 1 and 2, if the triangles are congruent, justify
with a triangle congruence theorem and indicate
corresponding vertices. Otherwise, write *not
enough information to know.*

1.

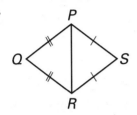

2.

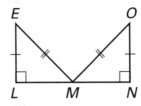

1. _____

_____

2. _____

_____

3. Refer to △*ABC* at the right.

a. Find m∠*A*.

b. Find m∠*B*.

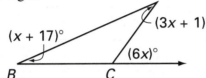

3. a. _____

b. _____

In 4 and 5, a triangle is drawn with certain measures indicated.
a. Are all triangles with these measures congruent?
b. Why or why not?

4.

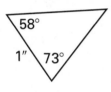

5.

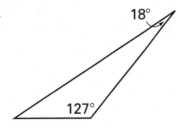

4. a. _____

b. _____

_____

5. a. _____

b. _____

_____

6. Refer to the figure at the right.
$\overline{WY}$ and $\overline{XZ}$ intersect at *A*.
If *AX* = 4, *AZ* = 4,
AW = 5, and *AY* = 5, is
WXYZ a parallelogram?
Explain your answer.

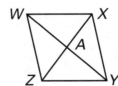

_____

_____

_____

► **CHAPTER 7 TEST, Form A** *page 2*

7. Refer to parallelogram *ABCD* at the right. If m∠*BAC* = 47 and m∠*ACB* = 31, find as many other angle measures as you can.

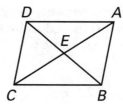

7. _____

_____

_____

_____

In 8 and 9, write an argument for the proof.

8. Given: ⊙*S* and ⊙*T* intersecting at *M* and *O*.
   To prove: △*MST* ≅ △*OST*.

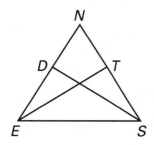

Conclusions	Justifications
_____	_____
_____	_____
_____	_____
_____	_____

9. Given: ∠*ETN* ≅ ∠*SDN*; $\overline{NT}$ ≅ $\overline{ND}$.
   To prove: ∠*NET* ≅ ∠*NSD*.

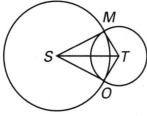

Conclusions	Justifications
_____	_____
_____	_____
_____	_____
_____	_____

10. The figure at the right shows vertical posts of equal length called *balusters* separating two railings of equal length, $\overline{AB}$ and $\overline{CD}$. Explain why $\overline{AB} \parallel \overline{CD}$.

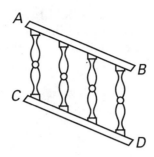

_____

_____

11. Refer to $\triangle JET$ at the right.

   a. Name the largest angle.

   b. Name the smallest angle.

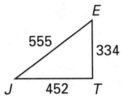

11. a. _____

    b. _____

12. Name the sides of $\triangle BOX$ at the right in order from shortest to longest.

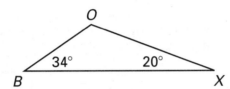

12. _____

13. In the figure at the right, $\overline{PR}$ and $\overline{PS}$ are ropes of equal length attached to the top of pole $\overline{PQ}$. $\overline{PQ}$ is perpendicular to $\overline{RS}$. Explain why $\angle 1 \cong \angle 2$.

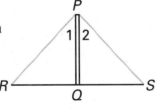

_____

_____

14. The tessellation below is part of a basket from Uganda. Trace a possible fundamental region.

14.

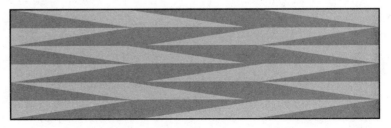

Check all your work carefully.

Name _____

CHAPTER 7 TEST, Form B

In 1 and 2, if the triangles are congruent, justify
with a triangle congruence theorem and indicate
corresponding vertices. Otherwise, write *not
enough information to know.*

1.

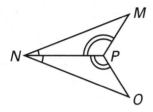

2.

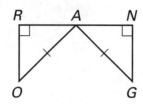

1. _____

_____

2. _____

_____

3. Refer to △*LMN* at the right.

    a. Find m∠*M*.

    b. Find m∠*N*.

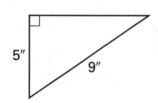

3. **a.** _____

    b. _____

In 4 and 5, a triangle is drawn with certain measures indicated.
a. Are all triangles with these measures congruent?
b. Why or why not?

4.

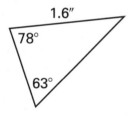

5.

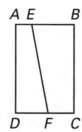

4. **a.** _____

    b. _____

    _____

5. **a.** _____

    b. _____

    _____

6. Refer to the figure at the right.
If $AD = 10$, $BC = 10$, $AE = 2$,
$EB = 5$, $DF = 4$, and $FC = 3$,
is *ABCD* a parallelogram?
Explain your answer.

      A E   B

      D F C

_____

_____

_____

7. Refer to parallelogram *WXYZ* at the right. If *WX* = 10, *XY* = 6, and *OX* = 7, find as many other lengths as you can.

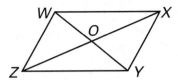

7. _____

_____

_____

_____

In 8 and 9, write an argument for the proof.

8. Given: *PARL* is a parallelogram. $\overline{MP} \cong \overline{NR}$.

     To prove: $\triangle MPA \cong \triangle NRL$.

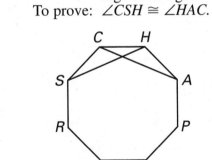

Conclusions	Justifications
_____	_____
_____	_____
_____	_____
_____	_____

9. Given: *CHAPTERS* is a regular octagon.

     To prove: $\angle CSH \cong \angle HAC$.

Conclusions	Justifications
_____	_____
_____	_____
_____	_____
_____	_____

10. The figure at the right shows a rectangular street blockade with alternating orange and white stripes. Each stripe has the same width at the top of the blockade as at the bottom. Explain why $\overline{AC} \parallel \overline{BD}$.

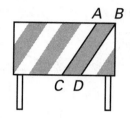

_____

_____

11. Refer to $\triangle TOM$ at the right.

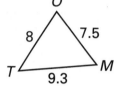
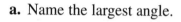

   a. Name the largest angle.

   b. Name the smallest angle.

11. a. _____

   b. _____

12. Name the sides of $\triangle SUN$ at the right in order from shortest to longest.

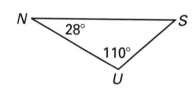

12. _____

13. In the figure at the right, posts $\overline{WX}$ and $\overline{YZ}$ are perpendicular to the water line $\overleftrightarrow{XZ}$, and rise to an equal height above it. $\overline{WV}$ and $\overline{YV}$ are ropes of equal length that connect the tops of the posts to a float at the water line. Explain why $\overline{XV} \cong \overline{ZV}$.

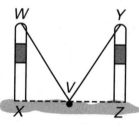

_____

_____

14. The tessellation below is part of a pattern of beadwork from Botswana. Trace a possible fundamental region.

14.

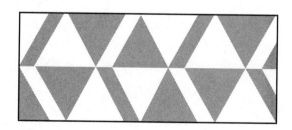

Check all your work carefully.

CHAPTER 7 TEST, Form C

1. Sketch a triangle and label it $\triangle ABC$. Then label three measures of your triangle in such a way that any other triangle with those same measures would be congruent to $\triangle ABC$. Explain how you know that any such triangle would be congruent.

2. Based on the theorems that you studied in this chapter, state as many facts as you can about the figure at the right.

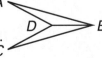

3. a. The only geometric tool that Clark has is a ruler. How could he use it to determine whether *JKLM* is a parallelogram?

   b. The only geometric tool Lois has is a protractor. How could she use it to determine whether *JKLM* is a parallelogram?

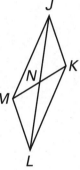

4. a. Name one regular polygon that tessellates the plane. Make a sketch of the tessellation.

   b. Name one regular polygon that does *not* tessellate the plane. Justify your answer.

5. Suppose you were asked to write a proof argument for each of the two situations shown at the right. Describe how your two proof arguments would be alike and how they would be different.

Given: $\overline{AB} \cong \overline{CB}$;
$\overline{AD} \cong \overline{CD}$.

To prove: $\triangle ABD \cong \triangle CBD$.

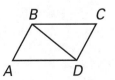

Given: $\overline{AB} \cong \overline{CD}$;
$\overline{AD} \cong \overline{CB}$.

To prove: $\angle A \cong \angle C$.

CHAPTER 7 TEST, Form D

In architecture, a *truss* is a rigid framework that supports a structure. A truss usually is made of wooden beams or steel bars.

The figures on this page show five styles of trusses that are used to support roofs and bridges.

a. Refer to the diagram of the scissors truss at the right. Name a pair of overlapping triangles that *appear* to be congruent to each other. Be sure to indicate corresponding vertices.

b. An architect's assistant has provided two specifications for the scissors truss: $AC = EC = 20$ feet, and $m\angle C = 66$.

  i. Explain why this is *not* enough information to guarantee that the triangles you named in Part **a** are congruent.

  ii. Supply one additional specification to guarantee that the overlapping triangles *are* congruent. (Be sure that any measures you supply are reasonable.)

  iii. Justify your response to Part ii with a triangle congruence theorem.

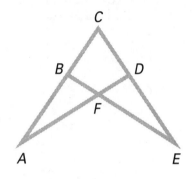

c. The scissors truss also contains a pair of triangles that are *not* overlapping. Write an argument to show that, if the overlapping triangles are congruent, these triangles also must be congruent.

d. Why is it important that the pairs of triangles you examined in Parts **a** through **c** be congruent?

e. Consider the king-post truss or queen-post truss shown on this page. Identify all the pairs of triangles that appear to be congruent. Be sure to indicate corresponding vertices.

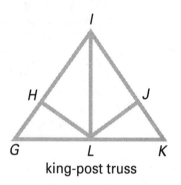

king-post truss

Now suppose you are an architect's assistant. Supply a set of specifications for the truss that would guarantee all the pairs of triangles you identified to be congruent. Be sure that the specifications are reasonable, and be careful to supply no more measures than are necessary. (Supplying too many measures is called *overdetermining* the figure. If you overdetermine a triangle, you run the risk of providing contradictory information.) For each pair of triangles, identify the triangle congruence theorem that you can use to prove them congruent.

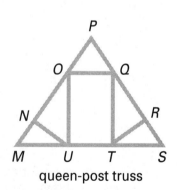

queen-post truss

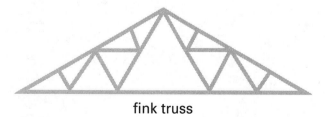

fink truss

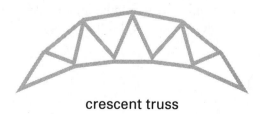

crescent truss

CHAPTER 7 TEST, Cumulative Form

1. Refer to the figure at the right. Are the triangles congruent? If so, justify with a triangle congruence theorem and indicate corresponding vertices. Otherwise, write *not enough information to know.*

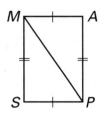

1. _____

2. A triangle is drawn at the right with certain measures indicated.

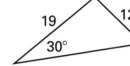

   a. Are all triangles with these measures congruent?

2. a. _____

   b. Why or why not?

   b. _____

   _____

3. Refer to parallelogram *PARL* at the right. Let *PA* = 4 and *RT* = 2.8.

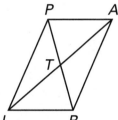

   a. What other segments have length 4?

3. a. _____

   b. What other segments have length 2.8?

   b. _____

4. a. Refer to quadrilateral *TRAP* at the right. Explain why *TRAP* is a trapezoid.

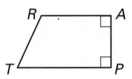

   _____

   _____

   b. If m∠*T* = 2*g*, then m∠*R* = ___?___.

   b. _____

5. a. In the figure at the right, what is the relationship between m∠*M* and m∠*PNO*?

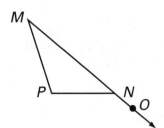

5. a. _____

   b. If m∠*M* = 4*t* and m∠*P* = 9*t*, then m∠*ONP* = ___?___.

   b. _____

6. Write an argument for this proof.

Given: $\overline{AB} \cong \overline{CD}$; $\overline{AC} \cong \overline{CE}$;   Conclusions   Justifications
$\overline{AB} \mathbin{/\mkern-5mu/} \overline{CD}$.
To prove: $\angle B \cong \angle D$.

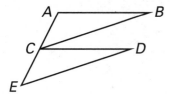

_____   _____

_____   _____

_____   _____

_____   _____

7. *Multiple choice.* Suppose m$\angle O = 4t$ and $\angle O$ is obtuse.   **7.** _____
Which *best* represents all possible values of *t*?

(a) $4t > 90$ (b) $t > 90$

(c) $0 < 4t < 180$ (d) $22.5 < t < 45$

8. a. Locate the center of symmetry of   **8. a.**
the logo at the right. Label it as point *R*.

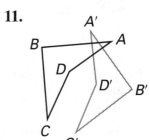

b. The logo in Part **a** has ___?___-fold rotation symmetry.   **b.** _____

9. Refer to quadrilateral *BATH* at   **9.** _____
the right. Find m$\angle THE$.

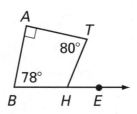

10. From the information given in   **10.** _____
the drawing at the right, what
quadrilateral is pictured? Be
as specific as possible.

11. In the figure at the right, draw and label the reflecting   **11.**
line *m* for which $r_m(ABCD) = A'B'C'D'$.

12. Write an argument for this proof.

Given: *PENTA* is a regular
pentagon.
To prove: △*PAT* ≅ △*NTA*.

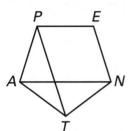

Conclusions   Justifications

_____   _____

_____   _____

_____   _____

_____   _____

13. Figures I and II at the right are
two views of the same seesaw.
The *fulcrum* $\overline{CD}$ is perpendicular
to the ground and bisects the
plank $\overline{AB}$. Explain why ∠*CAD*
in figure I is congruent to
∠*CBD* in figure II.

Figure I   Figure II

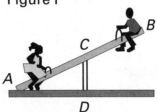 

_____

_____

14. The figure at the right shows several
strands of pasta. A pasta machine is
used to make cuts $\overline{MP}$ and $\overline{NO}$
that are parallel and equal in
length. Explain why $\overline{MN} \cong \overline{PO}$.

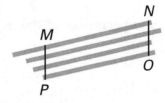

_____

_____

15. *True or false.* Every square is a rectangle.   **15.** _____

16. *Multiple choice.* In △*ABC*, which is uniquely determined?   **16.** _____

   (a)   a line that bisects ∠*A* and bisects $\overline{BC}$

   (b)   a line that bisects ∠*B* and is perpendicular to $\overline{AC}$

   (c)   a line that passes through *C* and is parallel to $\overline{AB}$

   (d)   a line that passes through $\overline{BC}$ at its midpoint

Check all your work carefully.

QUIZ

1. Explain the difference between the *perimeter* of a polygon and its *area*.

_____

_____

_____

2. Find the perimeter of a regular heptagon in which one side has length $4t$.

2. _____

3. The length of one side of a square is $\frac{3}{4}$ foot.

   a. Find its perimeter.

   3. **a.** _____

   b. Find its area.

   b. _____

4. Estimate the area of the Salton Sea in California using the grid at the right.

4. _____

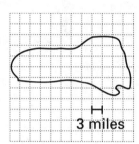

3 miles

In 5 and 6, find the area and perimeter of the polygon.

5.
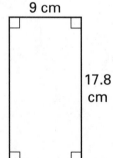
9 cm

17.8 cm

6.
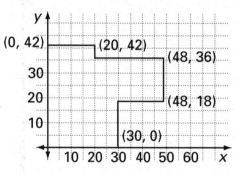

5. _____

_____

6. _____

_____

7. A homeowner is planning to carpet a rectangular room that is 24 feet long and 18 feet wide. The price of the carpeting is $12 per square yard, including installation. What will be the cost of carpeting the room?

7. _____

8. *True or false.* If two rectangles have the same perimeter, then they also have the same area.

8. _____

Name _____

QUIZ

In 1 and 2, calculate the area of the figure.

1.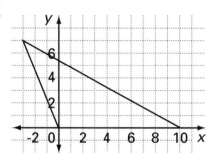

2.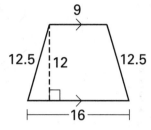

1. _____

2. _____

3. A rectangular piece of cloth is 20 cm long and 15 cm wide. Three triangular pieces are cut from its corners as shown at the right. What is the area of the cloth that remains?

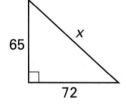

3. _____

In 4 and 5, find the length of the missing side.

4.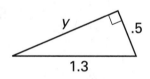

5.

4. _____

5. _____

6. Could the numbers 2, 3, and $\sqrt{13}$ be the lengths of the sides of a right triangle? Give a reason for your answer.

6. _____

   _____

   _____

   _____

7. A 12-foot ladder rests against a wall so that the bottom is 2.2 feet from the base of the wall. To what height does the ladder reach up the wall?

7. _____

8. The length of the hypotenuse of a right triangle is 45 mm and the length of one leg is 27 mm. Find the area of the triangle.

8. _____

CHAPTER 8 TEST, Form A

1. Kite *RSTU* with ends
   R and *T* has lengths of
   sides as shown at the right.
   Find its perimeter.

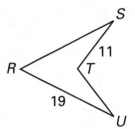

1. _____

In 2 and 3, calculate the area of the figure.

2.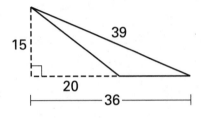

3.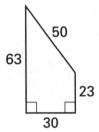

2. _____

3. _____

4. Find the perimeter of a regular decagon in which one
   side has length 3*p*.

4. _____

5. Find the area of
   parallelogram
   PARL, shown at
   the right.

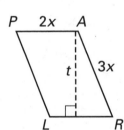

5. _____

6. Find the exact
   circumference and area
   of the circle at the right.

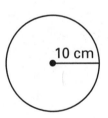

10 cm

6. _____

In 7 and 8, find the length of the missing side.

7.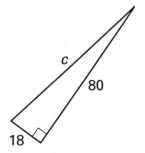

c
80
18

8.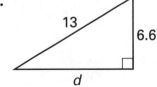

13   6.6
d

7. _____

8. _____

▶ **CHAPTER 8 TEST, Form A** *page 2*

9. The two legs of a right triangle have lengths 10 and 18.75. What is the perimeter of the triangle?

9. _____

10. In ⊙O at the right, m$\widehat{XNY}$ = 240°
    and OY = 18.

    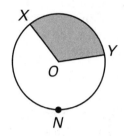

    a. Find the length of $\widehat{XY}$.

    10. a. _____

    b. Find the area of the shaded sector.

    b. _____

11. Find the perimeter of a square with area 64,516 km².

11. _____

12. A rectangular pool is 24 feet wide and 30 feet long. It is surrounded by a walk that is 2 ft wide, as shown at the right. What is the outer perimeter of the walk?

    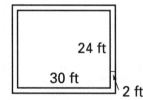

12. _____

13. A rectangular bathroom floor is 5 feet wide and 6 feet long. It is to be covered with square tiles that measure 6 inches on each side and cost $1.80 apiece. The tiles are to be laid with no space between them. What will be the total cost of the tiles?

13. _____

14. Find the area of the octagon on the coordinate axes at the right.

    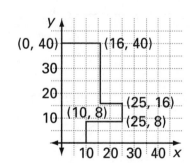

14. _____

15. A rope has been used to tie a boat to a dock, as shown at the right. To the nearest tenth of a foot, what is the horizontal distance from the boat to the base of the dock?

    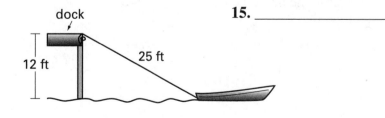

15. _____

16. *RSTU* at the right is a square with side 18 units. A semicircle is placed so its diameter lies along one side of the square and is equal in length to the side of the square. To the nearest tenth of a unit, what is the area of the shaded region?

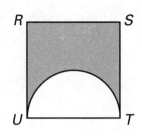

16. _____

17. Could the numbers 16, 24, and 25 be the lengths of the sides of a right triangle? Give a reason for your answer.

17. _____

_____

_____

_____

18. Find the area of the quadrilateral on the coordinate axes at the right.

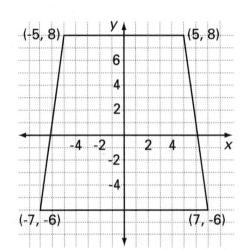

18. _____

19. An archery target is shown at the right. If an arrow hits this target at random, what is the probability that it hits the bull's-eye? Round your answer to the nearest hundredth.

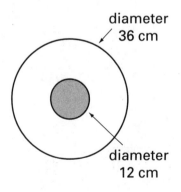

diameter 36 cm

diameter 12 cm

19. _____

20. Estimate the area of Lake
Winnebago in Wisconsin
using the grid at the right.

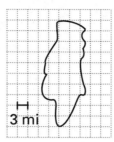

20. _____

21. The listening area for a radio station extends 55 miles in
every direction from its signal tower. To the nearest square
mile, what is the size of the station's listening area?

21. _____

22. The area of a triangle is 36 square units. The length of
one side is 16 units. Find the length of the altitude to
that side.

22. _____

Check all your work carefully.

CHAPTER 8 TEST, Form B

1. Kite *ABCD* with ends
   B and *D* has lengths of
   sides as shown at the right.
   Find its perimeter.

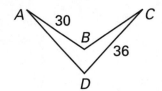

1. _____

In 2 and 3, calculate the area of the figure.

2.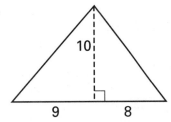

3.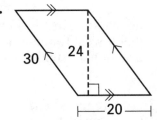

2. _____

3. _____

4. Find the length of one side of a regular octagon whose
   perimeter is *h*.

4. _____

5. Find the area of
   trapezoid *TRAP*,
   shown at the right.

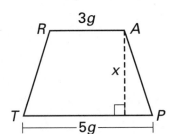

5. _____

6. Find the exact
   circumference and area
   of the circle at the right.

6. _____

   _____

In 7 and 8, find the length of the missing side.

7.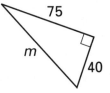

8.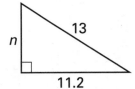

7. _____

8. _____

9. The two legs of a right triangle have lengths 6.25 and 15. What is the perimeter of the triangle?

9. _____

10. In $\odot O$ at the right, $m\overset{\frown}{ABC} = 210°$ and $OB = 12$.

    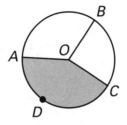

    a. Find the length of $\overset{\frown}{ADC}$.

    10. a. _____

    b. Find the area of the shaded sector.

    b. _____

11. Find the perimeter of a square with area 24,336 m².

11. _____

12. A rectangular pasture is 32 feet wide and 50 feet long. As shown at the right, one side of the pasture is against a barn wall. There is a 7-foot gate in the adjacent side. The rest of the pasture is enclosed by a wooden fence. What is the total length of the wooden fence?

    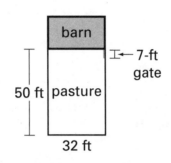

12. _____

13. A rectangular hall floor is 3 feet wide and 15 feet long. It is to be covered with square tiles that measure 9 inches on each side and cost $2.30 apiece. The tiles are to be laid with no space between them. What will be the total cost of the tiles?

13. _____

14. Find the area of the octagon on the coordinate axes at the right.

    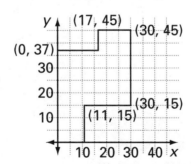

14. _____

15. There are two different paths you can use to cross the rectangular park shown at the right. One path is laid out along a diagonal of the park. The other path is laid out along two adjacent sides. To the nearest tenth of a meter, how much shorter is the diagonal path than the path along the two adjacent sides?

    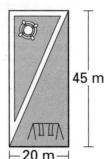

15. _____

16. *JKLM* at the right is a square with side 24 units. Two semicircles are placed so their diameters lie along one side of the square. The two diameters together are equal in length to the side of the square. To the nearest tenth of a unit, what is the area of the shaded region?

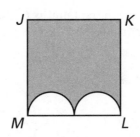

16. _____

17. Could the numbers 8, 6, and 9 be the lengths of the sides of a right triangle? Give a reason for your answer.

17. _____

_____

_____

_____

18. Find the area of the quadrilateral on the coordinate axes at the right.

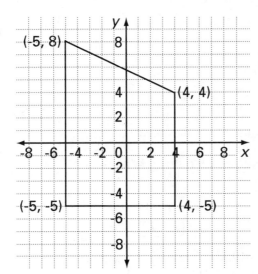

18. _____

19. A standard dart board is shown at the right. If a dart hits this board at random, what is the probability that it hits the circular bull's-eye at the center? Round your answer to the nearest thousandth.

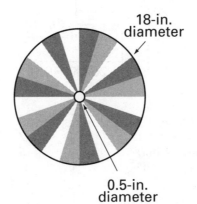

18-in. diameter

0.5-in. diameter

19. _____

20. Estimate the area of the Waterton-Glacier International Peace Park (located in Montana and Alberta, Canada) using the grid at the right.

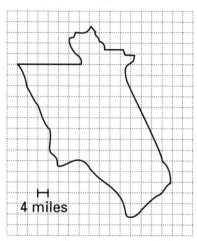

4 miles

20. _____

21. The listening area for a radio station extends 45 miles in every direction from its signal tower. To the nearest square mile, what is the size of the station's listening area?

21. _____

22. The area of a triangle is 33 square units. The length of one side is 12 units. Find the length of the altitude to that side.

22. _____

Check all your work carefully.

CHAPTER 8 TEST, Form C

1. Explain why this statement is not true.

If two kites have the same perimeter, then they are congruent.

Make a true statement by replacing "kite" with the name of a different quadrilateral.

2. Sketch a triangle that is equal in area to parallelogram *QRST* at the right.

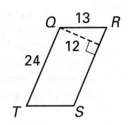

3. State as many facts as you can about quadrilateral *ABCD* below.

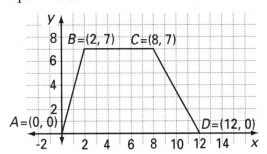

4. The sketch below shows three circular disks cut from a rectangular sheet of metal. Explain how you can tell that the sketch is labeled incorrectly. How do you think the sketch should be labeled? Using your labels, calculate the amount of metal that is wasted.

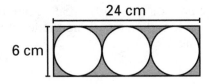

24 cm

6 cm

5. Joel wants to dig a rectangular garden and enclose it entirely with a low fence. He has 30 feet of fencing, and he wants to use it all. Give the dimensions of two different rectangles he could enclose with it. Which of these rectangles has the greater area?

6. Explain the difference between the Pythagorean Theorem and the Pythagorean Converse Theorem. Give an example of how you might use each theorem.

CHAPTER 8 TEST, Form D

The large plot of land shown at the bottom of the page has been donated to the town of Mulberry to be made into a public park. The town council has begun discussing possible ways to landscape the park.

a. One councilor wants a fence placed around the entire plot of land.

   i. What would be the total length of fence needed?

   ii. Suppose it would cost $5.19 per foot to construct the fence. What would be the total cost?

b. Another councilor has suggested that a 3-foot-wide walkway be laid across the park from the corner labeled *A* to the corner labeled *B*.

   i. What would be the length of this walkway to the nearest foot?

   ii. Suppose it would cost $7.59 per *square foot* to pave the walkway with concrete. What would be the approximate total cost?

c. A third councilor is interested in constructing a children's play area that is circular in shape.

   i. What is the greatest diameter possible for such a play area?

   ii. Suppose it would cost $2.75 per square foot to cover the play area with sand. What would be the total cost of the sand for the largest possible play area?

d. Estimate the area occupied by Hobson Pond.

e. Suppose you are one of the councilors. Draw a plan for landscaping the entire park. You may use some of the ideas above if you wish, but you must also incorporate some original ideas. At the right is a list of some possible features of the park and their costs. (If you use a feature that is not on this list, make a reasonable estimate of its cost.) Then prepare a report in which you present your plan to the town council together with an estimate of its total cost.

Landscape Features	
fencing	$5.19/ft
concrete walkways	$7.59/sq ft
sand	$2.75/sq ft
grass	$3.25/sq ft
flower beds	$10.39/sq ft

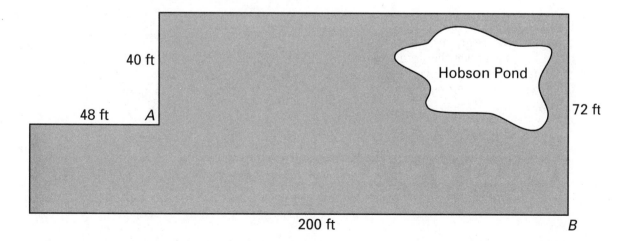

CHAPTER 8 TEST, Cumulative Form

1. Find the perimeter of a regular pentagon in which one side has length 3*s*.

1. _____

In 2 and 3, calculate the area of the figure.

2.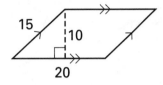

3.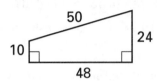

2. _____

3. _____

In 4 and 5, refer to ⊙*O* at the right, where $\overline{BD}$ is a diameter and m∠*AOF* = m∠*FOE* = m∠*EOD*.

4. Find m$\widehat{ED}$.

4. _____

5. Find m$\widehat{FCD}$.

5. _____

6. Is the network shown at the right traversable?

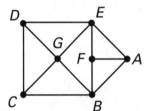

6. _____

7. Refer to △*OPE* at the right. Find m∠*P*.

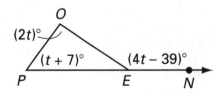

7. _____

8. Refer to the figure at the right. If the triangles are congruent, justify with a triangle congruence theorem and indicate corresponding vertices. Otherwise, write *not enough information to know.*

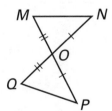

8. _____

9. Find the exact circumference and area of the circle at the right.

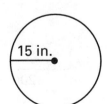

15 in.

9. _____

_____

In 10 and 11, find the length of the missing side.

10.
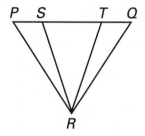

11.
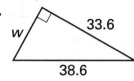

10. _____

11. _____

12. Write an argument for this proof.

Given: $\triangle PQR$ is isosceles
with base $\overline{PQ}$;
$\angle PRS \cong \angle QRT$.
To prove: $\overline{PS} \cong \overline{QT}$.

Conclusions	Justifications
_____	_____
_____	_____
_____	_____
_____	_____
_____	_____

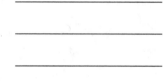

13. A patio is square-shaped and has a perimeter of 14 meters.   13. _____
What is its area?

14. The shape of a tile is a parallelogram. Can a floor be covered
using tiles of this shape? Explain your answer.

_____

_____

15. *Multiple choice.* Given that $r_\ell(\overline{PT}) = \overline{QT}$,
which statement justifies the
conclusion that $r_\ell(\overline{QT}) = \overline{PT}$?

(a) definition of reflection

(b) Figure Reflection Theorem

(c) Flip-Flop Theorem

(d) definition of congruent figures

15. _____

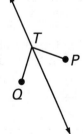

16. When Gus walks his dog, he uses a retractable leash attached to his dog's collar. He holds the leash at a height 1 foot above the height of the dog's collar. How far from Gus is his dog when the leash has been pulled out to its full 25-foot length?

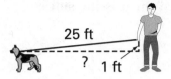

25 ft

? 1 ft

16. _____

17. The diameter of ⊙O at the right is 40 km.

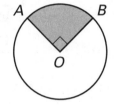

A   B

O

a. Find the length of $\overset{\frown}{AB}$.

b. Find the area of the shaded sector.

17. a. _____

    b. _____

18. Find the area of the triangle on the coordinate axes at the right.

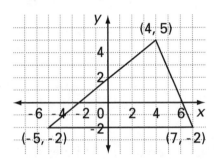

y

(4, 5)

4

2

-6 -4 -2 0   2   4   6   x

-2

(-5, -2)   (7, -2)

18. _____

19. The listening area for a radio station extends 30 miles in every direction from its signal tower. To the nearest square mile, what is the size of its listening area?

19. _____

20. The length of each side of a square is tripled.

a. What happens to its area?

b. What happens to its perimeter?

20. a. _____

    b. _____

21. Could 35, 84, and 91 be the lengths of the three sides of a right triangle? Give a reason for your answer.

_____

_____

_____

22. *Multiple choice.* Erik drew a triangle with one side having length 5.5 cm and two angles having measures 115 and 25. The triangle he drew

    (a) is uniquely determined.

    (b) is not uniquely determined.

    (c) may or may not be uniquely determined.

22. _____

23. Refer to parallelogram *ABCD* at the right. If *ED* = 2*a*, what is the length of $\overline{BD}$?

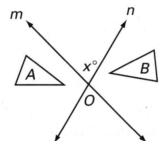

23. _____

In 24 and 25, use the figure below, in which
$\mathbf{r}_n \circ \mathbf{r}_m(A) = (B)$.

24. *Multiple choice.* $\mathbf{r}_n \circ \mathbf{r}_m$ is a

    (a) reflection.

    (b) rotation.

    (c) translation.

    (d) glide reflection.

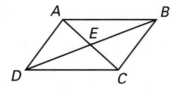

24. _____

25. The magnitude of $\mathbf{r}_n \circ \mathbf{r}_m$ is
    ___?___.

25. _____

26. In the figure at the right, $\overrightarrow{TR}$ bisects ∠*STL*.
If m∠*STR* = *x* + *y*,
then m∠*STL* = ___?___.

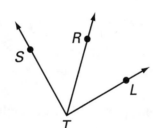

26. _____

Check all your work carefully.

QUIZ   **Lessons 9-1 Through 9-4**

You will need a ruler for this quiz.

1. *True or false.* If two different planes intersect, they can have exactly one point in common.

   1. _____

2. If a line is perpendicular to at least __?__ line(s) in a plane, then it is perpendicular to the plane.

   2. _____

3. The figure at the right below is a right pentagonal prism.

   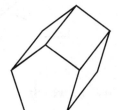

   a. How many lateral faces does the prism have?

      3. a. _____

   b. What is the shape of each lateral face?

      b. _____

   c. How many bases does the prism have?

      c. _____

   d. How many edges does it have?

      d. _____

4. A pyramid has a total of 15 faces.

   a. What shape is its base?

      4. a. _____

   b. How many edges does the pyramid have?

      b. _____

5. In the space at the right, draw an oblique cylinder.

   5.

In 6–8, use the regular pentagonal pyramid at the right below.

6. The length of which segment is the slant height of the pyramid?

   6. _____

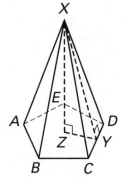

7. The length of which segment is the height of the pyramid?

   7. _____

8. Let $XY = 82$ and $XZ = 80$. Find ZY.

   8. _____

QUIZ

You will need a ruler for this quiz.

In 1–2, use the right cone at the right.

1. a. Sketch a plane section not parallel to and not intersecting the base.

1. a.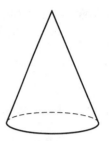

b. Name the shape of the section you drew in Part **a**.

b. _____

2. How many symmetry planes does the right cone have?

2. _____

3. The area of the great circle of a sphere is 36π. What is the diameter of the sphere?

3. _____

4. The figure at the right is a regular triangular pyramid.

a. Does the figure have bilateral symmetry?

b. How many symmetry planes does the figure have?

4. a. _____

b. _____

5. In the spaces designated, draw front, side, and top views of the school bus shown below.

5.

FRONT   SIDE   TOP

6. In the space at the right, draw a net for a right cone.

6.

Name

CHAPTER 9 TEST, Form A

You will need a ruler for this test.

In 1 and 2, draw the figure in the space at the right.

1. two intersecting planes

   1.

2. an oblique pentagonal prism

   2.

3. In the figure at the right, line m lies in plane T and $\ell \perp m$. Is line ℓ necessarily perpendicular to plane T? Explain your answer.

   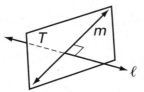

   3. _____

   _____

   _____

   _____

   _____

   _____

In 4–6, use the right square pyramid at the right.

4. **a.** Sketch a plane section not parallel to and not intersecting the base.

   4. **a.**

   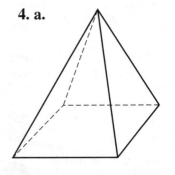

   b. Name the shape of the section you drew in Part **a** as precisely as possible.

   b. _____

5. As precisely as possible, name the shape of any plane section that is parallel to the base.

   5. _____

6. How many symmetry planes does this figure have?

   6. _____

7. *True or false.* A Mercator projection is an accurate representation of the relative size of land masses on Earth.

   7. _____

8. In the spaces designated, draw front, side, and top views
   of the regular hexagonal pyramid shown below.

   8.

   FRONT   SIDE   TOP

In 9 and 10, use the net shown below.

9. As specifically
   as possible, name the
   figure that would be
   formed from the net.

   9. _____

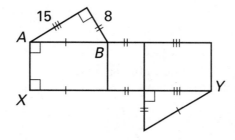

10. **a.** Find *AB*.

    b. Find *XY*.

    10. a. _____

    b. _____

11. In the right cylinder
    shown at the right,
    OB = 14. Find the area
    of a base of the cylinder.
    Give an exact value.

    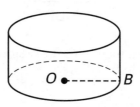

    11. _____

12. **a.** In the space at the right, draw a sphere with radius
    1.5 cm. Sketch a great circle of the sphere.

    12. a.

    b. What is the circumference of the great circle? Round
    to the nearest tenth of a centimeter.

    b. _____

13. In the spaces designated, draw front, side, and top views
    of the dresser shown below.

    13.

    FRONT   SIDE   TOP

14. In the right square pyramid at the right, $EH = 50$ and $ET = 54$.

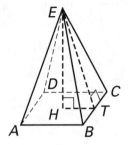

    a. Find the area of $\triangle EHT$.

    b. Find the area of the base.

14. a. _____

    b. _____

15. In the space at the right, draw a net for a cylinder.

15.

16. Give as specific a name as possible to the surface studied in this chapter with these views.

16. _____

    FRONT   TOP   SIDE

17. In the space at the right, draw a map with four regions that needs two colors in order to be colored.

17.

In 18 and 19, tell which three-dimensional figure most resembles the real-world object. Give as specific a name as you can, distinguishing solids from surfaces.

18. a shoe box

18. _____

19. a log cut from a tree trunk

19. _____

20. Use the given views of the building.

    FRONT   SIDE   TOP

    a. How tall in stories is the building?

20. a. _____

    b. Where is the tallest part of the building located?

    b. _____

    c. How long in sections is the building from front to back?

    c. _____

Check all your work carefully.

CHAPTER 9 TEST, Form B

You will need a ruler for this test.

In 1 and 2, draw the figure in the space at the right.

1. a line perpendicular to a plane

   1.

2. a right pentagonal pyramid

   2.

3. In the figure at the right, points A and B lie in plane T and point A lies on $\overleftrightarrow{BC}$. Does point A necessarily lie in plane T? Explain your answer.

   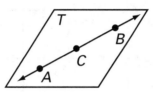

   3. _____
   _____
   _____
   _____
   _____

In 4–6, use the oblique cylinder at the right.

4. **a.** Sketch a plane section not parallel to and not intersecting the bases.

   4. a.
   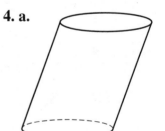

   b. Name the shape of the section you drew in Part **a** as precisely as possible.

   b. _____

5. As precisely as possible, name the shape of any plane section that is parallel to the bases.

   5. _____

6. How many symmetry planes does this figure have?

   6. _____

7. *True or false.* A Mercator projection map is made by projecting the surface of Earth onto the lateral face of a cone.

   7. _____

Name _____

8. In the spaces designated, draw front, side, and top views   **8.**
   of the regular triangular prism shown below.

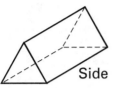

                        FRONT   SIDE   TOP

In 9 and 10, use the net shown below.

9. As specifically   **9.** _____
   as possible, name the
   figure that would be
   formed from the net.

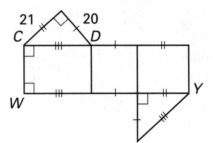

10. **a.** Find CD.   **10. a.** _____

   b. Find WY.   **b.** _____

11. In the right cylinder shown at   **11.** _____
    the right, $PQ = 19$. Find
    the exact value of the
    circumference of a base of
    the cylinder.

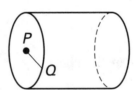

12. **a.** In the space at the right, draw a sphere with radius   **12. a.** _____
    1.7 cm. Sketch a great circle of the sphere.

   b. What is the area of the great circle? Round to the   **b.** _____
    nearest tenth of a centimeter.

13. In the spaces designated, draw front, side, and top views   **13.**
    of the desk shown below.

                        FRONT   SIDE   TOP

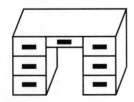

14. In the right square pyramid at the right, $XT = 32$ and $OT = 68$.

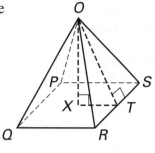

a. Find the area of $\triangle OXT$.

b. Find the area of the base.

14. a. _____

b. _____

15. In the space at the right, draw a net for a regular triangular pyramid.

15.

16. Give as specific a name as possible to the surface studied in this chapter with these views.

16. _____

FRONT   SIDE   TOP

17. In the space at the right, draw a map with four regions that needs four colors in order to be colored.

17.

In 18 and 19, tell which three-dimensional figure most resembles the real-world object. Give as specific a name as you can, distinguishing solids from surfaces.

18. an empty soup can

18. _____

19. a wooden plank

19. _____

20. Use the given views of the building.

FRONT   SIDE   TOP

a. How long in sections is the building from front to back?   20. a. _____

b. How tall in stories is the building?   b. _____

c. Where is the tallest part of the building located?   c. _____

Check all your work carefully.

CHAPTER 9 TEST, Form C

1. In this chapter, you studied ways that two planes can be related to each other. How are these relationships similar to the relationships that can exist between two lines? How are they different?

2. Explain the difference between a *cylindric solid* and a *cylindric surface*. Give a real-world example of each.

3. Draw a 3-dimensional figure of your choice. Then do the following

   a. Identify the number of symmetry planes.

   b. Give the top, front, and right-side views of the figure.

   c. Draw a net for the surface of the figure.

4. Maps A, B, and C below each consist of four congruent L-shaped regions. Does this mean that the same number of colors is required to color each map? Explain your reasoning.

   A   B   C

5. The figure at the right is a right square pyramid. If $TU = 24$ and $PS = 20$, give as many additional measures as you can.

   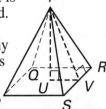

6. Why is it useful to give three views of a 3-dimensional figure rather than one or two views? Make a sketch to illustrate your answer.

CHAPTER 9 TEST, Form D

Two people you know have decided to become managers of a local music store. They have asked for your help in planning the layout of the store and in designing attractive displays and bins to hold the merchandise.

The sketch at the right shows a view of the empty store from above, as if the ceiling were removed.

a. Recall that architects often draw exterior views of a building, which are called *elevations.* Draw an elevation of the east side of the store.

b. Your friends want a carpenter to build several bins and racks for holding and displaying CDs, tapes, records, videos, and other merchandise in the center of the store. Below are three views of a bin they plan to use for holding CDs. Use these views to make a drawing of the bin.

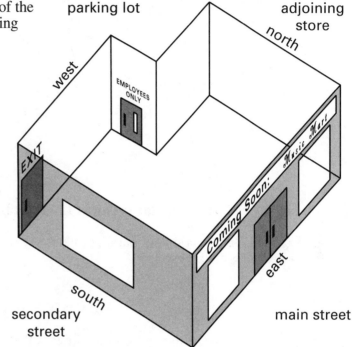

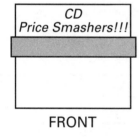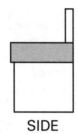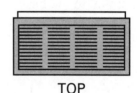

FRONT   SIDE   TOP

c. What suggestions do you have about how your friends might arrange the displays and the merchandise? Use you suggestions to do the following.

- Draw a view of the store from the top. Show all the displays that you would place.

- Make your own original design for a display rack or a bin that can be used in the center of the store. Draw three views of the bin that a carpenter could use in constructing it.

CHAPTER 9 TEST, Cumulative Form

You will need a ruler for this test.

In 1 and 2, draw each figure in the space at the right.

1. a right triangular prism

1.

2. an oblique square pyramid

2.

In 3–5, use the right rectangular prism at the right below.

3. a. Sketch a plane section not parallel to and not intersecting the bases.

3. a.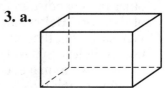

b. Name the shape of the section you drew in Part **a** as precisely as possible.

b. _____

4. As precisely as possible, name the shape of any plane section that is parallel to the base.

4. _____

5. How many symmetry planes does this figure have?

5. _____

6. Find the area of the octagon on the coordinate axes at the right.

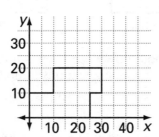

6. _____

7. A rectangular wall is 15 feet long and 10 feet high. It is to be covered with square tiles that measure 10 inches on each side. How many tiles will be needed to cover the wall completely?

7. _____

8. *True or false.* A discrete line is dense.

8. _____

9. In the space at the right, draw front, side, and top views of the regular pentagonal pyramid shown below.

FRONT   SIDE   TOP

10. Quadrilateral *TRAP* at the right is an isosceles trapezoid. Find its area.

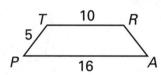

10. _____

11. Use the figure at the right. Supply justifications in the argument.

Given: $\overline{AD} \perp \overline{DC}; \overline{BC} \perp \overline{DC}.$
To prove: *ABCD* is a trapezoid.

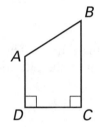

a. 0. $\overline{AD} \perp \overline{DC}; \overline{BC} \perp \overline{DC}$

b. 1. $\overline{AD} /\!/ \overline{BC}$

c. 2. *ABCD* is a trapezoid.

11. a. _____

b. _____

c. _____

12. From the information given in the drawing at the right, what quadrilateral is pictured? Be as specific as possible.

12. _____

In 13 and 14, use the net drawn below. Assume that
$\odot Q \cong \odot P$ **and that** XY **= circumference of** $\odot Q$ **= 12.**

13. As specifically as possible, identify the figure that would be formed from the net.

13. _____

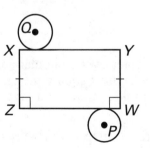

14. a. What is the circumference of $\odot P$?

14. a. _____

b. What is ZW?

b. _____

15. Suppose $PQRS \cong POMN$. If $PS = 18$, which other segment has length 18?

15. _____

16. *True or false.* A Mercator projection preserves distance.

16. _____

17. In the space at the right, draw front, side, and top views
of the lunch box shown below.

FRONT   SIDE   TOP

18. In the right square pyramid at the
right, $XY = 90$ and $YH = 48$.

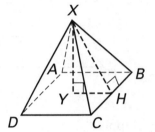

   a. Find XH.

   18. a. _____

   b. Find the area of $\triangle XBC$.

      b. _____

19. The area of a triangle is 80 square units. The length of one
side is 10 units. Find the length of the altitude to that side.

19. _____

20. In the space at the right, draw a net for a
triangular pyramid.

20.

21. Which 3-dimensional figure most resembles a
compact disc? Give as specific a name as you can,
distinguishing a surface from a solid.

21. _____

22. In the space at the right, draw and label a figure so that
$r_t(A) = A$.

22.

23. A lawn sprinkler can spray water over a circular area about
5 meters in diameter. To the nearest square meter, how
much lawn area can this sprinkler cover at a given time?

23. _____

24. In the space at the right, draw a map with five regions
that requires four colors to be colored.

24.

Check all your work carefully.

Name _____

COMPREHENSIVE TEST, Chapters 1–9

You will need a ruler for this test.

In 1–26, *multiple choice*. Give the letter of the correct answer.

1. Which statement is true in Euclidean geometry?   1. _____

   (a) The Point-Line-Plane Postulate is assumed true.

   (b) Lines are dense.

   (c) Through a point not on a line, there is exactly one line parallel to the given line.

   (d) All of the above statements are true in Euclidean geometry.

2. If A, B, and D are coplanar, $BD = 46$, $AD = 13$, and $AB = 59$, you can conclude that   2. _____

   (a) B is between A and D.

   (b) A is between B and D.

   (c) D is between A and B.

   (d) A, B, and D are vertices of a triangle.

3. Consider this conditional: *If two discrete lines intersect, then they intersect in a point.* The figure at the right below is   3. _____

   (a) an instance of the conditional

   (b) a counterexample to the conditional

   (c) neither an instance of nor a counterexample to the conditional.

   (d) none of the above.

4. Which is a correct way to read the statement $p \Rightarrow q$?   4. _____

   (a) if p, then q (b) if q, then p

   (c) p if and only if q (d) p and/or q

5. Which is a nonconvex octagonal region?   5. _____

   (a)   (b)   (c)   (d)

6. Which is the most specific name possible for the figure shown at the right?   6. _____

   (a) kite   (b) square

   (c) rhombus   (d) rectangle

▶ **COMPREHENSIVE TEST,** **Chapters 1–9** *page 2*

---

7. In the figure at the right, $\overrightarrow{BD}$ bisects $\angle ABC$. What is m$\angle ABC$?

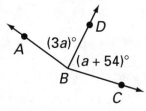

   (a) 18   (b) 27

   (c) 81   (d) 162

7. _____

8. Consider the figure at the right, where $\ell \parallel p$. Which of the following must be true?

   (a) $\angle 7$ and $\angle 9$ are supplementary angles.

   (b) m$\angle 9 = $ m$\angle 14$

   (c) $\angle 8$ and $\angle 14$ are vertical angles.

   (d) m$\angle 10 = $ m$\angle 7$

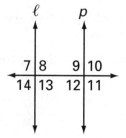

8. _____

9. In the figure at the right, $r_m(A) = B$. Which of the following is true?

   (a) $AX = BX$.

   (b) m is the $\perp$ bisector of $\overline{AB}$.

   (c) $r_m(B) = A$

   (d) All of the above are true.

9. _____

10. In the figure at the right, $r_t \circ r_s$ has magnitude ___?___.

   (a) $35°$ (b) $70°$

   (c) $-70°$ (d) $-140°$

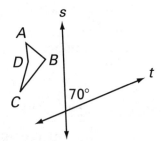

10. _____

11. In the diagram at the right, what type of isometry maps Figure I onto Figure II?

   (a) translation   (b) reflection

   (c) rotation   (d) glide reflection

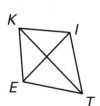

11. _____

12. Quadrilateral *KITE* at the right is a kite with ends *K* and *T*. If m$\angle EKT = 40$, what is m$\angle KTI$?

   (a) 100   (b) 80

   (c) 140   (d) cannot be determined

12. _____

13. Which is the image of (-5, 4) under the translation   13. _____
by the vector (2, -1)?

    (a) (-7, 5)   (b) (-3, 3)   (c) (3, 3)   (d) (-3, 5)

14. If $ABCDE \cong ZYWXV$, which is a true statement?   14. _____

    (a) $\overline{ED} \cong \overline{VX}$ (b) $AD = XZ$

    (c) $\angle C \cong \angle W$ (d) All of these statements are true.

15. Quadrilateral *RECT* at the right   15. _____
is a rectangle. If m$\angle ETC = 31$,
what is m$\angle TEC$?

    (a) 31   (b) 59

    (c) 69   (d) cannot be determined

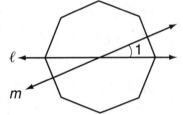

16. Lines ℓ and m are symmetry lines   16. _____
of the regular octagon at the right.
What is m$\angle 1$?

    (a) 22.5   (b) 30

    (c) 45   (d) 67.5

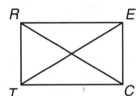

17. The measure of each interior angle of a regular *20-gon* is ___?___ .   17. _____

    (a) 164   (b) 162   (c) 160   (d) 158

18. Given the figure at the right as marked,   18. _____
which congruence theorem justifies the
conclusion that $\triangle ABC \cong \triangle ADC$?

    (a) SAS   (b) ASA

    (c) AA   (d) HL

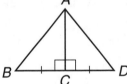

19. In the figure at the right, it is given that   19. _____
$\overline{PS} \cong \overline{PT}$. To prove $\triangle PSR \cong \triangle PTQ$ by the
ASA Congruence Theorem, what additional
information is sufficient?

    (a) $\angle P \cong \angle P$

    (b) $\overline{PR} \cong \overline{PQ}$

    (c) $\overline{SQ} \cong \overline{TR}$

    (d) $\angle PTQ \cong \angle PSR$

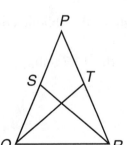

20. What is the perimeter of a regular decagon in which one side has length $\frac{1}{2}g$?

    (a) $10g$ (b) $5g$ (c) g (d) $\frac{1}{2}g$

    20. _____

21. What is the area of $\triangle PQR$ at the right?

    (a) 75 units^2 (b) 135 units^2

    (c) 85 units^2 (d) 150 units^2

    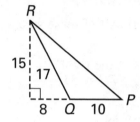

    21. _____

22. What is the area of parallelogram *PARL* at the right?

    (a) $21x$ units^2 (b) $21x^2$ units^2

    (c) $28x^2$ units^2 (d) $22x$ units^2

    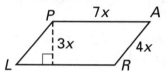

    22. _____

23. What is the perimeter of $\triangle ABC$ at the right?

    (a) 16.1 in.   (b) 25.74 in.

    (c) 28.6 in.   (d) 48 in.

    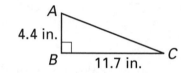

    23. _____

24. Pictured at the right is a right square pyramid. How many symmetry planes does it have?

    (a) 2   (b) 3

    (c) 4   (d) 5

    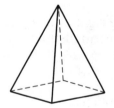

    24. _____

25. What is the height of the oblique cone at the right?

    (a) 15 units   (b) 13.7 units

    (c) 12 units   (d) 9 units

    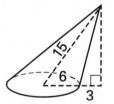

    25. _____

26. The intersection of a sphere and a plane that contains the center of the sphere is called a ___?___ of the sphere.

    (a) diameter   (b) radius   (c) circle   (d) great circle

    26. _____

In 27–29, refer to the figure at the right below. Choose among the following to supply justifications in the argument.

    (a) definition of congruent figures   **(b) Flip-Flop Theorem**

    (c) Figure Reflection Theorem   **(d) definition of reflection**

Given: $r_\ell(P) = P'$
To prove: $\overline{PT} \cong \overline{P'T}$

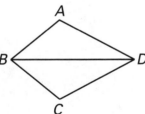

Conclusions	Justifications
0. $r_\ell(P) = P'$	0. Given
1. $r_\ell(T) = T$	1. ___?___
2. $r_\ell(\overline{PT}) = \overline{P'T}$	2. ___?___
3. $\overline{PT} \cong \overline{P'T}$	3. ___?___

27. The justification for step 1 of the proof is ___?___ .   **27.** _____

28. The justification for step 2 of the proof is ___?___ .   **28.** _____

29. The justification for step 3 of the proof is ___?___ .   **29.** _____

30. Write an argument for this proof.

Given: $\overline{AD} \cong \overline{CD}$;
            $\angle ADB \cong \angle CDB$.
To prove: $\overline{AB} \cong \overline{CB}$.

Conclusions	Justifications
_____	_____
_____	_____
_____	_____
_____	_____

31. In the space at the right below, draw front, side, and top views of the right cone shown below.

                                FRONT   SIDE   TOP

Check all your work carefully.

QUIZ

1. What is the volume of a cube with an edge length of 4π cm?

1. _____

2. Find the lateral area of the right hexagonal prism shown at the right.

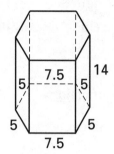

2. _____

3. Consider the right cone below. Find its

   a. lateral area.

   b. surface area.

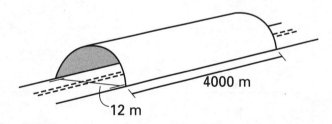

3. a. _____

   b. _____

4. Calculate $\sqrt[3]{120}$ to the nearest hundredth.

4. _____

5. A tunnel is to be lined with ceramic tiles of area 1 square meter. The tunnel, as shown below, is half a cylinder with length 4000 m and diameter 12 m. About how many tiles will be needed to line the tunnel?

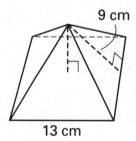

5. _____

6. The right square pyramid at the right has a slant height of 9 cm. A side of the base measures 13 cm. Find its surface area.

6. _____

Name _____

1. A box has dimensions ℓ, w, and h. How is the volume changed if the length and width are each multiplied by 5 and the height remains the same?

1. _____

2. *True or false.* The volume formula $V = Bh$ can be used with cones and cylinders.

2. _____

3. Find the area of the rectangle below.

3. _____

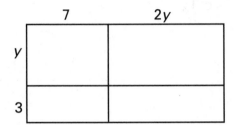

4. The volume of a prism with square base is 1032 mm³. Its height is 12 mm.

   a. Find the area of its base.

4. a. _____

   b. Find the length of a side of the base.

     b. _____

5. Find the volume of the oblique cylinder at the right.

5. _____

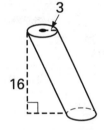

6. Based on Cavalieri's Principle, two 3-dimensional figures of the same height will have the same ___?___ if every plane parallel to the bases intersects the figures in sections with the same ___?___ .

6. _____

_____

7. A right pyramid has slant height s and its five base sides have equal lengths b. Find a formula for its lateral area in terms of s and b.

7. _____

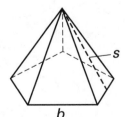

CHAPTER 10 TEST, Form A

1. The right prism at the right has right triangular bases. The height of the prism is 15″.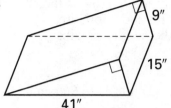

   a. Find its volume.

   b. Find its surface area.

   1. a. _____

   b. _____

2. Find the exact volume of the right cylinder at the right.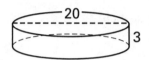

   2. _____

3. A pyramid has a square base. Its volume is 810 cm³ and the length of a base edge is 9 cm. Find the height of the pyramid.

   3. _____

4. Find the lateral area of the cone at the right.

   4. _____

5. A box for tissues is made from cardboard. If the area of the hole in the box is 69.7 cm², how much cardboard is needed for each box?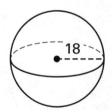

   5. _____

6. A cube has volume 512 mm³. Find its lateral area.

   6. _____

7. Consider the sphere at the right.

   a. Find its surface area.

   b. Find its volume.

   7. a. _____

   b. _____

8. Do the rectangular and triangular prisms at the right have the same volume? Explain your answer.

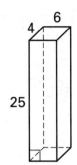 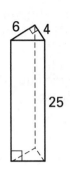

8. _____

_____

_____

_____

9. Find the volume of the cone at the right.

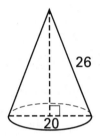

9. _____

10. A regular decagonal prism has base edge *t* and height 2*s*. Give a formula for the lateral area.

10. _____

11. Find the cube root of 630 to the nearest hundredth.

11. _____

12. The surface area of a sphere is 500 in². Give the radius of the sphere to the nearest tenth of an inch.

12. _____

13. **a.** Express the volume of the box at the right as a product of three binomials.

   b. Expand the product.

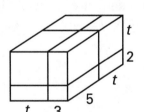

13. **a.** _____

_____

   b. _____

_____

In 14 and 15, consider the cone-shaped paper cup pictured below. It is 2.5″ high and the diameter of its top is 2″.

14. Ignoring any overlap, about how much paper does it take to make the cup? Round your answer to the nearest whole number.

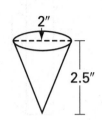

14. _____

15. If the cup is filled to the top, how many cubic inches of water will it hold? Round your answer to the nearest whole number.

15. _____

16. Each edge of a cube is multiplied by 7.

    a. What happens to the volume of the cube?

    16. a. _____

    b. What happens to the surface area of the cube?

    b. _____

17. A dome is hemispheric in shape and has diameter 25 m. How many square meters of gold leaf are needed to cover it?

17. _____

18. A plastic straw is 14 cm long and has a radius of 0.2 cm. If filled, how much will the straw hold? Round your answer to the nearest tenth.

18. _____

19. An oblique cone has height *h* and base radius *r*. Give a formula for its volume in terms of *h* and *r*.

19. _____

Check all your work carefully.

Name _____

CHAPTER 10 TEST, Form B

1. The bases of the right prism at the right are right triangles.

   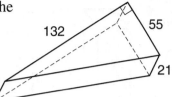

   a. Find its volume.

   b. Find its surface area.

   1. a. _____

   b. _____

2. Find the exact volume of the oblique cylinder at the right. Its height is 21″.

   2. _____

3. A pyramid has a square base. Its volume is 1536 mm³ and the height is 18 mm. Find the length of a base edge.

   3. _____

4. Find the lateral area of the cone at the right.

   4. _____

5. A jewelry box is to be painted with gold paint. If one jar of paint will cover 100 square inches, how many jars are needed to paint the jewelry box? Assume that all sides are to be painted.

   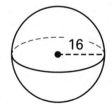

   5. _____

6. A cube has lateral area 169 ft². Find its volume.

   6. _____

7. Consider the sphere at the right.

   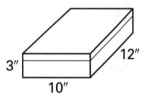

   a. Find its surface area.

   b. Find its volume.

   7. a. _____

   b. _____

8. Do the rectangular and triangular prisms at the right have the same volume? Explain your answer.

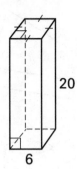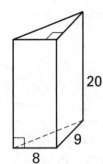

20 20 8 6 9

8. _____

_____

_____

_____

9. Find the volume of the cone at the right.

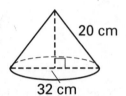

20 cm

32 cm

9. _____

10. A regular octagonal prism has base edge *g* and height 3*f*. Give a formula for the lateral area.

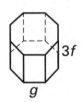

3*f*

g

10. _____

11. Find the cube root of 750 to the nearest hundredth.

11. _____

12. The volume of a sphere is 6000 in^3. Give the radius of the sphere rounded to the nearest hundredth.

12. _____

13. **a.** Express the volume of the box at the right as a product of three binomials.

b. Expand the product.

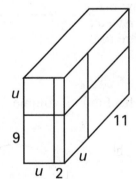

u

9

u 2

u

11

13. **a.** _____

_____

b. _____

_____

Name _____

**In 14 and 15, consider the waffle cone below.
The diameter of its top is 3.5″ and it is 8″ high.**

14. Assuming there is no overlap, how much waffle does it take to make the cone? Round your answer to the nearest tenth of a square inch.

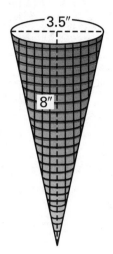

14. _____

15. If the cone is packed full, how many cubic inches of ice cream will it hold? Round your answer to the nearest cubic inch.

15. _____

16. The radius of a sphere is multiplied by 20.

   a. What happens to the volume of the sphere?

   16. a. _____

   b. What happens to the surface area of the sphere?

   b. _____

17. A planter is hemispheric in shape. If its diameter is 60 cm, what is the surface area of the planter?

17. _____

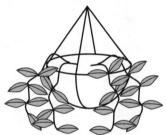

18. Pencil lead comes in two sizes: .7 mm in diameter and .5 mm in diameter. The length of a piece of pencil lead is 40 mm. How much more material does a .7-mm lead contain than a .5-mm lead? Round your answer to the nearest tenth.

18. _____

19. An oblique square pyramid has height h and base edge of length e. Give a formula for its volume in terms of h and e.

19. _____

Check all your work carefully.

CHAPTER 10 TEST, Form C

1. Draw and label a right square prism whose volume is equal to the volume of the right cone shown at the right. Give the exact volume of the figure you drew. Then compare the surface areas of the two figures.

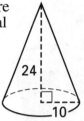

2. Looking at the cubes at the right, Janine said that cube B is twice as big as cube A. Lamar said that cube B is four times as big as cube A. Chris said that cube B is eight times as big as cube A. With whom do you agree? Explain your reasoning.

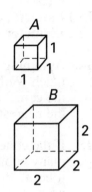

3. The general formula for the lateral area of a right cylindric surface is L.A. $= ph$. What does each variable in this formula represent? Give a formula for a more specific figure that you can derive from this formula. Identify the specific figure and show how the two formulas are related.

4. Explain what is represented by the picture at the right.

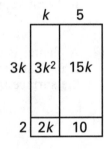

5. Write a real-world problem that you could solve by using the formula S.A. $= 4\pi r^2$. Then show how to solve your problem.

6. Make a sketch that illustrates Cavalieri's Principle. Write a brief paragraph to explain your sketch.

CHAPTER 10 TEST, Form D

All your friends love your Bountiful Brownies, which you make from an old family recipe. You and your friends are exploring the possibility of starting a small business making and selling the brownies.

a. You bake each batch of brownies in a rectangular pan that is 13 inches long and 9 inches wide. The average height of the baked brownies is $\frac{1}{2}$ inch. What is the total volume of the baked brownies in each batch?

b. Usually you create the individual brownies by making cuts as shown in the diagram at the right.

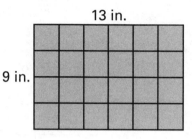

13 in.

9 in.

   i. Give the dimensions of each individual brownie.

   ii. Suppose you want to make small "brownie cakes" by frosting the top and sides of each individual brownie. What is the total surface area that you must frost?

   iii. On the average, the frosting would be spread to a thickness of $\frac{1}{8}$ inch. What would be the dimensions of a frosted brownie?

c. Boxes like the one shown at the right are available at a local bakery supply store. One of your friends said that, since the volume of the box is greater than the volume of a batch of unfrosted brownies, it is possible to fit an entire batch in the box. Do you agree or disagree? Explain you reasoning.

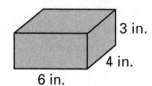

3 in.

4 in.

6 in.

d. The figure at the right shows the dimensions of a one-cup measure that you have in your kitchen. It is cylindrical in shape.

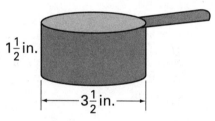

$1\frac{1}{2}$ in.

$3\frac{1}{2}$ in.

   i. What is the volume of this measuring cup?

   ii. Suppose you use this cup to measure one cup of chopped nuts, then add the nuts to the brownie batter before baking. Estimate the effect this might have on the average height of the baked brownies. (Your answer can be only an estimate, because the nuts cannot be packed tightly in the measuring cup.)

e. Make a plan for baking at least one type of brownie and packaging it so that one batch fits into the box shown in Part **c**. Standard sizes of baking pans are shown at the right. You may consider baking a batch in any of these, or you may suggest having a different size of pan custom-made. Present your plan in a report that includes the following.

Standard Sizes of Baking Pans

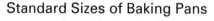
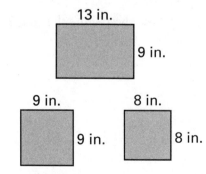

13 in.

9 in.

9 in.

9 in.

8 in.

8 in.

   • the size of the baking pan

   • the dimensions of each baked brownie

   • a diagram illustrating how the brownies will be packed into the box

CHAPTER 10 TEST, Cumulative Form

1. A cube has a volume of 3500 cm³. To the nearest hundredth, what is the length of an edge of the cube?

1. _____

2. Name the figure that could be made from the net at the right.

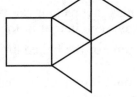

2. _____

3. Find the lateral area of the regular prism below.

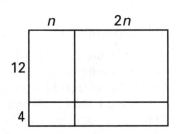

7 in.

2 in.

3. _____

4. If m∠AXE = 4y − 15 and m∠MXE = 2y + 27,

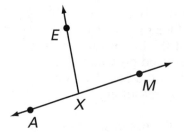

E

M

X

A

a. find m∠AXE.

b. find m∠MXE.

4. a. _____

b. _____

5. Show two ways to represent the area of the rectangle at the right.

n   2n

12

4

5. _____

_____

_____

6. In the space at the right, draw

a. two perpendicular planes.

6. a.

b. a triangular pyramid.

b.

7. Write a proof argument
using △*ABC* at the right.

   Given: m∠*A* = 2*x*,
               m∠*MRS* = *x*, and
               m∠*MNS* = 3*x*.

To prove: $\overleftrightarrow{MN}$ // $\overleftrightarrow{RS}$.

7.

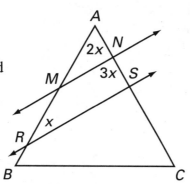

8. Consider the right cone pictured at
the right.

   a. Find its surface area.

   b. Find its volume.

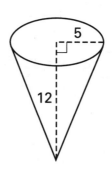

8. a. _____

    b. _____

9. The Montoya family is decorating a model of a giant
soup can which they plan to enter in the Good Food/
Good Health parade. They want to decorate the can
completely so that no spot is bare.

   a. If the can is 15 feet tall and has a radius of 5 feet,
how much *curved* surface will be decorated?

   b. How much area would be decorated if the top and
bottom of the can are covered as well?

9. a. _____

    b. _____

10. Does a right cone have bilateral symmetry? If so, how
many symmetry planes does the cone have?

10. _____

_____

11. Draw the vanishing point for the roof, drawn in
perspective below.

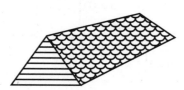

12. The right square pyramid at the right has height h and a base side of length b. Give a formula for its surface area using h and b.

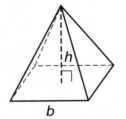

12. _____

13. Given the information at the right, is *QUAD* a parallelogram? Explain your reasoning.

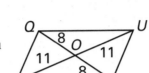

13. _____

_____

_____

14. A sphere has a surface area of exactly 8281π in². Find its diameter.

14. _____

15. The right square pyramid at the right has edge lengths $MO = 17$ and $ON = 16$.

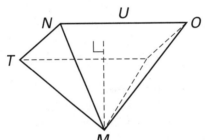

a. Find the perimeter of its base.

15. a. _____

b. Find its total surface area.

b. _____

16. State Cavalieri's Principle in your own words.

_____

_____

_____

17. A vertical cross section of a hemisphere-domed building is pictured at the right. Calculate the perimeter of this cross section of the building.

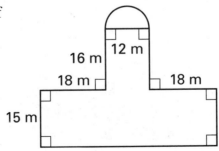

17. _____

18. Refer to the box at the right.

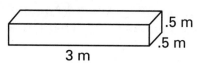

.5 m
.5 m
3 m

   a. What happens to the volume if the length of every edge is multiplied by $\frac{1}{2}$?

   b. Find the surface area of the new box.

18. a. _____

    b. _____

19. At the right, draw a map with five regions that needs four colors in order to be colored.

19.

20. The climatron in Shaw's Garden in St. Louis, Missouri, is a geodesic-domed greenhouse, shaped roughly like a hemisphere with diameter 384 feet. Estimate its volume to the nearest thousand cubic feet.

20. _____

Check all your work carefully.

QUIZ

In 1 and 2, two statements are given. a. What (if anything) can you conclude using both statements? b. What law(s) of reasoning have you used?

1. (1) If a figure is a square, then it is a parallelogram.

 (2) *MNOP* is a square.

1. a. _____

b. _____

2. (1) If $y = 7$, then $x = 2$.

 (2) $x = 11$

2. a. _____

b. _____

3. A conditional and its contrapositive are either ___?___ or ___?___ .

3. _____

_____

4. A statement is given. a. Write its inverse. b. Write its converse. c. Write its contrapositive.

If you ride the bus on Saturday, then you will pay a reduced fare.

a. _____

b. _____

c. _____

d. If the given statement is true, which other statement is also true?

4. d. _____

5. Use the following clues to decide which Great Lakes Andrew and Kara will visit.
  (1) Kara and Andrew will each visit a different Great Lake this summer: Superior, Huron, Erie, Michigan, or Ontario.
  (2) They will not go to Erie or Ontario.
  (3) Andrew will visit only Superior or Huron.
  (4) Kara will visit Michigan if Andrew visits Superior.
  (5) Andrew will not visit Huron if Kara does not visit Erie.

5. _____

6. Write an indirect proof to show that $\sqrt{8} \neq 2.83$.

6.

Name

QUIZ

1. Find the distance between points $P = (3, 4)$ and $Q = (8, 15)$.

    1. _____

2. Prove that quadrilateral *EFGH* below is *not* a rectangle.

    2.

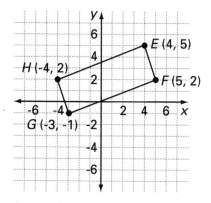

3. Kevin lives three blocks west and two blocks north of the grocery store. He lives one block east and six blocks north of his school.

    a. If he stops at the store on the way home from school, how far is his trip home?

    3. a. _____

    b. How far would it be if he could walk straight from school to the store to home without having to walk along the streets?

    b. _____

4. Write an equation for the circle with center $(4, 2)$ and radius 7.

    4. _____

5. Write an equation for the circle at the right.

    5. _____

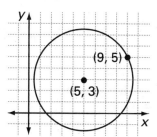

6. On the coordinate axes at the right, draw a right triangle in a convenient location and name its vertices.

    6.

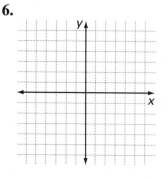

CHAPTER 11 TEST, Form A

You will need a ruler for this test.

In 1 and 2, $X = (9, 22)$ and $Y = (-7, 2)$.

1. Find XY.

    1. _____

2. Find the midpoint of $\overline{XY}$.

    2. _____

In 3 and 4, two statements are given. a. What (if anything) can you conclude using both statements? b. What law(s) of reasoning did you use?

3. (1) If $p \parallel r$, then $r \perp q$.
   (2) r is not perpendicular to q.

   a.   _____

   b.   _____

4. (1) If $xy = 0$, then either $x = 0$ or $y = 0$.
   (2) $xy = 0$ and $y \neq 0$.

   a.   _____

   b.   _____

5. $QRST$ is located on the coordinate plane at the right.

   a. Prove that $QRST$ is a rhombus.

   b. Show that its diagonals bisect each other.

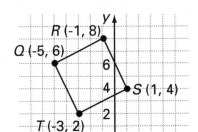

   5. a.

      b.

In 6 and 7, consider the sphere with equation $(x - 9)^2 + (y + 5)^2 + (z - 2)^2 = 49$.

6. What is its center?

    6. _____

7. *True or false.* $(3, -3, 5)$ is on the sphere.

    7. _____

8. A box measures 9 in. by 16 in. by 6 in. What is the longest drumstick, to the nearest inch, that fits in the box?

    8. _____

9. On the coordinate axes at the right, draw a kite in a convenient location and label its vertices.

9.

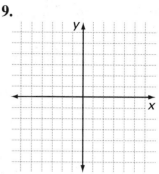

10. Use an indirect proof to prove that trapezoid *MNOP* below is *not* isosceles.

10.

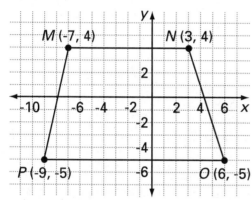

In 11 and 12, consider this conditional statement:
If you do not ride your bicycle, then you will walk.

11. a. Write its converse. b. Write its inverse. c. Write its contrapositive.

a. _____

b. _____

c. _____

12. Assuming the original statement is true, which (if any) of Parts **a–c** in Question 11 is (are) also true?

12. _____

In 13 and 14, let *Z* = (-2, 4, 5).

13. At the right, draw a 3-dimensional coordinate system and plot *Z*.

13.

14. Calculate *ZX* if *X* = (7, -1, 7).

14. _____

In 15 and 16, consider the circle with center (-3, 6) and radius 5.

15. Give an equation for this circle.

15. _____

16. Graph the circle at the right.

16.

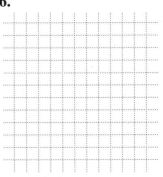

17. Larry left home and walked 10 blocks north and 3 blocks west to a playground. He then left the playground and walked 7 blocks east and 3 blocks north to a store. Finally, he walked 5 blocks east and 4 blocks south to the movie theater. Traveling by air, how far is Larry from home?

17. _____

In 18 and 19, use $\triangle STU$ **with midpoints** *E, F,* **and** *G* **below.**

18. Explain why $\angle UFG \cong \angle UTS$.

18. _____

_____

_____

_____

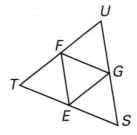

19. If $SE = 8.2$ cm, find *FG*.

19. _____

20. Stacy, Raul, and Kiyo must meet together to do a history project.
    (1) They must meet Thursday, Friday, Saturday, or Sunday.
    (2) Raul will be out of town on Sunday.
    (3) Stacy is available only on Thursday, Saturday, and Sunday.
    (4) Kiyo must work all day on Friday and Saturday.
    What can you conclude?

_____

21. Write an indirect proof to show that $\sqrt{242} \neq 16$.

21.

Check all your work carefully.

CHAPTER 11 TEST, Form B

You will need a ruler for this test.

In 1 and 2, $P = (2, 25)$ and $M = (9, 5)$.

1. Find PM.

    1. _____

2. Find the midpoint of $\overline{PM}$.

    2. _____

In 3 and 4, statements are given. a. What (if anything) can you conclude using all the statements? b. What law(s) of reasoning did you use?

3. (1) If $a = 0$ and $b = 0$, then $\frac{a}{b}$ is not defined.

    (2) $\frac{a}{b}$ is not defined.

    a. _____

    b. _____

4. (1) If two lines don't intersect, then they are either parallel or skew.
    (2) If two lines are parallel, then they lie in the same plane.
    (3) Lines p and q do not intersect and do not lie in the same plane.

    a. _____

    b. _____

5. $MNOP$ is located on the coordinate plane at the right.

    a. Prove that $MNOP$ is a rhombus.

    b. Show that its diagonals bisect each other.

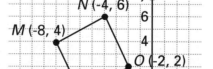
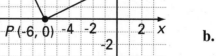

5. a.

    b.

In 6 and 7, consider the sphere with equation $(x + 7)^2 + (y - 4)^2 + (z + 2)^2 = 81$.

6. What is its center?

    6. _____

7. *True or false.* $(-5, 9, 5)$ is on the sphere.

    7. _____

8. A box measures 60 cm by 120 cm by 75 cm. What is the longest pole, to the nearest centimeter, that fits in the box?

    8. _____

9. On the grid at the right, draw a rectangle in a convenient location and label its vertices.

9.

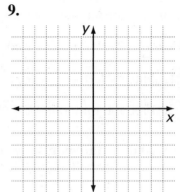

10. Use an indirect proof to prove that quadrilateral *QRST* below is *not* a kite.

10.

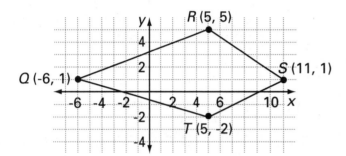

In 11 and 12, consider this conditional statement:
If you are in a brass band, then you do not play the violin.

11. a. Write its converse. b. Write its inverse. c. Write its contrapositive.

a. _____

b. _____

c. _____

12. Assuming the original statement is false, which (if any) of Parts **a–c** in Question 11 is (are) also false?

12. _____

In 13 and 14, let $V = (4, -3, 7)$**.**

13. At the right, draw a 3-dimensional coordinate system and plot *V*.

13.

14. Calculate *UV* if $U = (-2, -8, 5)$.

14. _____

In 15 and 16, consider the circle with center (1, 4) and radius 6.

15. Give an equation for this circle.

15. _____

16. Graph the circle at the right.

16.

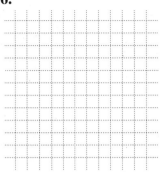

17. Two airplanes have left the Atlanta airport. Plane A is 100 miles north and 340 miles west of Atlanta, approximately over Memphis, while plane B is 400 miles south and 90 miles east of Atlanta, approximately over St. Petersburg. About how far apart are the two planes?

17. _____

In 18 and 19, use △*KLM* with midpoints *X, Y,* and *Z* below.

18. Explain why ∠*KZX* ≅ ∠*KMY*.

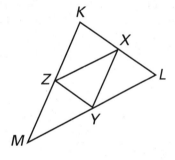

18. _____

19. If *YZ* = 4.9 in., find *KX*.

19. _____

20. Amy, Carolyn, and Jeremy want to meet for lunch next week. Their favorite restaurant is open only on Mondays, Tuesdays, and Thursdays.
  (1) Carolyn will be out of town on Monday of next week.
  (2) Amy fasts every Thursday and Friday.
  (3) Jeremy works on Thursdays and Saturdays.
  What can you conclude?

_____

21. Write an indirect proof to show that $\sqrt{43} \neq 6.6$.

21.

Check all your work carefully.

CHAPTER 11 TEST, Form C

1. In △*ABC* at the right, *X* is the midpoint of $\overline{AB}$ and *Y* is the midpoint of $\overline{BC}$. State as many other facts as you can about the figure.

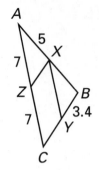

2. On the coordinate axes below, draw two circles that each have the same radius, but have different center points. Give an equation for each circle that you drew.

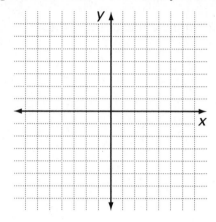

3. How is finding the distance between two points in a 3-dimensional coordinate system similar to finding the distance between two points on the coordinate plane? How is it different? Give examples to illustrate your answer.

4. State two laws of logic that you studied in this chapter. Then give an example of how each law might be applied to a real-world situation.

5. When studying for a test, Mari came across this torn page in her notebook. She knows the diagram concerns a proof, but she can't remember what she was trying to prove or how to prove it. Can you help her?

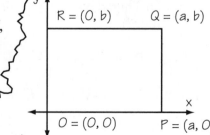

CHAPTER 11 TEST, Form D

Throughout your study of geometry in this course, you have been
presented with several different types of proof. In this activity, you
are asked to make a study guide for yourself in which you summarize
what you have learned.

a. How is the process of proving a statement to be true
different from proving a statement to be false?

b. Explain the difference between direct reasoning and
indirect reasoning.

c. What is the meaning of "two-column form"?

d. At the right are two situations, labeled I and II.

    i. How are the situations alike? How are they
different?

    ii. Give a proof argument for each situation.

e. Create a "proof study guide" for direct, indirect, and
coordinate proofs. Specifically, do the following for
each type of proof.

  • Write a brief description of the type of proof,
being sure to identify those characteristics that
distinguish it from other types of proof.

  • Give an example of how this type of proof can
be used to prove a statement about a geometric
figure.

f. Which type of proof do you find easiest to write?
hardest? Which type of proof did you like most?
least? Write a brief report that contains your answers
to these questions, being sure to give reasons for
your answers.

I.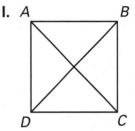

Given: *ABCD* is a square.
To prove: $\overline{AC} \cong \overline{BD}$.

II.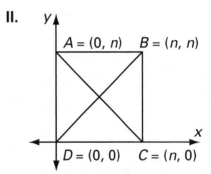

Given: *ABCD* is a square.
To prove: $\overline{AC} \cong \overline{BD}$.

CHAPTER 11 TEST, Cumulative Form

You will need a ruler for this test.

In 1 and 2, two points are given. a. Find the midpoint of the segment joining them. b. Find the distance between them.

1. (3, -8) and (-5, -2)

1. a. _____

    b. _____

2. (5, 0, 3) and (3, -2, 0)

2. a. _____

    b. _____

3. At the right, draw a 3-dimensional coordinate system and plot the points of Question 2.

3.

4. *E, F, G* are midpoints of the sides of isosceles triangle *ABC* with *AB = AC*. Classify △*EFG* as precisely as possible. Justify your answer.

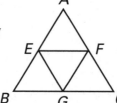

4. _____

_____

_____

_____

5. Two statements are given. a. What can you conclude from both statements? b. What law(s) of reasoning have you used?

(1) Anke eats eggs or drinks milk for breakfast every day.

(2) Anke did not drink milk today.

a. _____

b. _____

6. A statement is given. a. Write its converse. b. Write its inverse. c. Write its contrapositive.

If a figure is a kite, then it is a rhombus.

a. _____

b. _____

c. _____

7. Tell which of Parts **a–c** in Question 6 is (are) true.

7. _____

Name _____

8. Use an indirect proof to show that a quadrilateral
cannot have four obtuse angles.

8.

In 9 and 10, use the figure at the right below.

9. Prove that $A = (-1, -1)$,
$B = (0, 1)$, $C = (2, 2)$,
and $D = (1, 0)$ are vertices
of a rhombus.

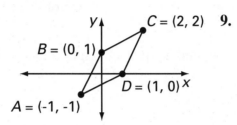

9.

10. Show that the figure's
diagonals are perpendicular
to each other.

10.

11. For the sphere $\left(x - \dfrac{1}{2}\right)^2 + \left(y + \dfrac{3}{2}\right)^2 + (z + 4)^2 = 5$, find

    a. the center.

11. a. _____

    b. the radius.

    b. _____

12. Write an equation for the
circle with center C
at the right.

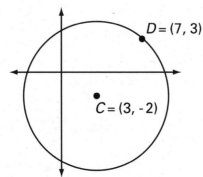

12. _____

13. A box has dimensions 3 ft, 4 ft, and 5 ft.

    a. Find its surface area.   **13. a.** _____

    b. Find its volume.   **b.** _____

14. Another box has edges which are three times as long as the edges of the box in Question 13.

    a. How does its surface area compare to that of the original?   **14. a.** _____

    b. How does its volume compare to that of the original?   **b.** _____

15. A regular triangular pyramid has a slant height of 5 cm and a height of 4 cm.

    a. Find the area of its base.   **15. a.** _____

    b. Find its total surface area.   **b.** _____

    c. Find its volume.   **c.** _____

16. Give two ways to represent the volume of the box at the right.   **16.** _____

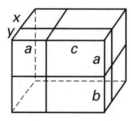

    _____

    _____

    _____

**In 17 and 18, refer to the figure below.
The top is a hemisphere with radius 4 cm.
The cylinder is 5 cm high.**

17. What is its volume?   **17.** _____

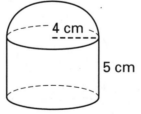

18. What is its surface area?   **18.** _____

19. In the figure at the right, $\overrightarrow{AD}$ is the bisector of $\angle BAC$. Find m$\angle BAC$.   **19.** _____

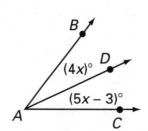

20. Use the drawing at the right. Draw the path of a ball that starts at *A* and bounces off walls *x, y,* and *z* in that order and then hits *B*.

20.

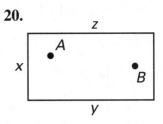

21. In the figure at the right, use the angle measures given to find *x*.

21. _____

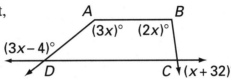

22. In the figure at the right, which is the shortest segment? Justify your answer.

22. _____

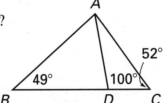

23. *Multiple choice.* Which set of numbers can be the lengths of sides of a right triangle?

23. _____

   (a) $1, \sqrt{2}, 3$ (b) $1, \sqrt{2}, \sqrt{3}$

   (c) $\sqrt{5}, 3, 4$ (d) $2, 4, \sqrt{19}$

24. Two spheres with the same radius *r* fit exactly in a rectangular box as shown at the right.

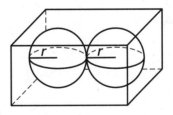

   a. Find the total volume of the two spheres.

24. a. _____

   b. Find the width of the box.

b. _____

   c. Find the length of the box.

c. _____

   d. Find the height of the box.

d. _____

   e. Find the volume of the box.

e. _____

   f. What percent of the box is filled by the two spheres?

f. _____

Check all your work carefully.

You will need a ruler for this quiz.

In 1–3, let $E = (-4, -2)$, $F = (-2, 1)$, $G = (2, 2)$, and $H = (3, -2)$.

1. Find the coordinates of the vertices of the image of *EFGH* under $S_{\frac{3}{2}}$.

   1. _____

2. Graph *EFGH* and $S_{\frac{3}{2}}(EFGH)$ on the coordinate axes at the right. Label the vertices.

   2.

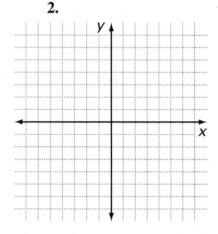

3. Let $Q = F'_{\frac{3}{2}}(F)$ and $G' = S_{\frac{3}{2}}(G)$. Show that $\overline{FG} \parallel \overline{F'G'}$.

   3.

4. In the figure at the right, A' is the image of A. Determine the center and the scale factor k for the size transformation.

   4. _____

5. A photo measures $4''$ by $6''$. If the shorter dimension of a similar photo is $14''$, what is the longer dimension?

   5. _____

6. At the right, $S(\triangle TRE) = \triangle LOG$.

   a. Find $m\angle G$.

   b. Find $\overline{LG}$.

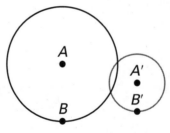

   6. a. _____

   b. _____

7. If $\frac{r}{s} = \frac{t}{u}$, then $ru = $ ___?___.

   7. _____

Name _____

CHAPTER 12 TEST, Form A

You will need a ruler for this test.

1. Draw the image of *QRTU* under a size change with center *T* and magnitude $\frac{3}{5}$.

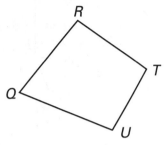

2. Draw the image of ∠*MAP* under a size change with center *O* and magnitude 2.5.

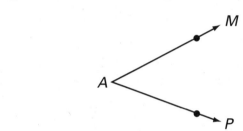

3. At the right are a circle in black and its size-change image in gray. Use a ruler to determine the center and size change factor *k*.

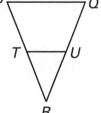

3. _____

In 4 and 5, use the figure at the right below.

4. △*PQR* ~ △*TUR*. If *PQ* = 12, *TU* = 5, and *QR* = 16, find *UR*.

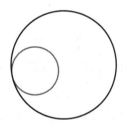

4. _____

5. *T* and *U* are midpoints of $\overline{PR}$ and $\overline{QR}$, respectively. Let S$_k$ be the size change such that S$_k$(△*TUR*) = △*PQR*.

   a. Is this size change an expansion or a contraction?

   5. a. _____

   b. What is the value of *k* in this size change?

   b. _____

6. *PENTA ~ FIVES* with sides and angle measures as indicated at the right. Find as many missing lengths and angle measures as possible.

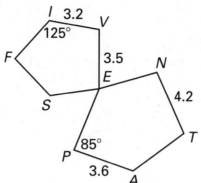

6. _____

_____

_____

_____

_____

7. *Multiple choice.* Size changes do *not* preserve

    (a) betweenness.   (c) angle measure.

    (b) distance.   (d) collinearity.

7. _____

8. An octagon has area 80 cm² and shortest side with length 5 cm. A similar octagon has shortest side of length 4 cm. What is the area of this similar octagon?

8. _____

9. If k is the size-change factor for two similar figures, how do their volumes compare?

9. _____

10. A water tower that stands 70 ft high holds 500,000 gallons of water. A similar tower is 95 ft high. How much water will it hold?

10. _____

11. A poster measures 120 cm by 80 cm. If a similar postcard is 10 cm on its shorter side, what is the length of the longer side of the postcard?

11. _____

12. If you ride your bicycle 26 km in 40 minutes, at that rate how many minutes would it take you to ride 60 km?

12. _____

13. A clay model of an automobile is 8 inches long and weighs 2 pounds. What would a full-size clay model of a similar automobile weigh if it were 12 feet long?

13. _____

In 14 and 15, use the figure and the grid at the right below.

14. Graph the image of *WHEN* under $S_{\frac{3}{4}}$ and give the coordinates of its vertices.

14. _____

   _____

   _____

   _____

15. What is $S_6(N)$?

15. _____

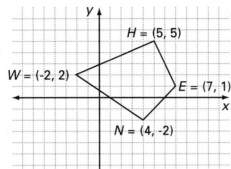

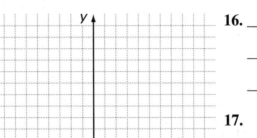

In 16 and 17, use the figure and the grid at the right below.

16. Graph the image of $\triangle MNO$ under S_4 and give the coordinates of its vertices.

16. _____

   _____

   _____

17. Verify that the distance between $S_4(M)$ and $S_4(O)$ is $4 \cdot MO$.

17.

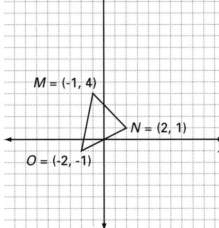

Check all your work carefully.

CHAPTER 12 TEST, Form B

You will need a ruler for this test.

1. Draw the image of *GREAT* under a size change with center *G* and magnitude $\frac{1}{2}$.

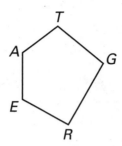

2. Draw the image of quadrilateral *HOME* under a size change with center *S* and magnitude 1.5.

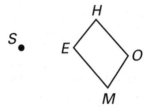

3. Given $\overline{XY}$ at the right in black and its size-change image in gray, use a ruler to determine the center and size-change factor *k*.

3. _____

In 4 and 5, use the figure below.

4. $\triangle DEF \sim \triangle DGH$. If $DE = 2.5$, $EG = 0.5$, and $EF = 0.95$, find *GH*.

4. _____

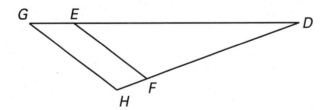

5. Let S be the size change such that $S_k(\triangle DEF) = \triangle DGH$.

   a. Is this size change an expansion or a contraction?

   5. a. _____

   b. What is the value of *k* in this size change?

   b. _____

6. *MARN ~ HTRO* with sides and angle measures as indicated below. Find as many missing lengths and angle measures as possible.

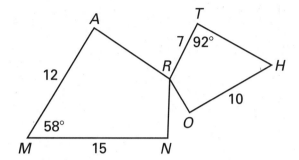

6. _____

_____

_____

_____

7. *Multiple choice.* Size changes preserve ___?___.

   (a) angle measure and area

   (b) collinearity and angle measure

   (c) distance and collinearity

   (d) betweenness and area

7. _____

8. A hexagon has an area of 96 cm², with its longest side 12 cm long. The longest side of a similar hexagon is 8 cm long. What is the area of this similar hexagon?

8. _____

9. *k* is the size-change factor for two similar figures. How do their areas compare?

9. _____

10. A swimming pool that is 14 m long holds 200,000 L of water. A similar pool is 25 m long. How much water will it hold?

10. _____

11. A photo measures 3 in. by 5 in. If the shorter side of a similar photo is 7.5 in., what is the length of the longer side of the photo?

11. _____

12. If a helicopter travels 180 miles in 2 hours, how long would it take to travel 495 miles at the same rate?

12. _____

13. A donut of radius 5 cm weighs 80 g. What would a similar donut of radius 8 cm weigh?

13. _____

Name _____

In 14 and 15, use the figure and the grid below.

14. Graph the image of $\triangle XYZ$ under $S_{\frac{3}{2}}$ and give the coordinates of its vertices.

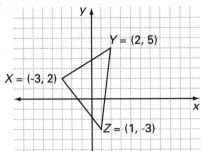

14. _____

_____

_____

15. What is $S_9(Z)$?

15. _____

In 16 and 17, use the figure and the grid below.

16. Graph the image of *CHAD* under $S_{.8}$ and give the coordinates of its vertices.

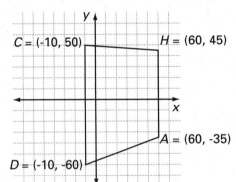

16. _____

_____

_____

_____

17. Verify that the distance between $S(D)$ and $S(A)$ is $.8 \cdot DA$.

17.

Check all your work carefully.

CHAPTER 12 TEST, Form C

1. In the space at the right, draw any size transformation image of △*ABC*. Then answer the following questions about your transformation.

   a. Where is the center?

   b. What is the magnitude?

   c. Is the transformation an expansion or a contraction?

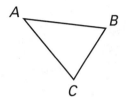

2. In the coordinate plane, the endpoints of $\overline{CD}$ are $C = (x, y)$ and $D = (m, n)$. $\overline{C'D'}$ is the image of $\overline{CD}$ under the transformation S_k. State as many relationships as you can between $\overline{CD}$ and $\overline{C'D'}$.

3. Your little cousin has a new doll house that is labeled "$\frac{1}{12}$ actual size." In a toy store, your cousin found a teapot that is $1\frac{3}{4}$ inches tall. Explain why this teapot is not appropriate for your cousin's doll house.

4. In the trapezoids at the right, explain how you can tell that *SHIP ~ BOAT* is a false statement. Then show how you can make it true by changing just one of the labeled measures.

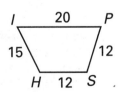

5. At the right is shown a standard-size box of corn flakes. The manufacturer plans to make a jumbo-size box that is similar to it, but is 15 inches high. Use the Fundamental Theorem of Similarity to describe the important characteristics of the jumbo-size box.

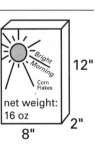

CHAPTER 12 TEST, Form D

The article below appeared in this morning's edition of *The Center City Tribune.*

Pelman board debates tower plans

Tempers flared at yesterday's meeting of the executive board of the Pelman Corporation, as architects from the firm of Madison & Lu presented preliminary plans for the new Pelmanco Plaza. The towering office building is to sit on a one-block lot in the heart of Center City and will serve as the new headquarters for the Pelman Corporation.

At issue is the amount of office space available on the eleven upper floors of the tower. At 2970 square feet each, the total area of these floors is just over 32,000 square feet. However, the director of the board contends that the rapidly expanding company will

need at least twice that amount. To provide the extra space, the director proposed "doubling the building's footprint" to 132 feet by 90 feet. The director claimed that this will double the office area on the upper eleven floors and should roughly double the cost of constructing and operating the tower. Since the company plans to rent space on the first floor to retail shops, the director claims that this also will double the income from rental of this space.

Several board members disagreed with the director's statements. A heated debate ensued, but no agreement was reached. The matter is being submitted to the company treasurer, who will analyze the issue and report to the board at their meeting next month.

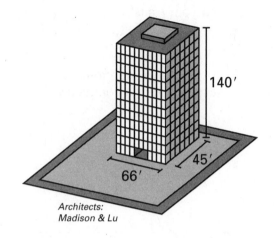

Architects:
Madison & Lu

Artist's rendering
of proposed
Pelmanco Plaza

a. Suppose the board accepted the director's suggestion and increased the "footprint" to 132 feet by 90 feet. Would the new footprint be similar to the one in the diagram above? Explain your reasoning.

b. The director claimed that changing the tower's footprint as described in Part **a** doubles the amount of retail area on the first floor and doubles the office area on the upper eleven floors. Explain why this is incorrect.

c. When analyzing the issue, the treasurer concluded that you can double the office area simply by doubling the height of the tower. Do you agree or disagree with this conclusion? Explain your reasoning.

d. Suppose the executive board decides that it likes both suggestions— "doubling the footprint" of the tower as described in Part **a** and doubling its height as described in Part **c**. You are the company treasurer. Write a report in which you predict how constructing and operating the larger tower would compare to constructing and operating it as specified in the diagram above. In your report, consider items such as the following.

- the cost of various types of building materials, such as windows, steel support beams, wallboard, and concrete for floors

- the area that will be available for office use and retail shops

- the amount of air to be heated in winter and air-conditioned in summer

CHAPTER 12 TEST, Cumulative Form

You will need a ruler and a protractor for this test.

In 1 and 2, $A = (5, -8)$, $B = (-6, 0)$, and $C = (-8, -4)$.

1. Graph $\triangle ABC$ and its image under $S_{\frac{1}{2}}$ on the coordinate axes at the right.

1.

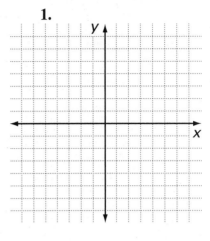

2. Describe the characteristics of $S_{\frac{1}{2}}(\triangle ABC)$.

_____

3. Draw the image of $\odot O$ under a size change with center A and magnitude .75.

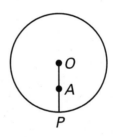

4. A picture with width 4 cm and length 11 cm is enlarged to have a new width of 6 cm.

   a. Find the size change factor of the expansion.

   4. a. _____

   b. Find the length of the enlargement.

   b. _____

   c. Find the area of the enlargement.

   c. _____

   d. The area of the enlargement is how many times the area of the original?

   d. _____

5. Let $A = (4, -7)$ and $B = (-5, 2)$. Suppose $\overline{A'B'} = S_3 \circ S_6(\overline{A'B'})$. Find the length of $\overline{A'B'}$.

5. _____

6. Below $\triangle ABC \sim \triangle DEF$. Find the length of $\overline{EF}$.

6. _____

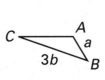

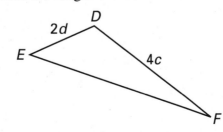

7. A green box has height 1.5 times the height of a blue box, and the length of the shorter side of its base is 0.5 times the corresponding length in the blue box. Could the boxes be similar? Explain your answer.

7. _____

_____

_____

_____

8. If there were a person 3.4 times as tall as you, the person would weigh __**a.**__ times as much. This weight would be supported by about __**b.**__ times the surface area.

8. a. _____

b. _____

9. If $A = (-4, 1)$ and $B = (2, 3)$, verify that the distance between $S_{10}(A)$ and $S_{10}(B)$ is $10 \cdot AB$.

9. _____

10. The preimage below is black and its size-change image is gray. Determine the center and size-change factor k.

10. _____

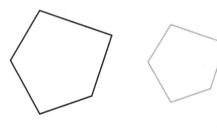

11. Given $A = (2, 1)$, $B = (-4, 5)$, and $C = (3.5, 0)$, let S be the size transformation of magnitude 3.

a. Find $S(A)$, $S(B)$, and $S(C)$.

11. a. _____

b. The distance between $S(A)$ and $S(B)$ is __?__ times the distance between A and B.

b. _____

c. Verify that the slope of $\overline{AB}$ equals the slope of the line through $S(A)$ and $S(B)$.

c. _____

12. Given the points $(0, 2, -3)$ and $(1, -4, 0)$,

a. find the midpoint of the segment joining them.

12. a. _____

b. find the distance between them.

b. _____

13. Consider this conditional: *If two lines are parallel, they must be in the same plane.* a. Write its converse. b. Write its inverse. c. Write its contrapositive. d. Tell which of a–c is (are) true.

a. _____

b. _____

c. _____

d. _____

14. Use an indirect proof to show that $\sqrt[3]{28} \neq 3$.　　　　**14.**

15. Consider the sphere with equation
$(x + 3)^2 + (y - 1)^2 + z^2 = 9.$

a. Name its center.　　　　　　　　　**15. a.** _____

b. Find the length of its radius.　　　　**b.** _____

c. Give the coordinates of two points on the sphere.　　**c.** _____

16. Three statements are given. a. What can you conclude?
b. What law(s) of reasoning have you used?

(1) Kelly and Markeith eat either a bagel or cereal for breakfast each morning.

(2) Kelly did not eat cereal today.

(3) Markeith always eats the breakfast item that Kelly does *not* eat.

a. _____

b. _____

17. Consider the triangle at the right. Are all
triangles with these measures congruent?
Why or why not?

17. _____

_____

_____

18. In the space at the right,
draw in perspective
a right cylinder.

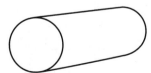

18.

19. Use Cavalieri's Principle to explain whether or not
the figures below have the same volume.

19. _____

_____

_____

_____

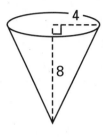

right cone   right rectangular pyramid

20. Calculate the volumes of the figures above to verify your
answer in Question 19.

20. _____

_____

21. The closed figure *ABCDEFGHI* below is the union of
segments and one semicircle. Find its area.

21. _____

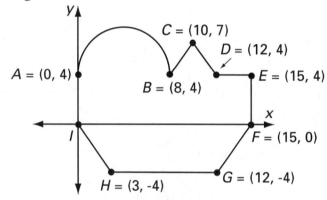

22. Draw the image of the quadrilateral at the
right under the composite $r_m \circ r_n$.

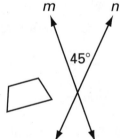

23. *Multiple choice.* Which set of numbers can be the
lengths of three sides of a triangle?

23. _____

(a) $\{1, 2, 3\}$ (b) $\{\frac{1}{2}, \frac{1}{3}, \frac{1}{4}\}$

(c) $\{2, 4, 6\}$ (d) $\{3, 4, 8\}$

24. Each line perpendicular to the line with equation
$3x + 2y = 5$ has slope ___?___.

24. _____

Check all your work carefully.

QUIZ

In 1 and 2, tell whether the two given triangles are similar. Justify your answer.

1. One triangle has sides 7, 11, and 12. A second triangle has sides 48, 28, and 44.

1. _____

_____

_____

_____

2.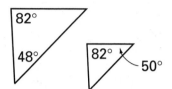

2. _____

_____

_____

_____

3. In △*ABC* at the right, $\overline{BC}$ // $\overline{MN}$. Find each length.

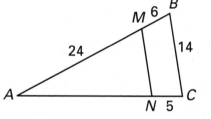

   a. *AN*

3. a. _____

   b. *MN*

   b. _____

4. A telephone pole casts a shadow that is 12 m long. At the same time, a person who is 1.5 m tall casts a shadow of 90 cm. How tall is the telephone pole?

4. _____

5. In the triangle below, *SY* = 1.7, *YT* = 0.5, *XU* = 0.4, and *SU* = 1.76. Is $\overline{UT}$ // $\overline{XY}$? Why or why not?

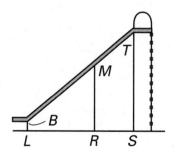

5. _____

_____

_____

_____

6. A slide has three parallel supports as shown at the right. If *LR* = 8 ft, *RS* = 5 ft, *MB* = 10 ft, *BL* = 1 ft, and *MR* = 7 ft, find

   a. *TS*.

6. a. _____

   b. *BT*.

   b. _____

QUIZ

1. In the drawing at the right, △*JMP* and △*JPR* are right triangles. If *PM* = 5 and *JM* = 3, find *MR*.

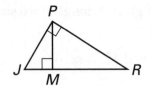

1. _____

2. In the figure at the right, *A* is on $\overline{ED}$ and *AB* = *x*. Find each length.

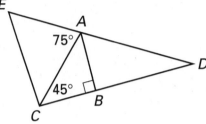

   a. *AD*

   b. *BC*

   c. *AC*

   d. *BD*

2. **a.** _____

  b. _____

  c. _____

  d. _____

3. Use △*WPM* at the right. Find

   a. the measure of ∠*P* to the nearest degree.

   b. the tangent of ∠*W*.

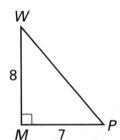

3. **a.** _____

  b. _____

4. Use the definition of tangent to give the tangent of ∠*B* in the triangle at the right.

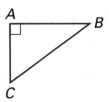

4. _____

5. Give the exact value of tan 45°.

5. _____

6. The pole $\overline{JK}$ supporting the front of the tent shown at the right is 6 ft tall. The measure of the angle between this pole and the wire $\overline{JL}$ is 62. How far from the base of the pole $\overline{JK}$ does the wire meet the ground?

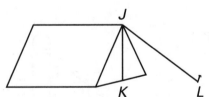

6. _____

CHAPTER 13 TEST, Form A

1. In the figure at the right, is $\overline{JE}$ // $\overline{BG}$? Why or why not?

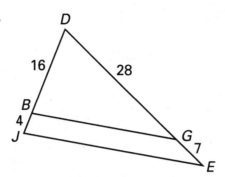

1. _____

   _____

   _____

2. Given $\triangle ABC$ at the right in which $\overline{BC}$ // $\overline{DE}$, find each length.

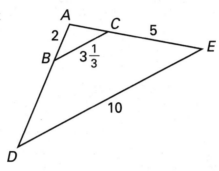

   a. BD

   b. AC

2. a. _____

   b. _____

3. In the figure at the right, $MP = 3$ and $OP = 6$.

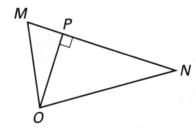

   a. Find PN.

   b. Find ON.

3. a. _____

   b. _____

4. In $\triangle PQR$ at the right, find

   a. PQ.

   b. QR.

4. a. _____

   b. _____

5. In $\triangle CDE$ at the right, find

   a. CD.

   b. CE.

5. a. _____

   b. _____

6. Give the exact value of sin 60°.

6. _____

7. Estimate tan 85° to the nearest thousandth.

7. _____

8. Of angles 1–4 in △*JKO* at the right, which has the greatest sine?

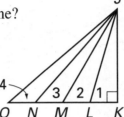

8. _____

9. Use △*JES* at the right

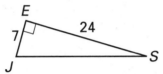

   a. Find tan *S*.

9. a. _____

   b. Find sin *J*.

     b. _____

10. Find the area of △*DEF* at the right.

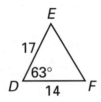

10. _____

In 11 and 12, are the triangles similar? Justify your answer.

11.

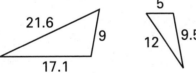

11. _____

_____

_____

12.

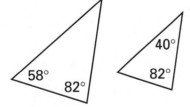

12. _____

_____

_____

13. In the figure at the right, *NR* = 10.5 and *FR* = 10. What is *UR*?

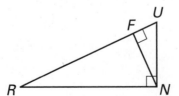

13. _____

In 14 and 15, use △*AIR* **at the right below.**

14. $\frac{IR}{AI}$ is the tangent of which angle?

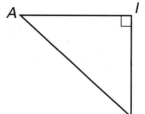

14. _____

15. $\frac{AI}{AR}$ is the ___?___ of angle *A*.

15. _____

16. An apartment building casts a shadow of 42 ft. At the same time, a 6-ft resident of the building casts a shadow of 3.5 ft. How tall is the building?

16. _____

17. In the roof at the right, beam $\overline{LT}$ is parallel to beam $\overline{NP}$ and splits the sides of the roof as shown. If *TP* = 4 m, *ST* = 3 m, *LN* = 5.2 m, and *NP* = 10.8 m, find

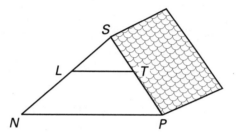

  a. *SL.*

17. a. _____

  b. *LT.*

  b. _____

18. Amy is flying her kite in the park. While she holds one end of the 60-foot kite string, the kite floats at an angle of elevation of 40°. How high is her kite?

18. _____

19. A cowboy must ride his horse across an open field to a point 4 km to the south and 16 km to the east of his present location.

  a. What direction must he ride?

19. a. _____

  b. How far will he need to ride?

  b. _____

Check all your work carefully.

1. In the figure at the right, is $\overline{MN} \parallel \overline{QR}$? Why or why not?

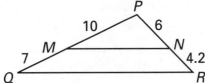

1. _____

_____

_____

2. Given $\triangle ZBA$ at the right in which $\overline{ER} \parallel \overline{ZA}$, find each length.

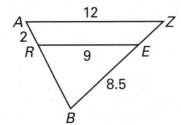

   a. ZE

   b. BR

2. a. _____

   b. _____

3. In the figure at the right, $IN = 8$ and $NS = 14$.

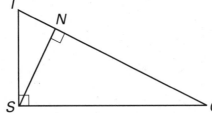

   a. Find NG.

   b. Find GS.

3. a. _____

   b. _____

4. In $\triangle ABC$ at the right, find

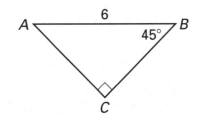

   a. AC.

   b. BC.

4. a. _____

   b. _____

5. In $\triangle SNO$ at the right, find

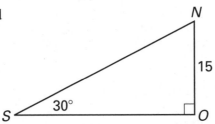

   a. SO.

   b. SN.

5. a. _____

   b. _____

6. Give the exact value of $\sin 45°$.

6. _____

7. Estimate $\sin 72°$ to the nearest thousandth.

7. _____

8. Of angles 1–3 in △*DEF* at the right, which has the least sine?

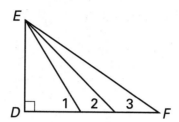

8. _____

9. Use △*TAF* at the right.

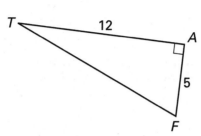

   a. Find tan *F.*

   b. Find cos *T.*

9. a. _____

  b. _____

10. Find the area of △*JKL* at the right.

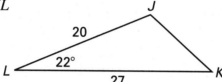

10. _____

In 11 and 12, are the triangles similar? Justify your answer.

11.

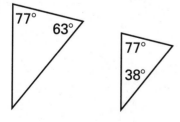

11. _____

_____

_____

12.

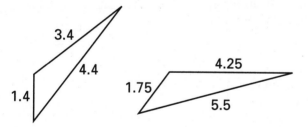

12. _____

_____

_____

13. In the figure at the right, *AL* = 20 and *LF* = 16. What is *BL?*

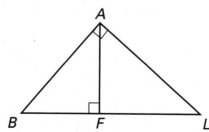

13. _____

In 14 and 15, use △*TUV* at the right below.

14. $\dfrac{VU}{UT}$ is the cosine of which angle?

14. _____

15. $\dfrac{VU}{TV}$ is the ___?___ of angle *T*.

15. _____

16. A billboard casts a shadow of 6 m. At the same time, a meter stick casts a shadow of 40 cm. How tall is the billboard?

16. _____

17. In the roof shown at the right, beam $\overline{BR}$ is parallel to beam $\overline{EF}$ and splits the sides of the roof as shown. If *FR* = 10 ft, *LF* = 24 ft, *BE* = 8 ft, and *BR* = 22 ft, find

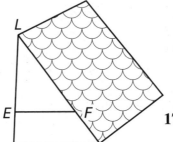

   a. *EL.*

17. a. _____

   b. *EF.*

   b. _____

18. The wire support for a telephone pole is 20 m long. If the angle of depression of the wire is 25°, how tall is the telephone pole?

18. _____

19. A storm cloud is traveling toward the center of a large city. It is currently 120 miles west and 35 miles south of the city. If it is to hit the city,

   a. what direction will it travel?

19. a. _____

   b. how far will it travel?

   b. _____

Check all your work carefully.

CHAPTER 13 TEST, Form C

1. In △*RST* at the right, $\overline{MN}$ // $\overline{RT}$ and $w \neq x \neq y \neq z$. Give a possible set of values for *w, x, y,* and *z*. Explain how you decided on those values.

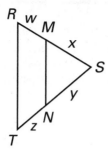

2. Describe at least one way in which the figure at the right illustrates the term *geometric mean*.

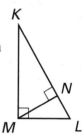

3. The formula for the area *A* of a triangle is $A = \frac{1}{2}ab$, where *b* is the length of the base and *a* is the altitude to that base. Sally says you cannot find the area of the triangle at the right because there is not enough information given. Do you agree? Explain your reasoning.

4. Marco performed these calculations to find the height of the tree shown at the right.

$$\cos 68° = \frac{x}{12}$$

$$x = \frac{\cos 68°}{12} \approx .03$$

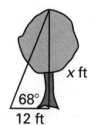

How can Marco tell that he made an error? What error(s) did he make? Correct the error(s) and calculate the height of the tree.

5. State one of the three triangle similarity theorems that you studied in this chapter. Draw and label two triangles that you can prove to be similar as a result of the theorem you chose.

6. Write a real-world problem that you can solve by finding the magnitude and direction of vector *OA* at the right. Then show how to solve your problem.

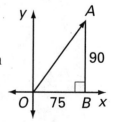

CHAPTER 13 TEST, Form D

Often the top layer of a quilt is made from many patches of colorful fabric sewn together to make an attractive design. The result, accordingly, is called a patchwork quilt. Some patchwork quilts may appear quite elaborate, but their basic designs often are based in relatively simple geometric figures.

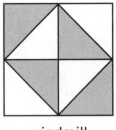

windmill

A set of patches that join together to form a basic unit of the design is called a *block*. At the right are blocks of some designs that feature triangular patches. Each block is a square with 8-inch sides.

Quiltmakers usually use stiff material such as cardboard, sandpaper, or plastic to make guides for outlining and cutting quilt patches. These guides are called *patterns* for the patches. In answering the questions that follow, imagine that you are responsible for preparing the patterns. When necessary, round the results of your calculations to the nearest hundredth.

pinwheel

a. The windmill design is made of eight congruent triangles.

  i. What special type of triangle are they?

  ii. Calculate the length of each side of one of these triangles.

b. The pinwheel design is made of three different types of triangles. The measure of the smallest angle in the design is 20. For each type of triangle, give the measures of each angle and the length of each side.

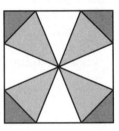

blossom

c. Choose one of the other three blocks. Identify all the different figures that make up the design. Then, for each figure, give the measure of each angle and the length of each side. *(Hints for the eight-pointed star design:* The length of each side of the middle square is about 1.46 inches, and each "point" of the star is a 30-60-90 triangle.)

d. Create your own original design for a patchwork quilt. Be sure to include one or more types of right triangles in your design. In creating your design, keep in mind not only the appearance of an individual block, but also the appearance of the entire quilt when several blocks are stitched together. For example, below is the result when several blocks of the eight-pointed-star design are stitched together.

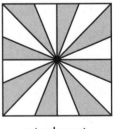

starburst

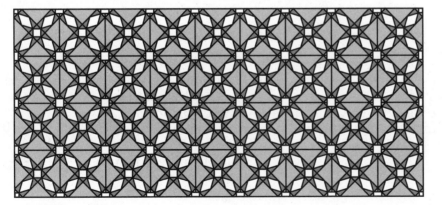

Make a careful drawing of one block of your design. Then give a detailed description of each figure in your design, including the measures of all angles and sides and how you arrived at them.

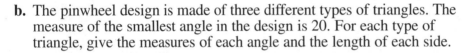

eight-pointed star

CHAPTER 13 TEST, Cumulative Form

You will need a ruler for this test.

1. In $\triangle DEF$ at the right, find

    a. EF.

    b. DE.

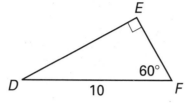

1. a. _____

    b. _____

2. *True or false.* In $\triangle ABC$ at the right, $\overline{DE} \parallel \overline{BC}$ and $\dfrac{AD}{DB} = \dfrac{AE}{EC} = \dfrac{DE}{BC}$.

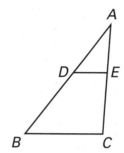

2. _____

3. Use the figure at the right.

    a. The numbered angle with the least cosine is ___?___.

    b. The numbered angle with the greatest tangent is ___?___.

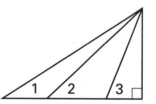

3. a. _____

    b. _____

4. Let $R = (-1, 3)$, $W = (2, 4)$, and $T = (0, 7)$. Give the coordinates of the vertices of the image of $\triangle RWT$ under $S_{\frac{3}{2}}$.

4. _____

5. At the right $\ell \parallel m$. Draw $r_{\ell} \circ r_{m}(GHI)$. What kind of transformation is $r_{\ell} \circ r_{m}$?

5. _____

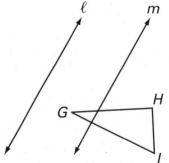

6. Hexagon $ABCDEF$ and $A'B'C'D'E'F'$ are similar with ratio of similitude k. $ABCDEF$ has perimeter p and area a. Find

    a. the perimeter of $A'B'C'D'E'F'$.

    b. the area of $A'B'C'D'E'F'$.

6. a. _____

    b. _____

**In 7 and 8, are the two triangles similar? Justify
your answer.**

7.

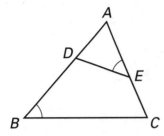

7. _____

_____

_____

8.

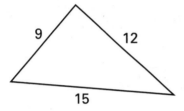

8. _____

_____

_____

9. Refer to the figure at the right.
The target is shot from
45 meters away. If a bullet
lands at random in the target
area, what is the probability
that it will hit the bull's-eye?

radius
200 mm

radius
15 mm

9. _____

10. In the figure at the right,
$LA = RA$, $AB = AT$,
$m\angle B = m\angle T$, $LA = 3$, and
$AB = 2$. Is $\triangle LAB \cong \triangle RAT$?
Justify your answer.

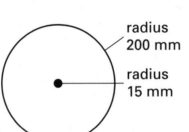

10. _____

_____

_____

_____

11. Refer to the figure at the
right. Find *AB*.

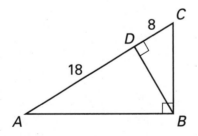

11. _____

12. A 32-ft ladder resting against a wall makes an angle of 75°
with the ground. How far is the foot of the ladder from
the base of the wall?

12. _____

13. In $\triangle DEF$, $DE = 17$, $EF = 5$, and $m\angle E = 78$. What is the
area of $\triangle DEF$?

13. _____

14. Provide an argument for the following proof.

14.

Given: ⊙O and ⊙P below intersect at S and T.
To prove: OSPT is a kite.

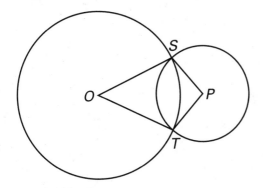

15. Refer to the figure at the right.

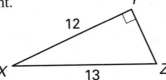

a. sin X = ___?___

15. a. _____

b. tan Z = ___?___

b. _____

16. A boat is traveling directly to a point 7.4 km north and 3.6 km west of its present location.

a. In what direction is it heading?

16. a. _____

b. How far will it travel?

b. _____

17. Write an equation for the line that passes through (0, 1) and is perpendicular to the line with equation $3x + 4y = 5$.

17. _____

18. Pentagon $P'E'N'T'A'$ at the right below is a size transformation image of pentagon *PENTA* with center O.

a. Find the magnitude of the size change.

18. a. _____

b. Find $N'T'$.

b. _____

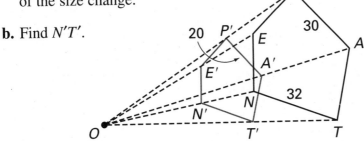

19. *True or false.* A size change does *not* preserve betweenness.

19. _____

20. A photograph is 5″ by 7″. If the shorter dimension of a similar photograph is 8″, what is its longer dimension?

20. _____

21. In the figure at the right, $GH = 2\sqrt{2}$ cm. Find *GI*.

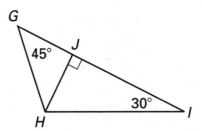

21. _____

22. At the right, draw the size-transformation image of hexagon *ABCDEF* with magnitude $\frac{1}{2}$ and center *A*.

22.

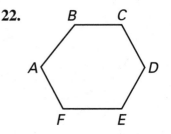

23. Find the surface area of a sphere with radius of 11 cm.

23. _____

24. From eye level 5 ft above the ground, a person has to look up at an angle of 40° to see the top of a tree 35 ft away. How tall is the tree?

24. _____

Check all your work carefully.

QUIZ

You will need a ruler and a protractor for this quiz.

In 1 and 2, use ⊙*H* at the right.
If m∠*EHF* = 74, find

1. m∠*EIF*.

2. m$\overarc{EG}$.

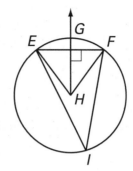

1. _____

2. _____

3. Suppose a circle has a radius of 14 mm. Find the length of a chord of a 120° arc.

3. _____

4. A photographer wants to take a photograph of a rectangular building which is 82 meters wide. He uses a camera with a picture angle of 85°. How far from the center of the building must he be if he stands on the perpendicular bisector of the face of the building?

4. _____

5. Given ⊙*O* at the right with *MA* = *MB* and m∠*EOB* = *y*. Explain why m$\overarc{EA}$ = *y*.

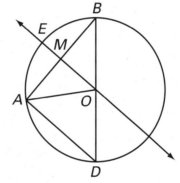

5. _____

   _____

   _____

6. Use the right-angle method to locate the center of the circle at the right.

6.

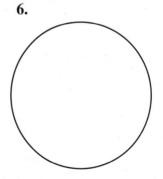

QUIZ

In 1 and 2, assume the radius of the earth is 3960 miles or 6375 kilometers and that there are no hills or obstructions.

1. About how far can a person see to the horizon from the top of the Space Needle in Seattle, 605 ft off the ground? (5280 feet = 1 mile)

1. _____

2. Mt. Etna is the tallest active volcano in Sicily. To the nearest kilometer, how far could a person see if it were possible to stand at the top of this 3.368-km-high volcano?

2. _____

In 3 and 4, use the diagram at the right below in which m∠A = 20 and m$\widehat{EF}$ = 100°.

3. **a.** What is m$\widehat{BC}$?

3. **a.** _____

   b. What is m∠BDC?

   b. _____

4. If m$\widehat{EB}$ = $(3x)°$ and m$\widehat{CF}$ = $(7x)°$, find m∠CDF.

4. _____

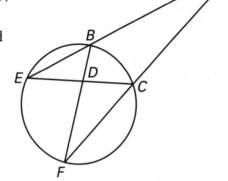

In 5–8, $\overleftrightarrow{NO}$ and $\overleftrightarrow{NQ}$ are tangents to ⊙P at O and Q, respectively.

5. If ON = 8 and QP = 6, what is the area of △OPN?

5. _____

6. If m∠ONQ = 80, what is m$\widehat{OR}$?

6. _____

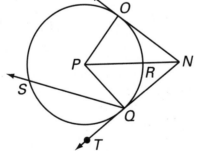

7. If m∠TQS = 55, find m$\widehat{QS}$.

7. _____

8. Prove that m∠ONQ + m$\widehat{OQ}$ = 180°.

8.

CHAPTER 14 TEST, Form A

You will need a ruler, a protractor, and a compass for this test.

1. *LMNO* is a square inscribed in
   ⊙*P* at the right. The radius of
   ⊙*P* = 5.

   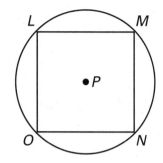

   a. Find *MN*.

   b. Find the length of $\overset{\frown}{LON}$.

   1. a. _____

   b. _____

2. In ⊙*E* at the right, m∠*ABE* = 55.
   Find m$\overset{\frown}{BC}$.

   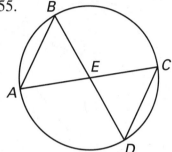

   2. _____

3. Given a circle with radius 7, find the chord length
   of a 132° arc.

   3. _____

4. Isosceles trapezoid *MAIN* at
   the right is inscribed in ⊙*E*.
   Diameter $\overline{XY}$ is perpendicular
   to $\overline{MA}$. Explain why $\overline{XY}$
   bisects $\overline{NI}$.

   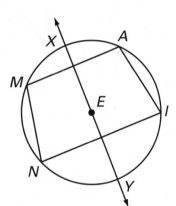

   4. _____

   _____

   _____

   _____

   _____

   _____

In 5 and 6, use the figure at the right below.

5. Suppose m$\overset{\frown}{RT}$ = 14°, and
   m∠*STU* = 39. Find m∠*Q*.

   5. _____

6. Suppose m∠*RVS* = 128
   and m$\overset{\frown}{TU}$ = 141°.
   Find m$\overset{\frown}{RS}$.

   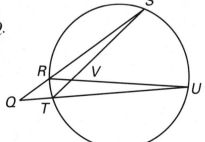

   6. _____

7. Use the right-angle method to locate the center of the circle at the right.

7.

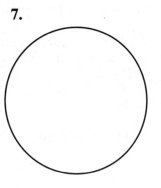

8. In the figure at the right, $AB = 4$, $BC = 11$, and $AE = 5$. What is DE?

8. _____

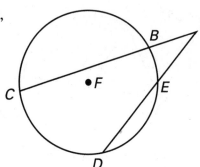

9. $\overrightarrow{OR}$ is tangent to $\odot N$ at R. If $OR = 18$ and $OE = 12$, find GE.

9. _____

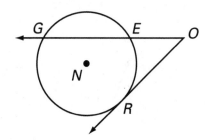

10. Use the figure at the right to write a proof argument.

Given: $\overleftrightarrow{WY}$ is tangent to $\odot Z$ at W.

To prove: $m\angle WYZ = 90 - m\widehat{WV}$.

10.

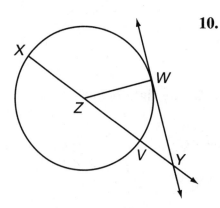

11. An object in space has a volume of 520 cm^3.

    a. What is the least possible surface area of an object with this volume?

    11. a. _____

    b. Name this figure.

    b. _____

    c. Calculate the surface area of the rectangular prism with this volume and the least possible surface area.

    c. _____

12. You have a camera with a lens that has a picture angle of 57°. During a visit to Jerusalem, you would like to take a picture of the famous Western (or Wailing) Wall, which measures about 50 m in length.

    a. At the right, draw a picture to indicate all the places where you can stand to fit the entire wall into your picture.

12. a.

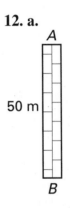

    b. If you stand on the perpendicular bisector of the line where the wall meets the ground, how far away from it will you need to be to fit the entire wall into your picture?

    b. _____

13. Assume that the radius of the earth is 6375 kilometers and that there are no hills or obstructions. If a bird were perched atop one of the towers of the Golden Gate Bridge, 228 meters above the water level, about how far could it see?

    13. _____

14. A wooden storage chest is to be a rectangular solid with a surface area of 100 ft^2. What is the maximum volume for this storage chest?

    14. _____

Check all your work carefully.

CHAPTER 14 TEST, Form B

You will need a ruler, a protractor, and a compass for this test.

1. $\triangle ABC$ is an equilateral triangle inscribed in $\odot D$ at the right. The radius of $\odot D = 8$.

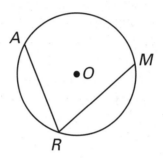

   a. Find AB.

   b. Find the length of $\overset{\frown}{BCA}$.

1. a. _____

    b. _____

2. In $\odot O$ at the right, $m\overset{\frown}{AR} = 104°$ and $m\overset{\frown}{MR} = 118°$. Find $m\angle ARM$.

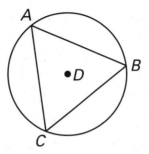

2. _____

3. Given a circle with radius 3.5, find the chord length of an 86° arc.

3. _____

4. Explain why, in $\odot I$ at the right, $m\angle EHF + m\angle DGE = 45$ if $m\overset{\frown}{HD} = 90°$.

4. _____

    _____

    _____

    _____

    _____

    _____

In 5 and 6, use the figure at the right below.

5. Suppose $m\overset{\frown}{UP} = 34°$ and $m\angle STO = 46$. Find $m\angle L$.

5. _____

6. Suppose $m\angle CRT = 138$ and $m\overset{\frown}{SO} = 103°$. Find $m\overset{\frown}{CUT}$.

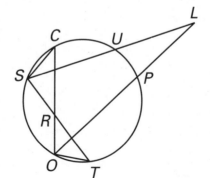

6. _____

7. Use the right-angle method to locate the center of the circle at the right.

7.

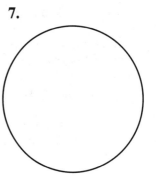

8. In ⊙*Q* at the right, *ST* = 16, *RS* = 52, and *TU* = 20. What is *UV*?

8. _____

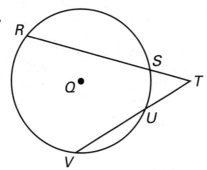

9. In ⊙*L* at the right, $\overrightarrow{SI}$ is tangent at *I*. If *SI* = 9 and *OS* = 7.2, what is *FO*?

9. _____

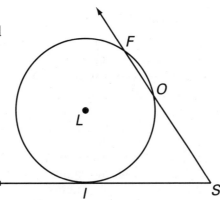

10. Use ⊙*P* at the right.

Given: $\overleftrightarrow{PR} \perp \overleftrightarrow{RO}$, $\overleftrightarrow{OE} \mathbin{/\!/} \overline{RP}$, and m$\widehat{RV}$ = 40°.

To prove: m$\widehat{ETR}$ = 220°.

10.

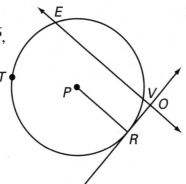

11. An object in space has a volume of 2000 cm³.

    a. What is the least possible surface area of an object   **11. a.** _____
    with this volume?

    b. Name this figure.   **b.** _____

    c. Calculate the surface area of the rectangular prism   **c.** _____
    with this volume and the least possible surface area.

12. You have a camera with a lens that has a 52° picture angle.
During a visit to Washington, D.C., you would like to take a
picture of the White House, which measures 168 ft across.

    a. At the right, draw a picture to indicate all the   **12. a.**
    places where you can stand so that $\overline{AB}$, the entire
    front of the White House, just fits into your picture.

    b. If you stand directly in front of the middle of   **b.** _____
    the White House, how far away from it will
    you need to be to fit the entire building into
    your picture?

13. If you are in hot-air balloon 2500 ft above sea level, how   **13.** _____
far on Earth could you see? Assume that the radius of the
earth is 3960 miles and that there are no obstructions.
(5280 feet = 1 mile)

14. A builder is planning some storage bins with rectangular   **14.** _____
bases, each of which is to occupy 150 square feet of
ground. What is the least perimeter that a bin can have?   _____
Why might the builder prefer the least perimeter?

                                                                       _____

Check all your work carefully.

CHAPTER 14 TEST, Form C

1. At the right are three figures, labeled I, II, and III. Assume that you are given the measures of all labeled arcs. For each figure, describe the procedure you could follow to find m∠*CAB*. How are your procedures alike? How are they different?

I.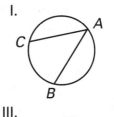

II.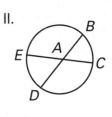

III.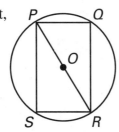

---

2. In the figure at the right, *PQRS* is a rectangle inscribed in ⊙*O*, m∠*QPR* = 60 and *PR* = 18. State as many additional facts about the figure as you can.

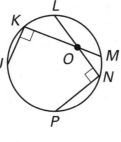

3. Give a set of possible values for the lengths labeled *a, b, c, d,* and *e* in the figure at the right. Explain how you decided on the values that you chose.

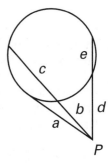

---

4. Jameel tried to find the center of a circle by the right angle method. His work is at the right. Clearly, the point he labeled *O* is not the center. Describe the error(s) he made. Then show how to correct the error(s).

5. Write a real-world problem that you can solve by applying one of the Isoperimetric Inequalities. Then show how to solve your problem.

CHAPTER 14 TEST, Form D

Line designs are geometric patterns consisting entirely of line segments. The segments are placed in such a way that they produce the illusion of a curve.

Each of the three line designs below, for example, consists of segments whose endpoints are ten *anchor points* equally spaced around a circle. (The circle is gray because it is used to place the points, but is not part of the final design.) Notice how the decagon at the center of the design appears more "curved" as the placement of the segments changes.

I.  II. 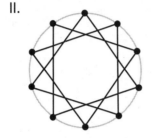 III.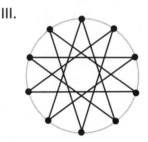

a. In each design above, the ten anchor points separate the circle into ten arcs. What is the measure of one of these arcs?

b. In each design above, each anchor point is the vertex of an inscribed angle of the circle. Show how to use the Inscribed Angle Theorem to find the measure of each of these angles.

c. Often line designs are made using string or yarn stretched between small nails placed at the anchor points. Suppose the designs above are to be made in this manner. If the diameter of the circle is 24 inches, calculate the total amount of string or yarn needed for each design.

d. For these questions, refer to Figure I only. Assume that the diameter of the circle is 24 inches.

   i. When two segments of the design intersect in the interior of the circle, two pairs of vertical angles are formed. Show how to use the Angle-Chord Theorem to find the measure of the larger angles.

   ii. Calculate the length of a segment whose endpoints are two anchor points.

   iii. Use your answers to parts i and ii to find the length of the smaller segments formed when two chords of the design intersect in the interior of the circle.

   iv. What is the length of each side of the decagon at the center of the design?

e. Create an original line design that uses points on a circle as its anchor points. Draw the design on paper. Specify a diameter for your circle, and calculate the amount of string or yarn that you would need if you were to make your design as described in Part **c** above. Then write a report in which you use the methods and theorems of this chapter to find as many angle measures and lengths in your design as you can.

CHAPTER 14 TEST, Cumulative Form

You will need a ruler, a protractor, and a compass for this test.

1. Use the right-angle method to locate the center of the circle at the right.

   1.

   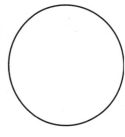

2. Draw the circle through points *E, F,* and *G.*

   2.

   E ●

   ● *F*   ● *G*

3. In the figure at the right, *RECT* is a rectangle inscribed in ⊙*O*. The distance from the center *O* to $\overline{RT}$ is 5, and the radius of the circle is 13. Find the area of the shaded region.

   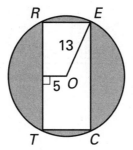

   3. _____

4. *True or false.* Of all the plane figures with the same perimeter, the circle has the least area.

   4. _____

5. Give the exact value for each trigonometric ratio.

   a. cos 30°

   5. a. _____

   b. tan 45°

   b. _____

6. Refer to the figure at the right. $\overline{YX}$ is tangent to ⊙*O*. Find the length of $\overline{YZ}$.

   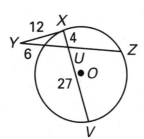

   6. _____

7. The figure at the right consists of three semicircles on the sides of right triangle *ABC*. The area of the semicircle of ⊙*G* is 4π. Find the total area of the figure.

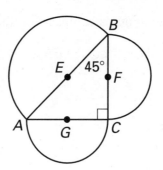

7. _____

8. In the figure at the right, $\overleftrightarrow{ST}$ is tangent to circle *C* at *T*. △*TRI* is inscribed in ⊙*C* and *RT* = *RI*. Write a proof argument to show that $\overline{RT}$ bisects ∠*STI*.

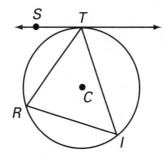

8.

In 9 and 10, are the triangles similar? Justify your answer.

9.

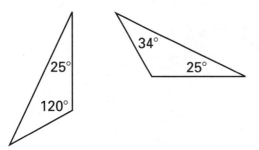

9. _____

_____

_____

10.

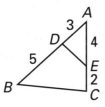

10. _____

_____

_____

11. In a circle with radius of 9, find the length of a chord of

  a. a 90° arc.   **b.** a 150° arc.

11. **a.** _____

  b. _____

12. Refer to the figure at the right. Is *DECF* a parallelogram? Why or why not?

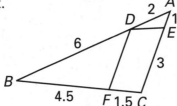

12. _____

_____

_____

13. $\overleftrightarrow{CA}$ is tangent to
⊙*O* at *A*. Find

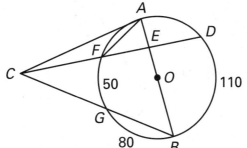

  a. m∠*DCB*.

  b. m∠*CAF*.

  c. m∠*DEB*.

13. a. _____

    b. _____

    c. _____

14. How far up a vertical wall can a 4.6-meter ladder reach
if the angle it makes with the ground is 73°?

14. _____

15. A boat is leaving the lake shore
in a straight line at an angle of
72° with a speed of 15 miles
per hour. How long will it
take the boat to be 39 miles
away from the lake shore?
Assume the shore of the lake
is straight.

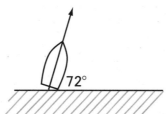

15. _____

16. At the right, m∠*BAD* = m∠*CAD*.
Write a proof argument to show that
△*ABC* is isosceles.

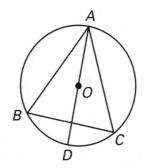

16.

17. *Multiple choice.* A rhombus is *not*

  (a) a kite.   (b) a trapezoid.

  (c) a square.   (d) a parallelogram.

17. _____

18. How far can you see from the top of a building
256 meters up? Assume the radius of the earth is
6374 kilometers and there are no hills or obstructions.

18. _____

19. Maria, John, Kim, Tanisha, and Thao attend Central High.
Among them, two are freshmen, one is a sophomore, and
two are juniors. Maria is either a freshman or a junior.
Tanisha is neither a freshman nor a sophomore. John is
not a junior. Kim is neither a freshman nor a junior. Thao
is not a freshman. Determine each person's year in school.

19. _____

    _____

    _____

    _____

20. A sphere and a cone both have volume 100 cubic feet.
Which one has less surface area? Explain why.

20. _____

    _____

21. Tell whether the network at the right is traversable or not.

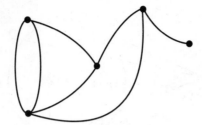

21. _____

22. At the right is a building viewed from the top. Locate all the points where a photographer could stand to exactly fit the east side of the building if the camera lens has a picture angle of 62°.

22.

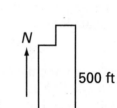

N

500 ft

23. Refer to the figure at the right. Find *AB* and *BC*.

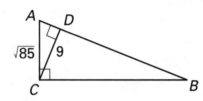

23. _____

24. A figure with area 81 is transformed into a figure with area of 9 under a size change of magnitude ___?___.

24. _____

25. At the right, *m* // *n*. Draw r$_m$ ∘ r$_n$ (△*ABC*).

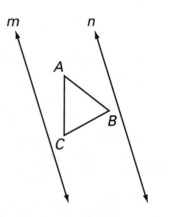

26. a. Find the greatest possible area for a rectangle with perimeter 33 meters.

26. a. _____

b. What is the name of this rectangle?

b. _____

Check all your work carefully.

COMPREHENSIVE TEST, Chapters 1–14

You will need a ruler and a protractor for this test.

1. The outside temperature goes from -17° to 8°. What is the change in temperature?

   (a) 9°   (b) -9°   (c) 25°   (d) -25°

   1. _____

2. If $\triangle ACE \cong \triangle DEC$, name the angle which corresponds to $\angle CEA$.

   (a) $\angle CED$ (b) $\angle CDE$ (c) $\angle EDC$ (d) $\angle ECD$

   2. _____

3. If Maple Road runs parallel to Oak Street, and Oak Street is perpendicular to Main Street, what can you conclude?

   (a) Maple Road is parallel to Main Street.

   (b) Maple Road is perpendicular to Main Street.

   (c) There is not enough information to draw a conclusion.

   3. _____

4. An obtuse triangular region is a d-dimensional figure, where $d =$

   (a) 1.   (b) 2.   (c) 3.   (d) zero.

   4. _____

5. The figure at the right is *not* a polygon because

   (a) it is not closed.

   (b) it is not the union of segments.

   (c) it has only three sides.

   (d) its sides intersect at more than one point.

   5. _____

6. Which figure below shows a pair of adjacent supplementary angles?

   6. _____

   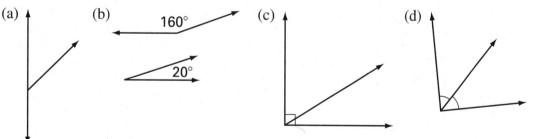
   (a)   (b) 160° 20°   (c)   (d)

7. Let $A = \{10, 17, 20, 27, 30, 37, 40, 47, 50\}$ and $B =$ the set of all integers greater than 20 that are multiples of 5. What is $A \cap B$?

   (a) $\{30, 40, 50\}$ (b) $\{20, 30, 40, 50\}$

   (c) $\{10, 20\}$ (d) $\{10, 20, 30, 40, 50\}$

   7. _____

8. In the quadrilateral at the right, find *x*.

   (a) 60   (b) 50

   (c) 54   (d) none of the above

8. _____

9. Arrange from the most general to the most specific: rhombus, quadrilateral, square, parallelogram.

   (a) quadrilateral, rhombus, parallelogram, square

   (b) quadrilateral, parallelogram, rhombus, square

   (c) square, rhombus, parallelogram, quadrilateral

   (d) square, parallelogram, rhombus, quadrilateral

9. _____

10. The figure at the right has *n*-fold rotation symmetry. *n* is ___?___.

    (a) zero   (b) 1

    (c) 2   (d) more than 2

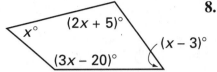

10. _____

11. In the figure at the right, which is the shortest segment?

    (a) $\overline{AD}$ (b) $\overline{BD}$

    (c) $\overline{DC}$ (d) $\overline{AB}$

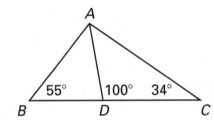

11. _____

12. In the figure at the right, $\overline{AC}$ and $\overline{BD}$ intersect at *E*. Which additional information is sufficient for the figure to be a parallelogram?

    (a) $AB = BC, AD = DC$

    (b) $AE = ED, BE = EC$

    (c) $\overline{AD} \mathbin{/\!/} \overline{BC}, AD = 3, BC = 3$

    (d) none of the above

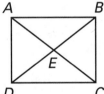

12. _____

13. Refer to the figure at the right. Three metal disks are cut out of a 10-m-by-30-m rectangular piece of metal. How much metal is wasted?

    (a) ≈ 235.62 m²   (b) ≈ 221.46 m²

    (c) ≈ 142.92 m²   (d) ≈ 64.38 m²

13. _____

14. Which can be the lengths of sides of a right triangle?   14. _____

    (a) 8, 31, 32   (b) 16, 20, 36

    (c) 1, 2, $\sqrt{5}$ (d) $\sqrt{3}$, $\sqrt{4}$, $\sqrt{5}$

15. is which view of the right square pyramid ?   15. _____

    (a) the top   (b) the front

    (c) the right side   (d) the left side

16. In the oblique cylinder at the right, $AC = 13$ cm, $BD = 12$ cm, and $CD = 7$ cm. What is the height of the cylinder?   16. _____

    (a) 8 cm   (b) 10 cm

    (c) 6 cm   (d) 12 cm

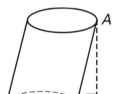

17. The diameter and the thickness of a pizza have been doubled. What is known about the new volume?   17. _____

    (a) It remains the same.   (b) It has been doubled.

    (c) It is four times the old one.   (d) It is eight times the old one.

18. The solids in which pair have the same volume?   18. _____

    (a)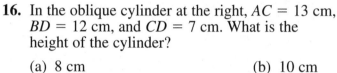

    (b)

    (c)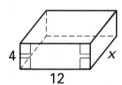

    (d)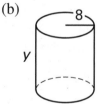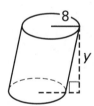

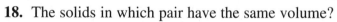

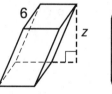
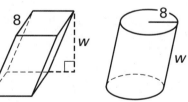

19. If the conditional $p \Rightarrow q$ is true, which of the following is also true?   19. _____

    (a) $q \Rightarrow p$ (b) $p \Rightarrow$ not-q

    (c) not-$p \Rightarrow$ not-q (d) not-$q \Rightarrow$ not-p

▶ **COMPREHENSIVE TEST, Chapters 1–14** *page 4*

20. The side of each small square is 1 unit. Which is the graph of $(x + 1)^2 + (y - 2)^2 = 4$?

20. _____

(a)

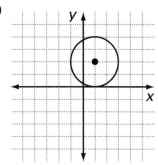

(b)

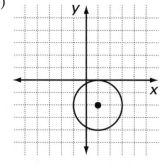

(c)

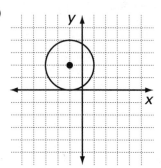

(d)

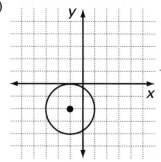

21. Which of the following is *not* preserved by a size change of magnitude $\frac{3}{2}$?

21. _____

  (a) collinearity   (b) angle measure

  (c) distance   (d) betweenness

22. In $\triangle ABC$ at the right, $\overline{BA} \perp \overline{CA}$ and $\overline{AD} \perp \overline{BC}$. If $AB = 3$ and $AC = 4$, which segment has a length of 2.4?

22. _____

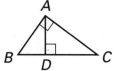

  (a) $\overline{BC}$ (b) $\overline{AD}$

  (c) $\overline{DC}$ (d) $\overline{BD}$

23. Use the figure at the right. Which angle has the greatest tangent?

23. _____

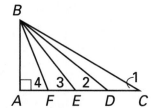

  (a) $\angle 1$ (b) $\angle 2$

  (c) $\angle 3$ (d) $\angle 4$

24. Assuming the following figures have the same perimeter, which has the greatest area?

24. _____

  (a) triangle   (b) square

  (c) circle   (d) regular

25. Assume the radius of the earth is 3960 miles and that there are no hills or obstructions. About how far can you see to the horizon from a plane 5 miles high?

    (a) 5 miles   (b) 25 miles

    (c) 200 miles   (d) 39,625 miles

25. _____

26. The composite of three reflections can be which of the following?

    (a) reflection or rotation   (b) translation or glide reflection

    (c) rotation or translation   (d) glide reflection or reflection

26. _____

27. To rotate $\triangle ABC$ -30° about a point O, you can reflect it over two lines that form an angle of ___?___ whose vertex is O.

    (a) 15°   (b) 30°   (c) 45°   (d) 60°

27. _____

28. The slope of a line which is perpendicular to the line with equation $2x + 3y = 5$ is ___?___ .

    (a) $-\dfrac{2}{3}$ (b) $-\dfrac{3}{2}$ (c) $\dfrac{2}{3}$ (d) $\dfrac{3}{2}$

28. _____

29. Write an argument to complete the proof below.

    Given: $AEFG$ is a trapezoid with bases $\overline{AE}$ and $\overline{GF}$; $\triangle GCF$ is an isosceles triangle with vertex C.

    To prove: $BDFG$ is an isosceles trapezoid.

29.

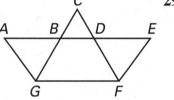

30. Schedule six teams for a round-robin tournament.

_____

_____

31. Find the exact volume of a sphere with radius 2 feet.

31. _____

32. An airplane is flying at 270 miles per hour in the direction 20° north of west. Draw this situation using a vector.

Check all your work carefully.

32.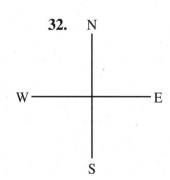

Answers and Evaluation Guides*

Quiz	Lessons 1-1 Through 1-3

1. (d) **2.** 475
3. oblique **4.** vertical
5.

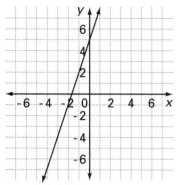

6. 109 miles
7. a. the buttons
   b. Sample: the outline of the shirt

Quiz	Lessons 1-4 Through 1-6

1. a dot, a location, an ordered pair (x, y), and a node of a network
2. 3 **3.** 5 **4.** 1
5. Yes. Sample: *NODNOD*
6. Sample:

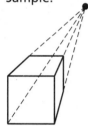

7. points
8. a. Sample:

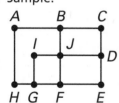

   b. No. The network has more than two odd nodes. In the sketch above, the odd nodes are *B, D, F,* and *G.*

Chapter 1 Test, Form A

1. 54
2. 114°F
3.

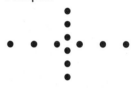

4. Sample:

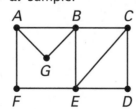

5. a. Sample: (0, -1), (1, 3)
   b, c.

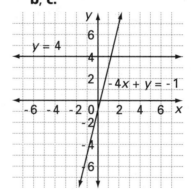

6. No. The network has more than two odd nodes (*A, B, C,* and *D*).
7. a. Sample:

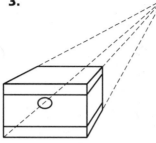

   b. Sample: In the sketch given in Part a, a traversable path would be *ABCDEFAGBEC*

8. 3
9. true
10. segment
11. vertical
12. oblique
13. $\overrightarrow{ON}$ or $\overrightarrow{OT}$
14. 54.7
15. Yes. Sample: Each consists of points *N* and *T* and all the points between *N* and *T.*
16. -58 and 22
17. 119 miles
18. points
19. Sample:

20. Sample:

In graph theory, the only points are the endpoints of arcs; there are no points in the middle of an arc. Arcs may be nonlinear; betweenness implies linearity.
21. Sample:
   a. the holes in the watch band
   b. the outline of the face of the watch

*Evaluation Guides for Chapter Tests, Forms C and D, are on pages 251–278.

ANSWERS

217

1. 112

2. 107°F

3.

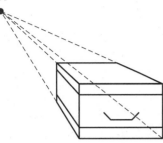

4. Sample:

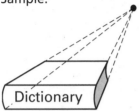

5. a. Sample: (0, -3), (5, -2)

b,c.

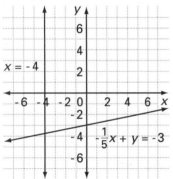

6. Yes. Sample: *NMNOMOPMP*

7. a. Sample:

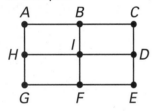

b. The network has more than two odd nodes. In the sketch above, the odd nodes are *B*, *D*, *F*, and *H*.

8. 3

9. true

10. ray

11. horizontal

12. oblique

13. $\overrightarrow{EI}$ or $\overrightarrow{EN}$

14. 43.8

15. No. Sample: $\overrightarrow{MT}$ consists of the points on $\overline{MT}$ and all points for which *T* is between the point and *M*. $\overrightarrow{TM}$ consists of the points on $\overline{MT}$ and all points for which *M* is between the point and *T*.

16. -84 and 38

17. 93 miles

18. points, plane, point

19. Sample:

20. Sample:

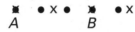

The diagram shows two different lines, one marked by dots (●) and the other marked by xs, that each pass through points *A* and *B*.

21. Sample:
a. the holes through which the spiral passes
b. the edges of the notebook

1. nonconvex

2. convex

3. a. A figure is a line.
b. It is a convex set.

4. a. If a figure is a convex set, then it is a line.
b. false

5. If a creature is an ostrich, then it has a long neck.

6. a. If $x \geq 25$, then $x > 30$; no
b. If $x > 30$, then $x \geq 25$; yes

7. Bettina will get her own phone.

8. No. Explanations may vary. Sample: In if-then form, the announcer said, "If a person attends the game on Friday, then he or she will receive a team poster." The converse is, "If a person receives a team poster then he or she attended the game on Friday." The converse describes Ari's situation. You cannot tell if the converse of a true statement is true. For example, Ari might have bought the poster. So it is impossible to tell if Ari attended the game on Friday.

Quiz   **Lessons 2-4**
Through 2-6

1. nonagon; nonconvex
2. Sample:

3. false
4. $\{E\}$
5. $\{\overline{NE}, \overline{ES}, \overline{ST}, \overline{TN}, \overline{ET}\}$
6. ∅
7. true
8. Samples: A good definition includes only words either commonly understood, defined earlier, or purposely undefined. A good definition accurately describes the idea being defined. A good definition includes no more information than is necessary.
9. $2x + 5 = 4x - 9$; $x = 7$; $GS = 38$

Chapter 2 Test, Form A

1. II
2. III
3. The temperature is above 100°F if and only if my car overheats.
4. It violates the property that "A good definition must include no more information than is necessary." For example, it is not necessary to include the information that the equal angles are called base angles.
5. If an angle is a straight angle, then its measure is 180. If the measure of an angle is 180, then it is a straight angle.
6. a. You don't water them.
   b. Flowers wilt.
7. a. Sample: $x = 10$
   b. Sample: $x = 13.5$
8. false
9. a. If a figure is an isosceles triangle, then it is a polygon with two equal sides.
   b. true
10. a. If a figure is a polygon with two equal sides, then it is an isosceles triangle.
    b. false
11. $\{\overline{NL}\}$
12. $\{\overline{NK}, \overline{KL}, \overline{LM}, \overline{MN}, \overline{NL}\}$
13. $\{N\}$
14. no
15. The distance is at least 36 miles and no more than 126 miles.
16. 238
17. 21

18.
```
              polygon
             /        \
      triangle      quadrilateral
         |
     isosceles
     triangle
         |
    equilateral
     triangle
```

19. a. Possible responses: $\overline{BO}$ and $\overline{OT}$; $\overline{OT}$ and $\overline{TH}$; $\overline{TH}$ and $\overline{HE}$; $\overline{HE}$ and $\overline{ER}$; $\overline{ER}$ and $\overline{RB}$; $\overline{RB}$ and $\overline{BO}$
    b. false
    c. $\overline{BT}$, $\overline{BH}$, and $\overline{BE}$
20. octagon
21. No. Sample: The converse of the statement made by Lupita's brother is, "If you got a dollar, then you did my chores." The converse describes Lupita's situation. You cannot tell if the converse of a true statement is true. For example, Lupita might have received the dollar as a gift. So it is impossible to tell if Lupita did her brother's chores.
22. between 5 inches and 95 inches

Chapter 2 Test, Form B

1. III
2. I
3. The power fails if and only if the lights go off.
4. It violates the property that "A good definition must include only words either commonly understood, defined earlier, or purposely undefined." For example, the meanings of the terms *normal, triangle,* and *special features* are not clear.
5. If an angle is an acute angle, then its measure is greater than 0 and less than 90. If the measure of an angle is greater than 0 and less than 90, then it is an acute angle.
6. **a.** You don't refrigerate it.
   b. The food will spoil.
7. **a.** Sample: $t = 19$
   b. Sample: $t = 20.5$
8. true
9. **a.** If a figure is an equilateral triangle, then it is a polygon with three sides of equal length.
   b. true
10. **a.** If a figure is a polygon with three sides of equal length, then it is an equilateral triangle.
    b. false
11. $\{\overline{OR}\}$
12. $\{\overline{NO}, \overline{OP}, \overline{PQ}, \overline{QR}, \overline{RS}, \overline{SN}, \overline{OR}\}$
13. $\varnothing$
14. yes
15. The distance is at least 35 miles and no more than 121 miles.
16. 184
17. 6

18.
```
            figure
      _____|_____
     |      |      |
  triangle quadri- octagon
     |     lateral
  scalene
  triangle
```
19. **a.** Possible responses: M and O; O and N; N and T; T and H; H and M
    b. true
    c. $\overline{MN}$, $\overline{MT}$
20. decagon
21. No. Sample: The converse of the statement made by Karl's father is "If you are tired tomorrow morning, then you stayed up late." The converse describes Karl's situation. You cannot tell if the converse of a true statement is true. For example, Karl may have been tired because he was sick. So it is impossible to tell if Karl stayed up late.
22. between 2 mm and 32 mm

Chapter 2 Test, Cumulative Form

1.

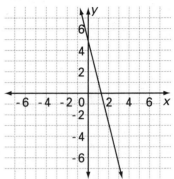

2. false
3. If a figure is a convex polygon, then it is a triangle.
4. false. Sample: A rectangle is a convex polygon, but it is not a triangle.
5. If a creature is a spider, then it has eight legs.
6. false
7. **a.** 9   **b.** 2
   c. yes
8. **a.** heptagon
   b. the borders of the garden
   c. the rose bushes
9. **a.** point   **b.** segment
10. **a.** (iii)   **b.** (i)
    c. (ii)
11. $\{\overline{PT}\}$
12. $\{\overline{PA}, \overline{AT}, \overline{TN}, \overline{NE}, \overline{EP}, \overline{PT}\}$
13. $\varnothing$ 14. -3
15. If $x \geq 2$, then $x \geq 3$.
16. Sample: $x = 4$
17. Sample: $x = 2.5$
18. No. Sample: The converse of Clare's statement is, "If you ground me for a week, then I stayed out past my curfew." The converse describes Clare's situation. You cannot tell if the converse of a true statement is true. For example, Clare may have been grounded because she did not do an important homework assignment. So it is impossible to tell if Clare stayed out past her curfew.

19. If an angle is an obtuse angle, then its measure is greater than 90 and less than 180. If the measure of an angle is greater than 90 and less than 180, then it is an obtuse angle.

20. 36   **21.** no

22. It violates the property that "A good definition must include no more information than is necessary." For example, it is not necessary to include the information that the polygon may be convex or nonconvex, nor is it necessary to include the information that the sum of the measures of the angles is 360.

23.

figure
|
polygon
/   \
triangle   pentagon

24. 26

25. The distance is at least 53 miles and no more than 181 miles.

26. a. It has brass buttons.
     b. A coat is handsome.

27. Sample:

28.

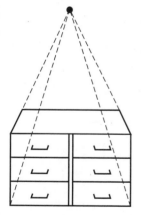

**Quiz   Lessons 3-1
               Through 3-3**

1.

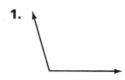

2. 51

3. a. Samples:
        ∠BOT and ∠TOR;
        ∠TOR and ∠ROM;
        ∠ROM and ∠MOB;
        ∠MOB and ∠BOT
   b. ∠BOT and ∠ROM;
        ∠MOB and ∠TOR

4. a. 24
   b. 156

5. 131

6. $90 - 2a$

7. 250°

8. -80°

**Quiz   Lessons 3-4
               Through 3-6**

1. For any real numbers a, b, and c, if $a = b$ and $b = c$, then $a = c$.

2. $m\angle R < m\angle P$

3. (a)

4. (b)

5. (d)

6. Substitution Property

7. ∠2

8. a. 129
   b. 51

9. $a = 22$

10. $-\frac{1}{3}$

6.

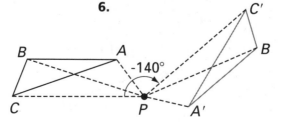

Chapter 3 Test, Form A

1. Sample:

2. Sample:

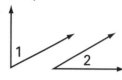

3. 41   **4.** $180 - 6n$

5. a. $j = 10$ **b.** 89

6. See below left.

7. 54   **8.** $s = 9.5$

9. $AD + OA = 10$ cm

10. $RO < 10$ cm

11. 108°

12.

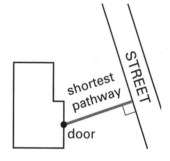

13. a. 117   **b.** 63°
     c. 243°

14. a. 50   **b.** 50
     c. 130

15. a. $u = 12$ **b.** 40

16. (c)

17. $m\angle PTS = 2(m\angle PTR) = 2(m\angle STR)$

18. 10   **19.** $\frac{10}{9}$; $-\frac{9}{10}$

20. $\frac{3}{4}$ **21.** (c)

22.

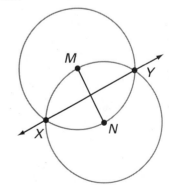

Chapter 3 Test, Form B

1. Sample:

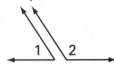

2. Sample:

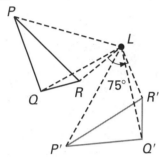

3. 102   **4.** $180 - 4t$

5. a. $r = 9$ **b.** 41

6.

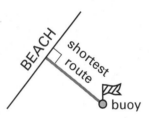

7. 43   **8.** $s = 5.5$

9. $m\angle NEL = m\angle AEG$

10. $m\angle 2 < 78$ **11.** $-210°$

12.

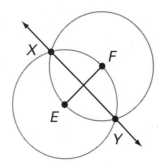

13. a. 34   **b.** 34°
     c. 214°

14. a. 107   **b.** 107
     c. 73

15. a. $d = 9$ **b.** 83

16. (d)

17. $VW = VX + XW = 2VX = 2XW$

18. $\frac{1}{5}$ **19.** $\frac{5}{8}, -\frac{8}{5}$

20. $-\frac{5}{2}$ **21.** (b)

22.

Chapter 3 Test, Cumulative Form

1.

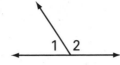

2. 149

3. $180 - 8b$

4. 151.5

5. between 114 cm and 296 cm

6. a. If an angle is a straight angle, then its measure is 180.
     b. true

7. See below.

8. a. An angle is a right angle if and only if its measure is 90.
     b. If an angle is a right angle, then its measure is 90. If the measure of an angle is 90, then it is a right angle.

9. The distance is at least 1.5 miles and no more than 3.9 miles.

10. Sample:

11. a. 106°
     b. 74
     c. 286°

12. 102

13. Answers will vary. Sample:

• • • • • • • • •

14. a. 33
     b. 147

15. 115.8

16. 2

17. (c)

7.

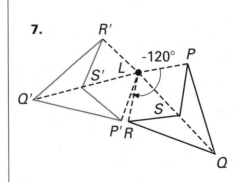

18. $m\angle 1 < m\angle MAN$

19. $\angle 1$ and $\angle 2$ are a pair of complementary angles.

20. false

21. vanishing point

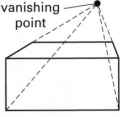

22. a. $s = 4$
     b. 48

23. oblique

24. $\frac{1}{3}$

25. a. $\{T\}$
     b. $\{ET\}$

26. true

27.

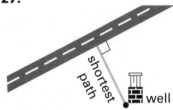

28. (c)

Comprehensive Test, Chapters 1–3

1. (d) **14.** (a)
2. (c) **15.** true
3. (b) **16.** (d)
4. (a) **17.** (b)
5. (b) **18.** (c)
6. (a) **19.** (d)
7. (a) **20.** (c)
8. (c) **21.** (d)
9. (b) **22.** (a)
10. (c) **23.** true
11. (d) **24.** (b)
12. (b) **25.** (c)
13. (d) **26.** (b)

27. No. Sample: The converse of the statement made by Frank's father is, "If you get a ticket, then you drove too fast." The converse describes Frank's situation. You cannot tell if the converse of a true statement is true. For example, Frank might have gotten a ticket for parking illegally. So it is impossible to tell if Frank drove too fast.

28.

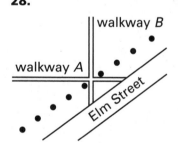

walkway B
walkway A
Elm Street

Quiz — Lessons 4-1 Through 4-3

1. Q
2. S
3. perpendicular bisector
4.

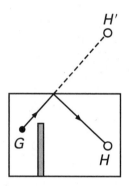

5. true
6. (b)
7. (a, -b)
8.

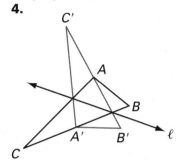

9. No. Sample: In a transformation each point in the preimage set has exactly one image. In correspondence T, however, preimage point A has two images, B and C. So T is not a transformation.

Quiz — Lessons 4-4 Through 4-6

1. a. translation
b. 5 cm
2. a. See below.
b. rotation; clockwise, -90°
3.

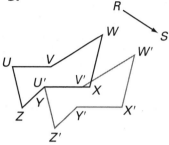

4. Samples: angle measure, betweenness, collinearity, distance, orientation
5. (-3, 8)

2. a.

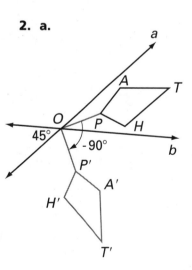

Chapter 4 Test, Form A

1. Sample:

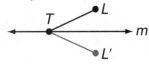

2.

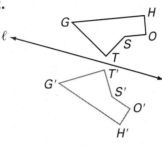

3. definition of reflection
4. Reflections preserve angle measure.
5. $(p - 5, q + 2)$
6. $P' = (0, 5)$, $Q' = (1, -4)$, $R' = (-3, 0)$
7. angle measure, betweenness, collinearity, distance
8. translation, rotation
9.

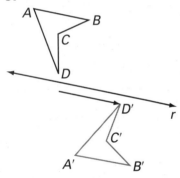

10. a.

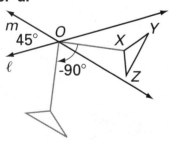

   b. rotation; clockwise, -90°

---

11. parallel; 2.9 cm
12. rotation; clockwise, -180° or counterclockwise, 180°
13. 48.5
14.

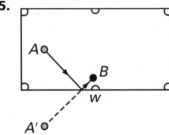

15.

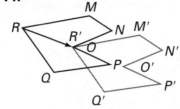

16. glide reflection
17. rotation
18. (b)

Chapter 4 Test, Form B

1. Sample:

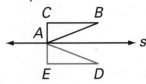

2.

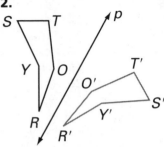

3. Reflections preserve distance.
4. definition of reflection
5. $(r + 3, s - 7)$
6. $X' = (3, 0)$, $Y' = (4, -5)$, $Z' = (0, 1)$
7. angle measure, betweenness, collinearity, distance, orientation
8. reflection, glide reflection
9.

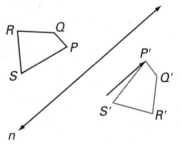

10. a.

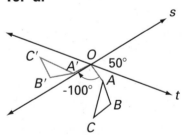

   b. rotation; clockwise, -100°

11. 80; N

12. translation; vertical, ≈1 inch (≈2.5 cm)

13. 56

14.

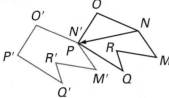

15.

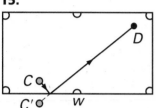

16. rotation

17. glide reflection

18. (a)

Chapter 4 Test, Cumulative Form

1.

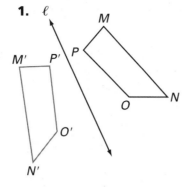

2. Point A lies on line p.

3. No. Sample: By the definition of betweenness, if T is between S and R, then T is on $\overline{SR}$. By the Distance Postulate, if T is on $\overline{SR}$, then $ST + TR = SR$. However, from the given information, $ST + TR = 119.61$ and $\overline{SR} = 119.58$. So, T is not between S and R. In fact, points S, T, and R determine a triangle.

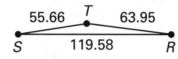

4. 4

5. false

6. Reflections preserve distance.

7. definition of reflection

8. Sample:

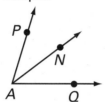

9. **a.** 7.2
 b. 48

10. $J' = (0, -4)$, $K' = (1, 4)$, $L' = (-5, 2)$

11. $(19, 44)$ **12.** $(9, 0)$

13. It violates the property that "A good definition must accurately define the idea being defined." For example, a right angle is larger than an acute angle, but it is not an obtuse angle.

14. **a.** (i)
 b. (iii)
 c. (ii)

15. true

16. false

17. **a.** If m is the perpendicular bisector of $\overline{PP'}$, then $r_m(P) = P'$.
 b. true

18. **a.** See below.
 b. rotation; counterclockwise, 76°

19. rotation; clockwise, -180° or counterclockwise, 180°

20.

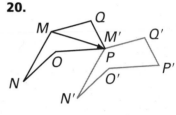

21.

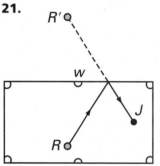

22. The distance is at least 513 miles and no more than 2393 miles.

23. no

24. rotation

25. glide reflection

26. 96

27. **a.** $w = 9$
 b. 96

18. **a.**

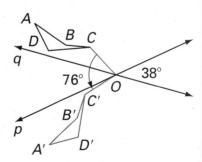

Quiz   Lessons 5-1 Through 5-3

1. $\angle W \cong \angle D$; $\angle E \cong \angle R$; $\angle T \cong \angle Y$; $\overline{WE} \cong \overline{DR}$; $\overline{ET} \cong \overline{RY}$; $\overline{WT} \cong \overline{DY}$
2. Two segments are congruent if and only if they have the same length.
3. true
4. 108
5. 11
6. (b)
7. $\overline{TF} \cong \overline{TR}$

Quiz   Lessons 5-4 Through 5-6

1. a. Given
   b. definition of reflection
   c. Figure Reflection Theorem
   d. definition of congruence
2. (c)
3. $m\angle 1 = 115$; $m\angle 2 = 142$
4. Transitive Property of Congruence
5.

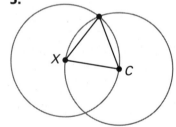

Chapter 5 Test, Form A

1. $\overline{CA}$
2. $m\angle A$
3. ST
4. a. $180 - 7k$
   b. $180 - 7k$
5. a. 19
   b. 15
6. a. Given
   b. definition of angle bisector
   c. Transitive Property of Congruence
7. 108
8. A two-column argument is shown. Paragraph form could also be accepted.

Conclusions	Justifications
0. R is the midpoint of $\overline{OP}$.	Given
1. $\overline{OR} \cong \overline{PR}$	definition of midpoint
2. $\overline{PQ} \cong \overline{PR}$	definition of circle
3. $\overline{OR} \cong \overline{PQ}$	Transitive Property of Congruence

9. $d = 19$; $m\angle T = 140$
10. $RQ = 19y$; $RG = 38y$

11. A two-column argument is shown. Paragraph form could also be accepted.

Conclusions	Justifications
0. $r_\ell(M) = K$; $r_\ell(A) = O$	Given
1. $r_\ell(B) = B$	definition of reflection
2. $r_\ell(\triangle BAM) = \triangle BOK$	Figure Reflection Theorem
3. $\triangle BAM \cong \triangle BOK$	definition of congruence

12. See below.
13. Yes. Sample: $\overline{AB}$ is a transversal that crosses $\overline{AD}$ and $\overline{CB}$, and $\angle DAB$ and $\angle CBA$ are a pair of alternate interior angles. Since $\angle DAB \cong \angle CBA$, $\overline{AD}$ // $\overline{CB}$ by the AIA $\cong$ $\Rightarrow$ // Lines Theorem.
14. true
15. yes
16. yes

12. Sample:

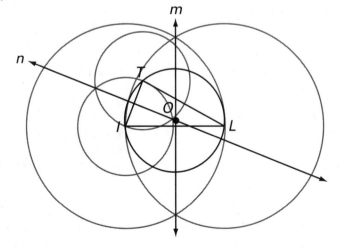

1. $\angle T$
2. RA
3. UE
4. a. $4h$
   b. $180 - 4h$
5. a. 8.2
   b. 3.5
6. a. Given
   b. definition of midpoint
   c. Transitive Property of Congruence
7. 96
8. A two-column argument is shown. Paragraph form could also be accepted.

Conclusions	Justifications
0. $\triangle WHY \cong$ $\triangle TOC$; $\triangle TOC \cong$ $\triangle PAL$	Given
1. $\triangle WHY \cong$ $\triangle PAL$	Transitive Property of Congruence
2. $\overline{WH} \cong \overline{PA}$	CPCF Theorem

9. $c = 23$; $m\angle G = 101$
10. $\overline{NT} = 14z$; $\overline{JT} = 28z$

11. A two-column argument is shown. Paragraph form could also be accepted.

Conclusions	Justifications
0. ℓ is the $\perp$ bisector of $\overline{MN}$.	Given
1. $r_\ell(A) = A$; $r_\ell(B) = B$; $r_\ell(M) = N$	definition of reflection
2. $r_\ell(\triangle AMB) =$ $\triangle ANB$	Figure Reflection Theorem
3. $\triangle AMB \cong$ $\triangle ANB$	definition of congruence

12. See below.
13. They are congruent. Sample: $\overline{AE}$ is a transversal that crosses $\overline{AB}$ and $\overline{DC}$, and $\angle BAE$ and $\angle AED$ are a pair of alternate interior angles. Since $\overline{AB} \parallel \overline{DC}$, $\angle BAE \cong \angle AED$ by the $\parallel$ Lines $\Rightarrow$ AIA $\cong$ Theorem.
14. true
15. yes
16. no

1. $\angle R$
2. true
3. a. $\angle 4$ and $\angle 9$
   b. $\angle 6$ and $\angle 9$
4. a. $2t$
   b. $180 - 2t$
5. $a = 10.5$; $m\angle 9 = 53.5$
6. a. $(-7, -12)$
   b. $(7, 12)$
7. rotation about O 154° counterclockwise
8. a. oblique
   b. vertical
9. a. It is cooked on a grill.
   b. A hamburger is tasty.
10. If a hamburger is tasty, then it is cooked on a grill.
11. (ii)
12. (iii)
13. (i)
14. a. (i)
   b. (ii)
15. 1260
16. 105
17.

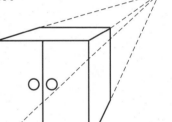

12. Sample:

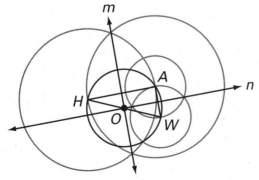

Chapter 5 Test, Cumulative Form, *continued*

18. a. Given
   b. Transitive Property of Congruence
   c. definition of midpoint

19. A two-column argument is shown. Paragraph form could also be accepted.

Conclusions	Justifications
0. $r_m(A) = E$; $r_m(B) = T$	Given
1. $r_m(G) = G$	definition of reflection
2. $r_m(\triangle GAB) = \triangle GET$	Figure Reflection Theorem
3. $\triangle GAB \cong \triangle GET$	definition of congruence

20. true

21. Sample:

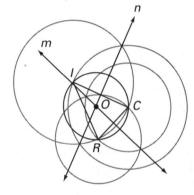

22. S
23. T
24. O

Quiz — Lessons 6-1 Through 6-3

1.

2. true
3. true
4. $m\angle T = 37$, $m\angle O = 106$
5. a. Given
   b. Isosceles Triangle Base Angles Theorem
   c. Vertical Angle Theorem
   d. Transitive Property of Equality (steps 1 and 2)
6. isosceles trapezoid
7. Sample:

Quiz — Lessons 6-4 Through 6-6

1. a. 10
   b. 90
   c. 71
   d. 94
2. parallelogram, rectangle, rhombus, square
3. a. definition of bases of a trapezoid
   b. Corresponding Angles Postulate
   c. Transitive Property of Equality
   d. definition of isosceles trapezoid
4. a.

   b. 4

Chapter 6 Test, Form A

1.

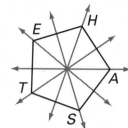

2. a.

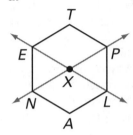

   b. 6
3. true
4. a. 73
   b. 17
5. parallelogram
6. $\overline{NG}$
7. a. 45
   b. 110
8. 73
9. $t = 5$, $m\angle P = 80$
10. a.

   b. rectangle
11. a. quadrilateral
   kite   parallelogram
   rhombus
   square
   b. true
12. a. Given
   b. definition of regular polygon
   c. definition of ends of a kite
   d. Transitive Property of Congruence
13. Sample: $\overline{TQ}$ and $\overline{UR}$
14. 70
15. 120

ANSWERS

16. A two-column argument is shown. Paragraph form could also be accepted.

Conclusions	Justifications
0. $\angle 1 \cong \angle B$	Given
1. $\overline{DA} \parallel \overline{CB}$	Corresponding Angles Postulate
2. $ABCD$ is a trapezoid.	definition of trapezoid

17. a. $\overline{AC}$
  b. 17.5
  c. 2
18. $AR = 15$, $LR = 9$
19. a. point A

  b. 5
20. (b)
21. Sample:
  week 1: A-B, E-C, D-F
  week 2: B-C, A-D, E-F
  week 3: C-D, B-E, A-F
  week 4: D-E, C-A, B-F
  week 5: E-A, D-B, C-F

Chapter 6 Test, Form B

1.

2. a.

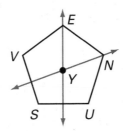

  b. 5
3. false
4. a. 20
  b. 90
5. isosceles trapezoid
6. $\overline{EC}$
7. a. 127
  b. 38
8. 36
9. $n = 5.5$, $m\angle Q = 81$
10. a.

  b. square

11. a. quadrilateral

  kite — trapezoid
  parallelogram
  square

  b. false
12. a. Given
  b. definition of rhombus
  c. definition of regular polygon
  d. Transitive Property of Congruence
13. Any two of $\overline{VY}$, $\overline{YT}$, $\overline{UZ}$, $\overline{VT}$, and $\overline{UX}$
14. 60
15. 120

16. A two-column argument is shown. Paragraph form could also be accepted.

Conclusions	Justifications
0. $\overline{LM} \parallel \overline{KJ}$; $\angle 1 \cong \angle K$	Given
1. $\overline{LK} \parallel \overline{MJ}$	AIA $\cong \Rightarrow$ $\parallel$ Lines Theorem
2. $JKLM$ is a parallelogram.	definition of parallelogram

17. a. $\overline{WY}$
  b. 18
  c. 2
18. $m\angle O = 72$, $m\angle 1 = 180$
19. a.

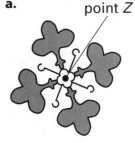

point Z

  b. 4
20. (a)
21. Sample:
  week 1: A-B, E-C, D bye
  week 2: B-C, A-D, E bye
  week 3: C-D, B-E, A bye
  week 4: D-E, C-A, B bye
  week 5: E-A, D-B, C bye

Chapter 6 Test, Cumulative Form

1. a, b.

2. 6

3.

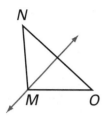

4. 42

5. $k = 4$, $m\angle M = 124$

6. kite

7. $x = 23$, $m\angle BOW = 88$

8. no

9. $m\angle R = 117$, $m\angle A = 63$, $m\angle P = 63$

10. a. Given

  b. Perpendicular Bisector Theorem

  c. definition of kite

11. $y = 45$, $m\angle 3 = 65$

12. No. Sample: By the Distance Postulate, if B is between A and C, then $AB + BC = AC$. However, $15.55 + 14.25 \neq 29.9$. So, B is not between A and C.

13. a. 7

  b. $m\angle WXZ = 17$, $m\angle WYX = 73$

14. 67.5

15. A two-column argument is shown. Paragraph form could also be accepted.

Conclusions	Justifications
0. $\angle 1 \cong \angle 2$	Given
1. $\overline{NA} \parallel \overline{EM}$	AIA $\cong \Rightarrow$ $\parallel$ Lines Theorem
2. $NAME$ is a trapezoid.	definition of trapezoid

16. a. Sample:

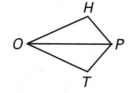

  b. $\overline{TO}$

17.

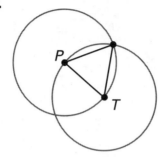

18. true

19.

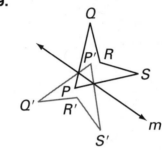

20. $7t$

21. 4

22. glide reflection

23. $z = 24$, $m\angle E = 124$

Comprehensive Test, Chapters 1–6

1. (a)   **11.** (c)
2. (b)   **12.** (c)
3. (a)   **13.** (a)
4. (b)   **14.** (b)
5. (b)   **15.** (d)
6. (b)   **16.** (d)
7. (d)   **17.** (a)
8. (a)   **18.** (c)
9. (d)   **19.** (c)
10. (d)   **20.** (c)

21. true

22. $\overline{KI}$ and $\overline{KE}$; $\overline{TI}$ and $\overline{TE}$; $\overline{IY}$ and $\overline{EY}$

23. No. Sample: Let T represent Tom's house, R represent Rosa's house, and A represent Abdul's house. By the definition of betweenness, if T is between R and A, then T is on $\overline{RA}$. By the Distance Postulate, if T is on $\overline{RA}$, then $RT + TA = RA$. However, from the given information, $RT + TA = 4.6$ miles and $RA = 4.5$ miles. So, T is not between R and A. In fact, points T, R, and A determine a triangle.

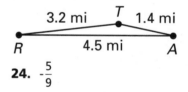

24. $-\dfrac{5}{9}$

25.

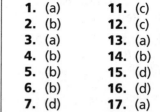

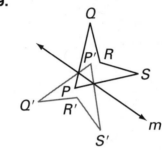

26. a.

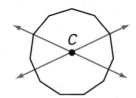

b. 11

27. a.

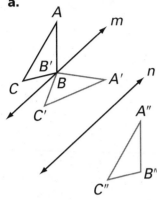

b. translation

28. a. Given
b. definition of reflection
c. Reflections preserve distance.
d. definition of kite

29. A two-column argument is shown. Paragraph form could also be accepted.

Conclusions	Justifications
0. ∠B ≅ ∠1	Given
1. ∠1 ≅ ∠BCA	Vertical Angles Theorem
2. ∠B ≅ ∠BCA	Transitive Property of Congruence

30. No. Sample: The converse of Laura's statement is, "If I take your turn doing dishes on Monday, then you took my turn on Sunday." The converse describes the given situation. You cannot tell if the converse of a true statement is true. For example, Laura's sister might have become ill and been unable to do the dishes for Laura on Sunday. So it is impossible to tell if Laura's sister did the dishes on Sunday.

31.

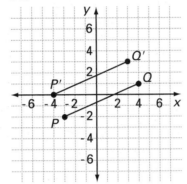

32.

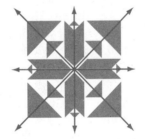

1. a. no
b. Sample: It is possible for two noncongruent triangles to each have two angles that measure 23 and 90.
2. a. yes
b. SSS Congruence Theorem
3. not enough information to know
4. ASA Congruence Theorem; △RYM ≅ △RAM
5. a. $\overline{ZY}$ and $\overline{XY}$
b. Isosceles Triangle Base Angles Converse Theorem
6. A two-column argument is shown. Paragraph form could also be accepted.

Conclusions	Justifications
0. $\overline{MN}$ ≅ $\overline{MP}$; $\overrightarrow{MO}$ bisects ∠NMP.	Given
1. ∠NMO ≅ ∠PMO	definition of angle
2. $\overline{MO}$ ≅ $\overline{MO}$	Reflexive Property of Congruence
3. △MNO ≅ △MPO	SAS Congruence Theorem
4. ∠MON ≅ ∠MOP	CPCF Theorem

ANSWERS

1. Sample:

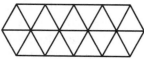

2. Samples:
△*TAP* and △*RPA*;
△*TRP* and △*RTA*;
△*TRP* and △*TAP*;
△*RTA* and △*RPA*

3. A two-column argument is shown. Paragraph form could also be accepted.

Conclusions	Justifications
0. *MNOP* is a kite with ends *P* and *N*;	Given
1. $\overline{PT} \cong \overline{PS}$	definition of ends of a kite
2. ∠*P* ≅ ∠*P*	Reflexive Property of Congruence
3. △*SMP* ≅ △*TOP*	SAS Congruence Theorem

4. SAS Congruence Theorem

5. HL Congruence Theorem

6. Sample: By the HL Congruence Theorem, △*ACD* ≅ △*BCD*. It follows that ∠*A* ≅ ∠*B* by the CPCF Theorem.

Chapter 7 Test, Form A

1. not enough information to know

2. HL Congr. Thm.; △*ELM* ≅ △*ONM*

3. a. 28
b. 26

4. a. yes
b. ASA Congr. Thm.

5. a. no
b. Sample: It is possible for two noncongruent triangles to each have two angles that measure 127 and 18.

6. Yes. Sample: Since *AX* = *AZ* = 4, *A* is the midpoint of $\overline{ZX}$. Since *AW* = *AY* = 5, *A* is the midpoint of $\overline{WY}$. So $\overline{ZX}$ and $\overline{WY}$ bisect each other, and they are the diagonals of *WXYZ*. So, by the Sufficient Conditions for a Parallelogram Theorem, *WXYZ* is a parallelogram.

7. m∠*DCA* = 47; m∠*DAC* = 31; m∠*DAB* = m∠*DCB* = 78; m∠*CDA* = m∠*ABC* = 102

8. A two-column argument is shown. Paragraph form could also be accepted.

Conclusions	Justifications
0. ⊙*S* and ⊙*T* intersecting at *M* and *O*	Given
1. $\overline{SM} \cong \overline{SO}$; $\overline{TM} \cong \overline{TO}$	definition of circle
2. $\overline{ST} \cong \overline{ST}$	Refl. Prop. of Congr.
3. △*MST* ≅ △*OST*	SSS Congr. Theorem

---

9. A two-column argument is shown. Paragraph form could also be accepted.

Conclusions	Justifications
0. ∠*ETN* ≅ ∠*SDN*; $\overline{NT} \cong \overline{ND}$	Given
1. ∠*N* ≅ ∠*N*	Refl. Prop. of Congr.
2. △*NET* ≅ △*NSD*	ASA Congr. Theorem
3. ∠*NET* ≅ ∠*NSD*	CPCF Theorem

10. Sample: From the given information, $\overline{AB} \cong \overline{CD}$ and $\overline{AC} \cong \overline{BD}$. By the Sufficient Conditions for a Parallelogram Theorem, a quadrilateral is a parallelogram if both pairs of opposite sides are congruent. So, *ABDC* is a parallelogram. By the definition of a parallelogram, $\overline{AB} \parallel \overline{CD}$.

11. a. ∠*T*
b. ∠*J*

12. $\overline{BO}, \overline{OX}, \overline{BX}$

13. Sample: Since $\overline{PQ} \perp \overline{RX}$, △*PRQ* and △*PSQ* are right triangles. You know that $\overline{PR} \cong \overline{PS}$ and *PQ* ≅ *PQ*, so △*PRQ* ≅ △*PSQ* by the HL Congruence Theorem. It follows that ∠1 ≅ ∠2 by the CPCF Theorem.

14. Sample:

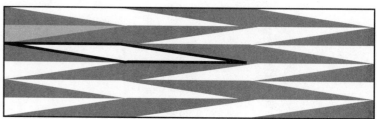

1. ASA Congr. Thm.;
   $\triangle NMP \cong \triangle NOP$
2. not enough information to know
3. **a.** 42
   b. 30
4. **a.** yes
   b. AAS Congr. Thm.
5. **a.** yes
   b. HL Congr. Thm.
6. Yes. Sample: From the given information, $AD = BC = 10$ and $AB = DC = 7$. Since $\overline{AD}$ and $\overline{BC}$ are opposite sides of $ABCD$, and $\overline{AB}$ and $\overline{DC}$ also are opposite sides of $ABCD$, both pairs of opposite sides of $ABCD$ are congruent. So, by the Sufficient Conditions for a Parallelogram Theorem, $ABCD$ is a parallelogram.
7. $ZY = 10$; $WZ = 6$; $OZ = 7$; $ZX = 14$
8. A two-column argument is shown. Paragraph form could also be accepted.

Conclusions	Justifications
0. $PARL$ is a parallelogram; $\overline{MP} \cong \overline{NR}$	Given
1. $\overline{PA} \cong \overline{RL}$; $\angle P \cong \angle R$	Properties of a Parallelogram Thm.
2. $\triangle MPA \cong \triangle NRL$	SAS Congr. Theorem

9. A two-column argument is shown. Paragraph form could also be accepted.

Conclusions	Justifications
0. $CHAPTERS$ is a regular octagon.	Given
1. $\overline{CS} \cong \overline{HA}$; $\angle HCS \cong \angle CHA$	definition of regular polygon
2. $\overline{CH} \cong \overline{HC}$	Refl. Prop. of Congr.
3. $\triangle CSH \cong \triangle HAC$	SAS Congr. Theorem
4. $\angle CSH \cong \angle HAC$	CPCF Theorem

10. Sample: Since the blockade is a rectangle, $\overline{AB} \parallel \overline{CD}$. Since each stripe has the same width at the top as at the bottom, $\overline{AB} \cong \overline{CD}$. By the Sufficient Conditions for a Parallelogram Theorem, a quadrilateral is a parallelogram if one pair of sides is both parallel and congruent. So $ABDC$ is a parallelogram. By the definition of a parallelogram, $\overline{AC} \parallel \overline{BD}$.
11. **a.** $\angle O$
    b. $\angle T$
12. $\overline{SU}$, $\overline{UN}$, $\overline{NS}$
13. Sample: Since the posts are perpendicular to the water line, $\triangle WXV$ and $\triangle YZV$ are right triangles. You know that $\overline{WV} \cong \overline{YV}$ and $\overline{WX} \cong \overline{YZ}$, so $\triangle WXV \cong \triangle YZV$ by the HL Congruence Theorem. It follows that $\overline{XV} \cong \overline{ZV}$ by the CPCF Theorem.
14. Sample:

1. SSS Congr. Thm.;
   $\triangle MSP \cong \triangle PAM$
2. **a.** no
   b. Sample: It is possible for two noncongruent triangles to each have two sides that measure 19 and 12 and an angle that measures 30. Consider the $\triangle ABC$ and $\triangle ABD$.

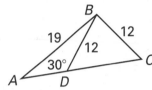

3. **a.** $\overline{LR}$ **b.** $\overline{PT}$
4. **a.** Sample: Since $\angle A$ and $\angle P$ are right angles, $\overline{RA} \perp \overline{AP}$ and $\overline{TP} \perp \overline{AP}$. By the Two Perpendiculars Theorem, it follows that $\overline{RA} \parallel \overline{TP}$. So, by the definition of trapezoid, $TRAP$ is a trapezoid.
   b. $180 - 2g$
5. **a.** $m\angle M < m\angle PNO$
   b. $13t$
6. A two-column argument is shown. Paragraph form could also be accepted.

Conclusions	Justifications
0. $\overline{AB} \cong \overline{CD}$; $\overline{AC} \cong \overline{CE}$; $\overline{AB} \parallel \overline{CD}$	Given
1. $\angle A \cong \angle DCE$	Corres. Angles Post.
3. $\triangle ABC \cong \triangle CDE$	SAS Congr. Theorem
4. $\angle B \cong \angle D$	CPCF Thm.

7. (d)
8. **a.**

point R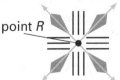

b. 4

9. 68
10. isosceles trapezoid
11.

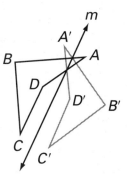

12. A two-column argument is shown. Paragraph form could also be accepted.

Conclusions	Justifications
0. *PENTA* is a regular pentagon.	Given
1. $\overline{PA} \cong \overline{NT}$; $\angle PAT \cong \angle NTA$	definition of regular polygon
2. $\overline{AT} \cong \overline{TA}$	Refl. Prop. of Congr.
3. $\triangle PAT \cong \triangle NTA$	SAS Congr. Theorem

13. Sample: Since $\overline{CD} \perp \overline{AD}$ and $\overline{CD} \perp \overline{BD}$, $\triangle CAD$ and $\triangle CBD$ are right triangles. Since $\overline{CD}$ bisects each plank, $\overline{AC} \cong \overline{BC}$. By the Refl. Prop. of Congr., $\overline{CD} \cong \overline{CD}$. So $\triangle CAD \cong \triangle CBD$ by the HL Congr. Thm. It follows that $\angle CAD \cong \angle CBD$ by the CPCF Thm.

14. Sample: From the given, $\overline{MP} /\!/ \overline{NO}$ and $\overline{MP} \cong \overline{NO}$. By the Sufficient Conditions for Parallelogram Thm., a quadrilateral is a parallelogram if one pair of sides is parallel and congruent. So, *MNOP* is a parallelogram. By the Properties of a Parallelogram Thm., opposite sides are congruent. So, $\overline{MN} \cong \overline{PO}$.

15. true
16. (c)

Quiz **Lessons 8-1 Through 8-3**

1. Sample: Perimeter is the sum of the lengths of the sides of the polygon; its measure is given in units of length. Area is a measure of the space covered by the polygon; this measure is given in square units.
2. 28*t*
3. **a.** 3 ft
    b. $\frac{9}{16}$ sq ft
4. Sample: ≈351 sq mi
5. area: 160.2 sq cm; perimeter: 53.6 cm
6. area: 1524 units^2; perimeter: 180 units
7. $576
8. false

Quiz **Lessons 8-4 Through 8-6**

1. 35 units^2
2. 150 units^2
3. 225 sq cm
4. 97 units
5. 1.2 units
6. Yes. Sample: By the Pythagorean Converse Theorem, *a*, *b*, and *c* can be the lengths of the sides of a right triangle if $a^2 + b^2 = c^2$. Since $2^2 + 3^2 = 13$, and $(\sqrt{13})^2 = 13$, the numbers 2, 3, and $\sqrt{13}$ can be the lengths of the sides of a right triangle.
7. ≈11.8 feet
8. 486 mm^2

Chapter 8 Test, Form A

1. 60 units
2. 120 units^2
3. 1290 units^2
4. 30*p* units
5. 2*tx* units^2
6. circumference: 20π cm; area: 100π cm^2
7. 82 units
8. 11.2 units
9. 50 units
10. **a.** 12π ≈ 37.7 units
    b. 108π ≈ 339.3 units^2
11. 1016 km
12. 124 ft
13. $216.00
14. 664 units^2
15. ≈21.9 ft
16. 196.8 units^2
17. No. Sample: By the Pythagorean Converse Theorem, *a*, *b*, and *c* can be the lengths of the sides of a right triangle if $a^2 + b^2 = c^2$. In this case, specifically, it would have to be true that $16^2 + 24^2 = 25^2$. However, $16^2 + 24^2 = 832$, and $25^2 = 625$. So, the numbers 16, 24, and 25 cannot be the lengths of the sides of a right triangle.
18. 168 units^2
19. $.11 = \frac{1}{9}$
20. Sample: ≈261 sq mi
21. ≈9503 sq mi
22. 4.5 units

Chapter 8 Test, Form B

1. 132 units
2. 85 units^2
3. 480 units^2
4. $\frac{h}{8}$ units
5. $4gx$ units^2
6. circumference: 24π ft; area: 144π sq ft
7. 85 units
8. 6.6 units
9. 37.5 units
10. **a.** $10\pi \approx 31.4$ units
    b. $60\pi \approx 188.5$ units^2
11. 624 m
12. 125 ft
13. $184.00
14. 929 units^2
15. ≈ 15.8 m
16. 462.9 units^2
17. No. Sample: By the Pythagorean Converse Theorem, a, b, and c can be the lengths of the sides of a right triangle if $a^2 + b^2 = c^2$. In this case, specifically, it would have to be true that $8^2 + 6^2 = 9^2$. However, $8^2 + 6^2 = 100$, and $9^2 = 81$. So, the numbers 8, 6, and 9 cannot be the lengths of the sides of a right triangle.
18. 99 units^2
19. .001
20. Sample: ≈ 2016 sq mi
21. ≈ 6362 sq mi
22. 5.5 units

Chapter 8 Test, Cumulative Form

1. $15s$ units
2. 200 units^2
3. 816 units^2
4. 30°
5. 300°
6. no
7. 53
8. SAS Congruence Theorem; $\triangle MNO \cong \triangle QPO$
9. circumference: 30π in.; area: 225π sq in.
10. 61 units
11. 19 units
12. A two-column argument is shown. Paragraph form could also be accepted.

Conclusions	Justifications
0. $\triangle PQR$ is isosceles with base $\overline{PQ}$; $\angle PRS \cong \angle QRT$	Given
1. $\overline{RP} \cong \overline{RQ}$	definition of the base of an isosceles triangle
2. $\angle P \cong \angle Q$	Isosceles Triangle Base Angles Theorem
3. $\triangle PRS \cong \triangle QRT$	ASA Congruence Theorem
4. $\overline{PS} \cong \overline{QT}$	CPCF Theorem

13. 12.25 sq meters

14. Yes. Sample: Any quadrilateral can be a fundamental region of a tessellation. So, a tile shaped like a parallelogram can be used to cover a floor with no gaps or overlaps. (Note: Some tiles at the sides of the floor will have to be cut to fit the available space, so, technically, some tiles will not be shaped like parallelograms.)
15. (c)
16. ≈ 24.98 ft
17. **a.** $10\pi \approx 31.4$ units
    b. $100\pi \approx 314.2$ units^2
18. 42 units^2
19. ≈ 2827 sq mi
20. **a.** It is multiplied by 9.
    b. It is tripled.
21. Yes. Sample: By the Pythagorean Converse Theorem, a, b, and c can be the lengths of the sides of a right triangle if $a^2 + b^2 = c^2$. Since $35^2 + 84^2 = 8281$, and $91^2 = 8281$, the numbers 35, 84, and 91 can be the lengths of the sides of a right triangle.
22. (a)
23. $4a$ units
24. (b)
25. $(-2x)°$
26. $2x + 2y$

Quiz   **Lessons 9-1**
               Through 9-4

1. false
2. two
3. **a.** 5
   b. rectangle
   c. 2
   d. 15
4. **a.** 14-gon
   b. 28
5. Sample:

6. $\overline{XY}$
7. $\overline{XZ}$
8. 18 units

Quiz   **Lessons 9-5**
               Through 9-7

1. **a.** Sample:

   b. ellipse
2. infinitely many
3. 12 units
4. **a.** yes
   b. 3
5. Sample:

FRONT

SIDE

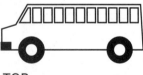

TOP

6. Sample:

Chapter 9 Test, Form A

1. Sample:

2. Sample:

3. No. Sample: By theorem, if a line is perpendicular to two different lines in space at the same point, then it is perpendicular to the plane that contains those lines. So, to know that line ℓ is perpendicular to plane T, you must know that line ℓ is perpendicular to two different lines in plane T at the same point.
4. **a.** Sample:

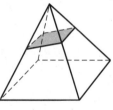

   b. parallelogram
5. square
6. 4
7. false
8.

FRONT

SIDE

TOP

9. right triangular prism
10. **a.** 17 units
    b. 40 units
11. 196π units^2
12. **a.** The figure below is drawn to actual size. The position of the great circle may vary from that shown.

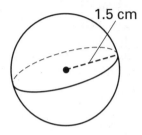

1.5 cm

    b. ≈ 9.4 cm
13. FRONT

SIDE

TOP

14. **a.** ≈ 509.9 units^2
    b. ≈ 1664 units^2
15. Sample:

16. right heptagonal pyramid or regular heptagonal pyramid
17. Sample:

18. right rectangular prism (surface)
19. solid right cylinder
20. **a.** 3
    b. right front
    c. 3

Chapter 9 Test, Form B

1. Sample:

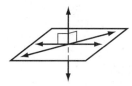

2. Sample:

3. Yes. Sample: By the Flat Plane Assumption, if two points lie in a plane, then the line containing them lies in the plane. This means that, since points B and C lie in plane T, $\overleftrightarrow{BC}$ lies in plane T. Since point A lies on $\overleftrightarrow{BC}$, it follows that point A lies in plane T.

4. a. Sample:

   b. ellipse
5. circle
6. 1
7. false
8. FRONT

   SIDE

   TOP

9. right triangular prism
10. a. 29 units
   b. 70 units
11. 38π units

12. a. The figure below is drawn to actual size. The position of the great circle may vary from that shown.

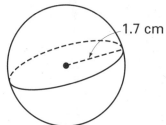

1.7 cm

   b. ≈9.1 sq cm
13. FRONT

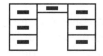

   SIDE

   TOP

14. a. 960 units²
   b. 4096 units²
15. Sample:

16. right pentagonal prism or regular pentagonal prism
17. Sample:

18. right cylinder (surface)
19. solid right rectangular prism
20. a. 3
   b. 3
   c. left front

Chapter 9 Test, Cumulative Form

1. Sample:

2. Sample:

3. 3
4. a. Sample:

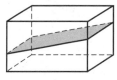

   b. rectangle
5. rectangle
6. 450 units²
7. 216 tiles
8. false
9. FRONT

   SIDE

   TOP

10. 52 units²
11. a. Given
   b. Two Perpendiculars Theorem
   c. definition of trapezoid
12. kite
13. right cylinder
14. a. 12 units
   b. 12 units
15. $\overline{PN}$
16. false

17. FRONT

SIDE

TOP

18. a. 102 units
    b. 4896 units^2
19. 16 units
20. Sample:

21. solid right cylinder
22. Sample:

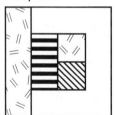

23. ≈79 sq meters
24. Sample:

Comprehensive Test, Chapters 1–9

1. (d)	**16.** (a)
2. (c)	**17.** (b)
3. (b)	**18.** (a)
4. (a)	**19.** (d)
5. (c)	**20.** (b)
6. (c)	**21.** (a)
7. (d)	**22.** (b)
8. (c)	**23.** (c)
9. (d)	**24.** (c)
10. (d)	**25.** (c)
11. (c)	**26.** (d)
12. (d)	**27.** (d)
13. (b)	**28.** (c)
14. (d)	**29.** (a)
15. (b)	

30. A two-column argument is shown. Paragraph form could also be accepted.

Conclusions	Justifications
0. $\overline{AD} \cong \overline{CD}$; $\angle ADB \cong \angle CDB$	Given
1. $\overline{BD} \cong \overline{BD}$	Reflexive Property of Congruence
2. $\triangle ABD \cong \triangle CBD$	SAS Congruence Theorem
3. $\overline{AB} \cong \overline{CB}$	CPCF Theorem

31. FRONT

SIDE

TOP

Quiz   Lessons 10-1 Through 10-3

1. $64\pi^3 \approx 1984.4$ cm^3
2. 490 units^2
3. a. $40\pi \approx 125.7$ units^2
    b. $44\pi \approx 138.2$ units^2
4. 4.93
5. ≈75,400 tiles
6. 403 cm^2

Quiz   Lessons 10-4 Through 10-6

1. multiplied by 25
2. false
3. $(2y + 7)(y + 3) = 2y^2 + 13y + 21$
4. a. 86 mm^2
    b. $\sqrt{86} \approx 9.3$ mm
5. $144\pi \approx 452.4$ units^3
6. volume; area
7. L.A. $= \frac{5}{2}sb$

Chapter 10 Test, Form A

1. a. 2700 in^3
    b. 1710 in^2
2. 300π units^3
3. 30 cm
4. $1224\pi \approx 3845.3$ units^2
5. 902.3 cm^2
6. 384 mm^2
7. a. $1296\pi \approx 4071.5$ units^2
    b. $7776\pi \approx 24,429$ units^3
8. No; the heights are the same, but the area of the base of the figure on the left is 24 units^2, while the area of the base of the figure on the right is 12 units^2.
9. $800\pi \approx 2513.3$ units^3
10. $20st$ units^2
11. 8.57
12. 6.3 in.
13. a. $(t + 3)(t + 5)(t + 2)$
    b. $t^3 + 10t^2 + 31t + 30$
14. 8 in^2
15. 3 in^3
16. a. It is multiplied by 7^3, or 343.
    b. It is multiplied by 7^2, or 49.
17. $312.5\pi \approx 981.7$ m^2
18. 1.8 cm^3
19. $V = \frac{1}{3}\pi r^2 h$

Chapter 10 Test, Form B

1. **a.** 76,230 units³
   b. 14,190 units²
2. 756π in³
3. 16 mm
4. 700π ≈ 2199.1 units²
5. 4 jars
6. 274.625 ft³
7. **a.** 1024π ≈ 3217.0 units²
   b. 5461.3π ≈
      17,157.3 units³
8. Yes; the heights are the same, and the area of each base is 36 units².
9. 1024π ≈ 3217.0 cm³
10. L.A. = 24fg
11. 9.09
12. 11.27 in.
13. **a.** $(u + 9)(u + 2)(u + 11)$
    b. $u^3 + 22u^2 + 139u + 198$
14. 45.0 in²
15. 26 in³
16. **a.** It is multiplied by 20³, or 8000.
    b. It is multiplied by 20², or 400.
17. 1800π ≈ 5654.9 cm³
18. 7.5 mm³
19. $\frac{1}{3}he^2$

Chapter 10 Test, Cumulative Form

1. 15.18 cm
2. right square pyramid
3. 70 in²
4. **a.** 97
   b. 83
5. Samples:
   $(n + 2n)(12 + 4) = 48n;$
   $12 \cdot n + 12 \cdot 2n + 4 \cdot n + 4 \cdot 2n = 48n$
6. **a.** Sample:

   b. Sample:

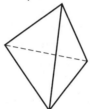

7. A two-column argument is shown. Paragraph form could also be accepted.

Conclusions	Justifications
1. m∠A = 2x; m∠MRS = x; m∠MNS = 3x	Given
2. m∠A + m∠AMN = m∠MNS	Exterior Angle Theorem
3. m∠AMN = x	Subtraction Property of Equality
4. $\overleftrightarrow{MN}$ // $\overleftrightarrow{RS}$	Corr. ∠s ≅ ⇒ // lines.

8. **a.** 90π ≈ 282.7 units²
   b. 100π ≈ 314.2 units³
9. **a.** 150π ≈ 471.2 ft²
   b. 200π ≈ 628.3 ft²
10. yes; infinitely many
11.

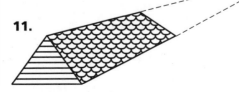

12. S.A. = $b^2 + 2b\sqrt{h^2 + \frac{b^2}{4}}$
13. yes; The diagonals bisect each other, so *QUAD* is a parallelogram.
14. 91 in.
15. **a.** 64 units
    b. 736 units²
16. Let I and II be two solids included between parallel planes. If every plane *P* parallel to the given planes intersects I and II in sections with the same area, then Volume(I) = Volume(II).
17. 146 + 6π ≈ 164.85 m
18. **a.** multiplied by $\left(\frac{1}{2}\right)^3 = \frac{1}{8}$
    b. .09375 m²
19. Sample:

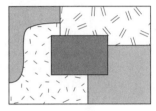

20. 14,824,000 ft³

ANSWERS

Quiz · Lessons 11-1 Through 11-4

1. **a.** *MNOP* is a parallelogram.
   b. Law of Detachment
2. **a.** $y \neq 7$
   b. Law of the Contrapositive
3. both true; both false
4. **a.** If you don't ride the bus on Saturday, then you won't pay a reduced fare.
   b. If you pay a reduced fare, then you ride the bus on Saturday.
   c. If you don't pay a reduced fare, then you don't ride the bus on Saturday.
   d. c, the contrapositive
5. Andrew: Lake Superior; Kara: Lake Michigan
6. Sample:
   Suppose $\sqrt{8} = 2.83$.
   Then $(\sqrt{8})^2 = (2.83)^2$.
   So $8 = 8.0089$, which is false. Therefore, $\sqrt{8} \neq 2.83$.

Quiz · Lessons 11-5 Through 11-7

1. $\sqrt{146} \approx 12.08$
2. Sample: Slope of
   $\overline{HG} = \dfrac{2-(-1)}{-4-(-3)} = \dfrac{3}{-1} = -3$
   and slope of
   $\overline{GF} = \dfrac{2-(-1)}{5-(-3)} = \dfrac{3}{8}$.
   $-3 \cdot \dfrac{3}{8} = -\dfrac{9}{8} \neq -1$, so $\angle G$ is not a right angle, and *EFGH* is not a rectangle.
3. **a.** 13 blocks
   b. 9.3 blocks
4. $(x-4)^2 + (y-2)^2 = 49$
5. $(x-5)^2 + (y-3)^2 = 20$
6. Sample:

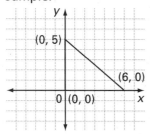

Chapter 11 Test, Form A

1. $4\sqrt{41} \approx 25.6$
2. $(1, 12)$
3. **a.** p is not $\parallel r$.
   b. Law of the Contrapositive
4. **a.** $x = 0$
   b. Law of Detachment and Law of Ruling Out Possibilities
5. **a.** $RQ = \sqrt{(-1+5)^2+(8-6)^2}$
   $= \sqrt{20} = 2\sqrt{5}$;
   $RS = \sqrt{(-1-1)^2+(8-4)^2}$
   $= \sqrt{20} = 2\sqrt{5}$;
   $ST = \sqrt{(1+3)^2+(4-2)^2}$
   $= \sqrt{20} = 2\sqrt{5}$;
   $QT = \sqrt{(-5+3)^2+(6-2)^2}$
   $= \sqrt{20} = 2\sqrt{5}$
   Since $RQ = RS = ST = QT$, *QRST* is a rhombus.
   b. Sample:
   Midpoint of $\overline{RT} =$
   $\left(\dfrac{-1+-3}{2}, \dfrac{8+2}{2}\right) = (-2, 5)$;
   Midpoint of $\overline{QS} =$
   $\left(\dfrac{-5+1}{2}, \dfrac{6+4}{2}\right) = (-2, 5)$.
   Since the midpoints of $\overline{RT}$ and $\overline{QS}$ are the same, $\overline{RT}$ and $\overline{QS}$ bisect each other.
6. $(9, -5, 2)$
7. true
8. 19 inches
9. Sample:

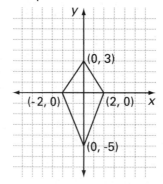

10. Assume trapezoid *MNOP* is isosceles. Then $MP = NO$.
    $MP = \sqrt{(-7+9)^2 + (4+5)^2}$
    $= \sqrt{85}$; and
    $NO = \sqrt{(3-6)^2 + (4+5)^2}$
    $= \sqrt{90}$. Since $MP \neq NO$, trapezoid *MNOP* is not isosceles.
11. **a.** If you walk, then you do not ride your bicycle.
    b. If you ride your bicycle, then you will not walk.
    c. If you do not walk, then you ride your bicycle.
12. c, the contrapositive
13.

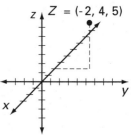

14. $\sqrt{110} \approx 10.5$
15. $(x + 3)^2 + (y - 6)^2 = 25$
16.

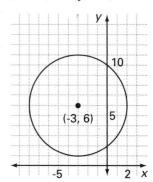

17. $9\sqrt{2} \approx 12.7$ blocks
18. Sample: Since *F* and *G* are midpoints, $\overline{FG}$ is parallel to $\overline{TS}$. $\parallel$ lines $\Rightarrow$ Corr. $\angle$s $\cong$, so $\angle UFG \cong \angle UTS$.
19. 8.2 cm
20. The students must meet on Thursday.
21. Sample:
    Suppose $\sqrt{242} = 16$.
    Then $(\sqrt{242})^2 = 16^2$, so $242 = 256$, which is false. Therefore, $\sqrt{242} \neq 16$.

Chapter 11 Test, Form B

1. $\sqrt{449} \approx 21.2$
2. $(5.5, 15)$
3. **a.** no conclusion
   b. none needed
4. **a.** Lines p and q are skew.
   b. Law of Detachment, Law of the Contrapositive, and Law of Ruling Out Possibilities
5. **a.** $MN = \sqrt{(-4+8)^2 + (6-4)^2}$
   $= \sqrt{20} = 2\sqrt{5};$
   $NO = \sqrt{(-4+2)^2 + (6-2)^2}$
   $= \sqrt{20} = 2\sqrt{5};$
   $OP = \sqrt{(-2+6)^2 + (2-0)^2}$
   $= \sqrt{20} = 2\sqrt{5};$
   $MP = \sqrt{(-8+6)^2 + (4-0)^2}$
   $= \sqrt{20} = 2\sqrt{5}$
   Since $MN = NO = OP = MP$, $MNOP$ is a rhombus.
   b. Sample:
   Midpoint of $\overline{NP} =$
   $\left(\dfrac{-4 + -6}{2}, \dfrac{6 + 0}{2}\right) = (-5, 3).$
   Midpoint of $\overline{MO} =$
   $\left(\dfrac{-8 + -2}{2}, \dfrac{4 + 2}{2}\right) = (-5, 3).$
   Since the midpoints of $\overline{NP}$ and $\overline{MO}$ are the same, $\overline{NP}$ and $\overline{MO}$ bisect each other.
6. $(-7, 4, -2)$
7. false
8. 153 cm
9. Sample:

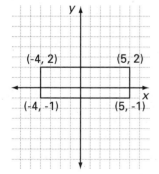

10. Suppose $QRST$ is a kite. Then $RS = TS$ and $QR = QT$.
    $RS = \sqrt{(5-11)^2 + (5-1)^2}$
    $= \sqrt{52} = 2\sqrt{13};$
    $TS = \sqrt{(5-11)^2 + (-2-1)^2}$
    $= \sqrt{45} = 3\sqrt{5}.$ Since
    $RS \neq TS$, $QRST$ is not a kite.
11. **a.** If you do not play the violin, then you are in a brass band.
    b. If you are not in a brass band, then you play the violin.
    c. If you play the violin, then you are not in a brass band.
12. c, the contrapositive
13.

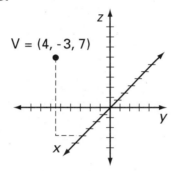

V = (4, -3, 7)

14. $\sqrt{65} \approx 8.1$
15. $(x-1)^2 + (y-4)^2 = 36$
16.

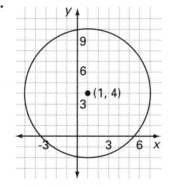

17. ≈ 659 miles
18. Sample: Since Z and X are midpoints, $\overline{ZX}$ is parallel to $\overline{ML}$. // lines $\Rightarrow$ Corr. $\angle$s $\cong$, so $\angle KZX \cong \angle KMY$.
19. 4.9 in.
20. The group will meet for lunch on Tuesday.
21. Sample: Suppose $\sqrt{43} = 6.6$. Then $(\sqrt{43})^2 = (6.6)^2$, so $43 = 43.56$, which is false. Therefore, $\sqrt{43} \neq 6.6.$

Chapter 11 Test, Cumulative Form

1. **a.** $(-1, -5)$
   b. 10
2. **a.** $(4, -1, 1.5)$
   b. $\sqrt{17}$
3.

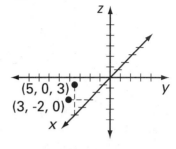

(5, 0, 3)
(3, -2, 0)

4. $\triangle EFG$ is isosceles; $AB = AC$, and E and F are midpoints. So $EB = FC$. $EG = \dfrac{1}{2}AC = FC$, and $FG = \dfrac{1}{2}AB = EB$. So $EG = FG$, and $\triangle EFG$ is isosceles by definition.
5. **a.** Anke ate eggs today.
   b. Law of Ruling Out Possibilities
6. **a.** If a figure is a rhombus, then it is a kite.
   b. If a figure is not a kite, then it is not a rhombus.
   c. If a figure is not a rhombus, then it is not a kite.
7. a, the converse; b, the inverse
8. Sample: Suppose quadrilateral $ABCD$ has four obtuse angles. Then $90 < m\angle A < 180$, $90 < m\angle B < 180$, $90 < m\angle C < 180$, and $90 < m\angle D < 180$. $90 + 90 + 90 + 90 < m\angle A + m\angle B + m\angle C + m\angle D < 180 + 180 + 180 + 180$. So $360 < m\angle A + m\angle B + m\angle C + m\angle D < 720$, which is false. So, a quadrilateral cannot have four obtuse angles.

9. Sample:
$$AB = \sqrt{(-1 - 0)^2 + (-1 - 1)^2}$$
$$= \sqrt{5};$$
$$BC = \sqrt{(0 - 2)^2 + (1 - 2)^2}$$
$$= \sqrt{5};$$
$$CD = \sqrt{(2 - 1)^2 + (2 - 0)^2}$$
$$= \sqrt{5};$$
$$DA = \sqrt{(1 + 1)^2 + (0 + 1)^2}$$
$$= \sqrt{5}.$$
Since $AB = BC = CD = DA$, A, B, C, and D are vertices of a rhombus.

10. Sample: Slope of $\overline{BD} =$
$$\frac{1 - 0}{0 - 1} = -1; \text{ slope of}$$

$$\overline{AC} = \frac{-1 - 2}{-1 - 2} = 1. \text{ Since}$$
$-1 \cdot 1 = -1$, $\overline{BD}$ and $\overline{AC}$ are perpendicular.

11. a. $\left(\frac{1}{2}, \frac{-3}{2}, -4\right)$

b. $\sqrt{5}$

12. $(x - 3)^2 + (y + 2)^2 = 41$

13. a. 94 ft²

b. 60 ft³

14. a. It is 3^2, or 9, times as great.

b. It is 3^3, or 27, times as great.

15. a. $27\sqrt{3} \approx 46.8$ cm²

b. $72\sqrt{3} \approx 124.7$ cm²

c. $36\sqrt{3} \approx 62.4$ cm³

16. $(a + c)(a + b)(x + y)$;
$a^2x + a^2y + abx + acx + bcx + aby + acy + bcy$

17. $\frac{368}{3}\pi \approx 385.4$ cm³

18. $88\pi \approx 276.5$ cm²

19. 24

20.

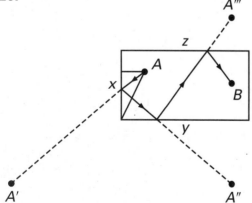

21. $x = 48$

22. Sample: $\overline{CD}$; in $\triangle ABD$, $\angle B$ is the smallest angle; so $\overline{AD}$ is the shortest side. In $\triangle ADC$, $\angle DAC$ is the smallest angle, so $\overline{DC}$ is the shortest side. Since $\overline{CD}$ is shorter than $\overline{AD}$, it is the shortest segment.

23. b

24. a. $\frac{8}{3}\pi r^3$

b. $2r$

c. $4r$

d. $2r$

e. $16r^3$

f. $\frac{\pi}{8} \approx 52\%$

Quiz 　　　　　　　　**Lessons 12-1**
　　　　　　　　　　Through 12-4

1. $E' = (-6, -3)$, $F' = (-3, \frac{3}{2})$, $G' = (3, 3)$, $H' = (\frac{9}{2}, -3)$

2.

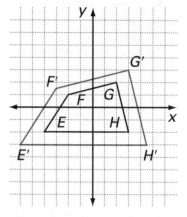

3. Slope of $\overline{FG} = \frac{2 - 1}{2 - (-2)} = \frac{1}{4}$;

slope of $\overline{F'G'} = \frac{3 - \frac{3}{2}}{3 - (-3)}$

$= \frac{\frac{3}{2}}{6} = \frac{1}{4}$

4. $k \approx \frac{1}{2} = .5$

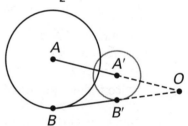

5. 21"

6. a. 37

b. $12\frac{6}{7} \approx 12.9$ units

7. st

Chapter 12 Test, Form A

1.

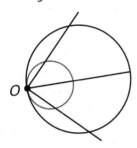

2. See below.

3. $k \approx \frac{4}{9} \approx .4$

4. $6\frac{2}{3} \approx 6.67$ units

5. a. expansion
b. $k = 2$

6. $m\angle E = 125$; $m\angle F = 85$; $FS = 3.0$; $EN = 3.84$

7. b

8. 51.2 cm^2

9. by k^3 or $\frac{1}{k^3}$

10. $\approx 1,249,818$ gallons

11. 15 cm

12. ≈ 92.3 minutes

13. 11,664 pounds

14.

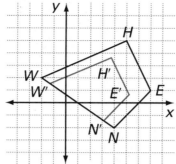

$$W' = \left(\frac{-3}{2}, \frac{3}{2}\right), H' = \left(\frac{15}{4}, \frac{15}{4}\right)$$

$$E' = \left(\frac{21}{4}, \frac{3}{4}\right), N' = \left(3, \frac{-3}{2}\right)$$

15. (24, -12)

16.

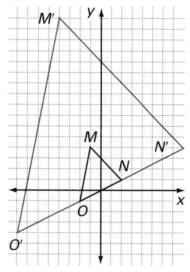

$M' = (-4, 16)$, $N' = (8, 4)$,
$O' = (-8, -4)$

17. $MO =$
$\sqrt{(-1 - (-2))^2 + (4 - (-1))^2}$
$= \sqrt{1 + 25} = \sqrt{26}$;
$M'O' =$
$\sqrt{(-4 - (-8))^2 + (16 - (-4))^2}$
$= \sqrt{16 + 400} = \sqrt{416} =$
$4\sqrt{26}$

Chapter 12 Test, Form B

1.

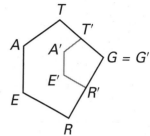

2.

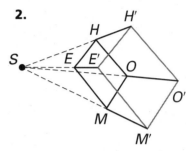

3. $k \approx \frac{4}{7} \approx .6$;

See below.

4. 1.14

5. a. expansion
b. $k \approx \frac{6}{5} = 1.2$

6. $m\angle H = 58$; $m\angle A = 92$; $TH = 8.0$; $AR = 10.5$

7. b

8. $42\frac{2}{3} \text{ cm}^2$

9. by k^2 or $\frac{1}{k^2}$

10. $\approx 1,138,848$

11. 12.5 in.

12. 5.5 hours

13. ≈ 328 g

2.

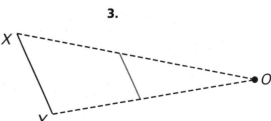

3.

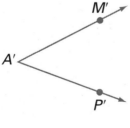

14.

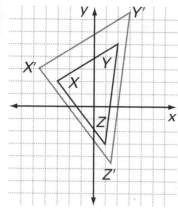

$X' = \left(-\frac{9}{2}, 3\right)$, $Y' = \left(3, \frac{15}{2}\right)$,

$Z' = \left(\frac{3}{2}, -\frac{9}{2}\right)$

15. (9, -27)

16.

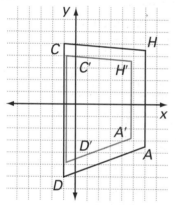

$C' = (-8, 40)$, $H' = (48, 36)$,
$A' = (48, -28)$, $D' = (-8, -48)$

17. $DA =$
$\sqrt{(-10-60)^2 + (-60-(-35))^2}$
$= \sqrt{5525} = 5\sqrt{221}$;
$D'A' =$
$\sqrt{(-8-48)^2 + (-48-(-28))^2}$
$= \sqrt{3536} = 4\sqrt{221} =$
$0.8(5\sqrt{221})$

1.

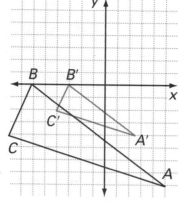

2. $\overline{AB} \parallel \overline{A'B'}$, $\overline{BC} \parallel \overline{B'C'}$,
and $\overline{AC} \parallel \overline{A'C'}$; $\overline{A'B'}$
$= \frac{1}{2}\overline{AB}$, $\overline{B'C'} = \frac{1}{2}\overline{BC}$,

and $\overline{A'C'} = \frac{1}{2}\overline{AC}$; angle
measure, betweenness,
and collinearity are
preserved.

3.

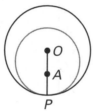

4. a. $k \approx \frac{3}{2} \approx 1.5$
   b. 16.5 cm
   c. 99 cm²
   d. $\left(\frac{3}{2}\right)^2 = \left(\frac{9}{4}\right) = 2.25$ times

5. $162\sqrt{2} \approx 229.1$
6. $\frac{6bd}{a}$
7. Sample: No; in order to
be similar, the dimensions
of the green box must
vary by the same factor
times the corresponding
dimension of the blue box.
8. a. $(3.4)^3 = 39.304$
   b. $(3.4)^2 = 11.56$
9. $AB = \sqrt{(-4-2)^2 + (1-3)^2}$
$= \sqrt{36+4} = 2\sqrt{10}$;
$S_{10}(A) = A' = (-40, 10)$;
$S_{10}(B) = B' = (20, 30)$;
$A'B' =$
$\sqrt{(-40-20)^2 + (10-30)^2}$
$= \sqrt{3600+400} = 20\sqrt{10}$

10. $K \approx .7$; See below.
11. a. $S(A) = (6, 3)$,
       $S(B) = (-12, 15)$,
       $S(C) = (10.5, 0)$
   b. 3
   c. Slope of $\overline{AB} = \frac{5-1}{-4-2} =$
       $\frac{4}{-6} = -\frac{2}{3}$;

       slope of $\overline{S(A)S(B)} =$
       $\frac{15-3}{-12-6} = \frac{12}{-18} = -\frac{2}{3}$

12. a. (0.5, -1, -1.5)
   b. $\sqrt{46} \approx 6.8$
13. a. If two lines are in the
       same plane, then they
       must be parallel.
   b. If two lines are not
       parallel, then they
       must not be in the
       same plane.
   c. If two lines are not in
       the same plane, then
       they are not parallel.
   d. c, the contrapositive
14. Sample:
   Suppose that $\sqrt[3]{28} = 3$.
   Then $(\sqrt[3]{28})^3 = 3^3$ and
   $28 = 27$, which is false.
   Therefore, $\sqrt[3]{28} \neq 3$.
15. a. (-3, 1, 0)
   b. 3
   c. Sample: (0, 1, 0),
       (-3, 1, 3)
16. a. Kelly ate a bagel;
       Markeith ate cereal.
   b. Law of Ruling Out
       Possibilities
17. Yes, by the SAS
   Congruence Theorem
18. Sample:

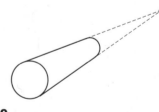

10.

19. Yes; the cross sections at corresponding heights have the same area.

20. cone: $\frac{1}{3} \cdot \pi \cdot 4^2 \cdot 8 = \frac{128}{3}\pi$

pyramid: $\frac{1}{3} \cdot 4\pi \cdot 4 \cdot 8 = \frac{128}{3}\pi$ units^3

21. $114 + 8\pi \approx 139.1$ units^2

22.

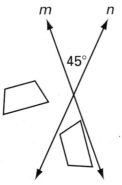

23. b

24. $\frac{2}{3}$

1. Yes; the ratios of the corresponding sides are equal: $\frac{7}{28} = \frac{11}{44} = \frac{12}{48} = \frac{1}{4}$; (SSS Similarity Theorem)

2. Yes; the measures of the angles in each triangle are 82, 50, and 48. (AA Similarity Theorem)

3. a. 20
    b. 11.2

4. 20 m

5. Yes; $\frac{ST}{YT} = \frac{1.7}{0.5} = 3.4$ and

$\frac{SX}{XU} = \frac{1.76 - 0.4}{0.4} = 3.4.$

By the Side-Splitting Converse Theorem, $\overline{UT} \parallel \overline{XY}$.

6. a. $11\frac{3}{8}$ ft

    b. $16\frac{1}{4}$ ft

1. $8\frac{1}{3}$

2. a. $2x$
    b. x
    c. $x\sqrt{2}$
    d. $x\sqrt{3}$

3. a. 49
    b. $\frac{7}{8} = 0.875$

4. $\frac{AC}{AB}$

5. 1

6. ≈ 11.3 ft

1. Yes; $\frac{DB}{BJ} = \frac{16}{4} = \frac{4}{1}$ and

$\frac{DG}{GE} = \frac{28}{7} = \frac{4}{1}$. By the

Side-Splitting Converse Theorem, $\overline{JE} \parallel \overline{BG}$.

2. a. 4
    b. $2\frac{1}{2}$

3. a. 12
    b. $6\sqrt{5} \approx 13.4$

4. a. $2\sqrt{2} \approx 2.8$
    b. $2\sqrt{2} \approx 2.8$

5. a. $3\sqrt{3} \approx 5.2$
    b. 6

6. $\frac{\sqrt{3}}{2}$

7. 11.430

8. $\angle 1$

9. a. $\frac{7}{24} \approx .29$

    b. $\frac{24}{25} = .96$

10. ≈ 106.03 units^2

11. Yes; $\frac{21.6}{12} = \frac{17.1}{9.5} = \frac{9}{5}$
(SSS Similarity Theorem)

12. Yes; measures of the angles in each are 58, 82, and 40. (AA Similarity Theorem)

13. ≈ 11.02

14. $\angle A$

15. cosine

16. 72 ft

17. a. 3.9 m
    b. ≈ 4.6 m

18. ≈ 38.6 ft

19. a. 76° east of south or 14° south of east
    b. ≈ 16.5 km

Chapter 13 Test, Form B

1. Yes; $\frac{7}{10} = \frac{4.2}{6} = .7$. By the Side-Splitting Converse Theorem, $\overline{MN} \parallel \overline{QR}$.
2. a. ≈2.8
   b. 6
3. a. 24.5
   b. ≈28.2
4. a. $3\sqrt{2} \approx 4.2$
   b. $3\sqrt{2} \approx 4.2$
5. a. $15\sqrt{3} \approx 26.0$
   b. 30
6. $\frac{\sqrt{2}}{2}$
7. 0.951
8. $\angle 3$
9. a. $\frac{12}{5} \approx 2.4$

   b. $\frac{12}{13} \approx .923$
10. ≈101.1 units²
11. Yes; $\frac{1.4}{1.75} = \frac{3.4}{4.25} = \frac{4.4}{5.5} = \frac{4}{5}$ (SSS Similarity Theorem)
12. No; corresponding angles are not congruent
13. 25
14. $\angle U$
15. tangent
16. 15 m
17. a. 19.2 ft
    b. ≈15.5 ft
18. ≈8.45 m
19. a. 73.7° east of north or 16.3° north of east
    b. ≈125 miles

Chapter 13 Test, Cumulative Form

1. a. 5
   b. $5\sqrt{3} \approx 8.7$
2. false
3. a. $\angle 3$
   b. $\angle 3$
4. $R' = \left(-\frac{3}{2}, \frac{9}{2}\right)$, $W' = (3, 6)$,

   $T' = \left(0, \frac{21}{2}\right)$
5. translation; See below.
6. a. kp
   b. $k^2 a$
7. Yes; $m\angle A = m\angle A$, $m\angle E = m\angle B$ (AA Similarity Theorem)
8. No; $\frac{12}{4} = \frac{15}{5} \neq \frac{9}{2}$
9. $\frac{9}{1600} = 0.005625$
10. Yes; SsA Congruence Theorem
11. $2\sqrt{117} \approx 21.6$
12. ≈8.3 ft
13. ≈41.6 units²
14. A two-column argument is shown. Paragraph form could also be accepted. Sample:

Conclusions	Justifications
1. $OS = OT$; $SP = TP$	definition of circle
2. $OSPT$ is a kite.	definition of kite

5.

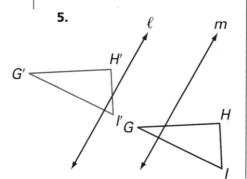

15. a. $\frac{5}{13} \approx .38$

    b. $\frac{12}{5} = 2.4$
16. a. ≈26° west of north or 64° north of west
    b. ≈8.2 km
17. $y = \frac{4}{3}x + 1$
18. a. $\frac{2}{3}$

    b. $21\frac{1}{3} \approx 21.3$
19. false
20. 11.2"
21. $2 + 2\sqrt{3} \approx 5.5$
22.

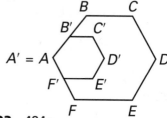

23. 484π ≈ 1521 cm²
24. ≈34.4 ft

Quiz   Lessons 14-1 Through 14-3

1. 37   **2.** 37°
3. $14\sqrt{3} \approx 24.25$
4. 44.7 m
5. Sample: $AM = BM$, $MO = MO$, and $BO = AO$ (radii of a circle), so $\triangle AMO \cong \triangle BMO$ by SSS Congruence Theorem. $m\angle BOM = m\angle AOM$ by CPCF Theorem, so $m\angle AOM = y$. Then $m\overset{\frown}{EA} = y°$ by definition of the measure of an intercepted arc.
6. Sample:

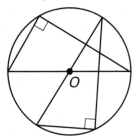

Quiz   Lessons 14-4 Through 14-6

1. ≈ 30 miles
2. ≈ 207.252 km
3. **a.** 60°   **b.** 80
4. $5x$
5. 24 units^2
6. 50°   **7.** 110°
8. Sample: $m\angle PON + m\angle ONQ + m\angle NQP + m\angle QPO = 360$. $\overleftrightarrow{NO}$ and $\overleftrightarrow{NQ}$ are tangents, so $m\angle PON$ and $m\angle NQP = 90$. Then $m\angle NQP + m\angle PON = 180$. Since $\angle QPO$ is a central angle, $m\angle QPO = m\overset{\frown}{OQ}$. Then. $m\angle ONQ + m\overset{\frown}{OQ} = 180°$.

Chapter 14 Test, Form A

1. **a.** $5\sqrt{2} \approx 7.1$
   b. $5\pi \approx 15.7$
2. 110°
3. 12.8
4. By definition of a trapezoid, $\overline{MA} \parallel \overline{NI}$. Since $\overline{XY} \perp \overline{MA}$, $\overline{XY} \perp \overline{NI}$. Then $\overline{XY}$ bisects $\overline{NI}$ by the Chord-Center Theorem.
5. 32
6. 115°
7. Sample:

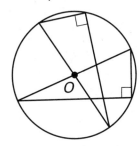

8. 7
9. 15
10. $\overrightarrow{WY}$ is tangent to $\odot Z$, so $\angle ZWY$ is a right angle. $m\angle WZY + m\angle WYZ = 90$ by the Triangle-Sum Thm. Since $\angle WZY$ is a central angle, $m\angle WZY = m\overset{\frown}{WV}$. Then $m\angle WYZ + m\overset{\frown}{WV} = 90°$, and $m\angle WYZ = 90 - m\overset{\frown}{WV}$.
11. **a.** ≈ 312.7 cm^2
    b. sphere
    c. ≈ 388 cm^2
12. **a.** anywhere on $\overset{\frown}{ABC}$; See below.
    b. ≈ 46.0 m
13. ≈ 53.89 km
14. ≈ 68.0 ft^3

12.

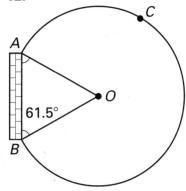

Chapter 14 Test, Form B

1. **a.** $8\sqrt{3} \approx 13.9$
   b. $\frac{32}{3}\pi \approx 33.5$
2. 69   **3.** ≈ 4.77
4. Sample: $m\overset{\frown}{HD} = 90°$, so $m\overset{\frown}{GF} = 90°$, $m\overset{\frown}{HG} = 90°$, and $m\overset{\frown}{DF} = 90°$. $m\overset{\frown}{DF} = m\overset{\frown}{DE} + m\overset{\frown}{EF} = 2m\angle EHF + 2m\angle DGE$. $m\angle EHF + m\angle DGE = \frac{1}{2}(90) = 45$.
5. 29   **6.** 173°
7. Sample:

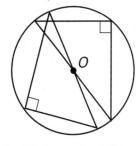

8. 34.4   **9.** 4.05
10. $m\overset{\frown}{RV} = 40°$, so $m\angle RPV = 40$. Since $\overleftrightarrow{OE} \parallel \overleftrightarrow{PR}$, and alternate interior angles are congruent, $m\angle PVE = 40$. In $\triangle PVE$, since $PV = PE$, $m\angle PEV = 40$. Then $m\angle PEV = 180 - (40 + 40) = 100$. $m\angle EPR = m\angle EPV + m\angle RPV = 100 + 40 = 140$. Then $m\overset{\frown}{EVR} = 140°$. $m\overset{\frown}{ETR} = 360° - m\overset{\frown}{EVR} = 360° - 140° = 220°$.
11. **a.** ≈ 767.7 cm^2
    b. sphere
    c. 952.44 cm^2
12. **a.** anywhere on $\overset{\frown}{ABC}$; See below
    b. ≈ 172.2 ft
13. ≈ 61.2 miles
14. ≈ 48.96 ft; he might save money on building materials.

12.

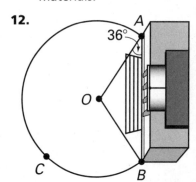

**Chapter 14 Test,
Cumulative Form**

1. Sample:

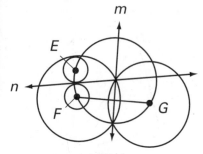

2. Sample:

3. $169\pi - 240 \approx$
290.9 units^2

4. false

5. **a.** $\frac{\sqrt{3}}{2}$ **b.** 1

6. 18

7. $16\pi + 16 \approx 66.3$ units^2

8. Sample: $RT = RI$, so
$m\angle RTI = m\angle TIR$. $m\angle I =$
$\frac{1}{2}m\widehat{TR}$, so $m\angle I = m\angle STR$.

Then by the Transitive
Property of Equality,
$m\angle STR = m\angle RTI$. By
definition of angle
bisector, $\overline{RT}$ bisects $\angle STI$.

9. No; angles in the
triangles are not
congruent.

10. Yes; $\frac{AE}{AB} = \frac{4}{8} = \frac{1}{2}$; $\frac{AD}{AC} =$

$\frac{3}{6} = \frac{1}{2}$; $\angle A \cong \angle A$

11. **a.** $9\sqrt{2} \approx 12.7$
   b. ≈ 17.4

12. Sample: Yes $\frac{AD}{DB} = \frac{2}{6} = \frac{1}{3}$

and $\frac{CF}{BF} = \frac{1.5}{4.5} = \frac{1}{3}$. Since

the ratios are the same,

$\overline{DF}$ // $\overline{AC}$. $\frac{AE}{EC} = \frac{1}{3}$ and

$\frac{AD}{DB} = \frac{1}{3}$, so $\overline{DE}$ // $\overline{FC}$. Since

both pairs of opposite
sides are parallel, *DECF* is
a parallelogram.

13. **a.** 30
   b. 25
   c. 80

14. ≈ 4.4 m

15. ≈ 2.7 hours

16. Sample: Since $m\angle BAD =$
$m\angle CAD$, $m\widehat{BD} = m\widehat{CD}$.
$\overline{AD}$ is a diameter, so
$m\widehat{ABD} = m\widehat{ACD} = 180°$.
$m\widehat{AB} = m\widehat{AC}$ by the
Subtraction Property of
Equality. $m\angle B = \frac{1}{2}m\widehat{AC}$

and $m\angle C = \frac{1}{2}m\widehat{AB}$. So

$m\angle B = m\angle C$. Then
$\triangle ABC$ is isosceles since
the base angles are
congruent.

17. c

18. ≈ 5.71 km

19. Maria, freshman;
John, freshman;
Kim, sophomore;
Tanisha, junior;
Thao, junior

20. the sphere; by the
Isoperimetric Theorem, of
all solids with the same
volume, the sphere has
the least surface area.

21. No

22.

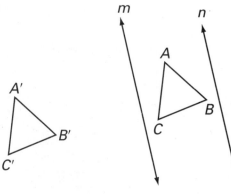

23. $AB = 42.5$,
$BC = 4.5\sqrt{85} \approx 41.5$

24. $\frac{1}{3}$

25. See below.

26. **a.** 68.0625 m^2
   b. square

25.

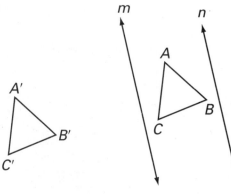

Comprehensive Test, Chapters 1–14

1. c	**15.** a
2. d	**16.** d
3. b	**17.** d
4. b	**18.** b
5. b	**19.** d
6. a	**20.** c
7. a	**21.** c
8. c	**22.** b
9. b	**23.** d
10. c	**24.** c
11. b	**25.** c
12. c	**26.** d
13. d	**27.** d
14. c	**28.** d

29. A two-column argument is shown. Paragraph form could also be accepted. Sample:

Conclusions	Justifications
1. $\angle CGF \cong \angle CFG$	Base angles of an isosceles triangle are congruent.
2. $BD \parallel GF$	definition of trapezoid
3. $BDFG$ is an isosceles trapezoid.	definition of isosceles trapezoid

30. Sample:

1-2	3-4	5-6
1-3	4-5	6-2
1-4	2-5	3-6
1-5	2-3	4-6
1-6	2-4	3-5

31. $\frac{32}{3}\pi$ ft^3

32.

1. In terms of the types of geometry studied in this chapter, how are figure *A* and figure *B* alike? How are they different?

figure *A*   figure *B*

Objectives A, F

- ☐ Understands how discrete lines are drawn.
- ☐ Understands properties of points and lines in discrete geometry and in synthetic geometry.
- ☐ Gives at least one significant likeness, such as: Both figures involve an oblique line crossing a horizontal line.
- ☐ Gives at least one significant difference, such as: The lines in figure *A* have no points in common. The lines in figure *B* have one point in common.

2. Points *A*, *B*, and *C* lie on $\overleftrightarrow{AB}$, $AB = 5.7$, and $BC = 9.2$. Janelle says this means that $AC = 14.9$. Roger says that $AC = 3.5$. Considering the given information, explain how both Janelle and Roger could be correct.

Objectives D, H

- ☐ Recognizes and correctly uses notation for lines, segments, and rays.
- ☐ Is able to apply the Distance Postulate properties of betweenness.
- ☐ Recognizes that Janelle is correct if point *B* is between point *A* and point *C*.
- ☐ Recognizes that Roger is correct if point *A* is between point *B* and point *C*.
- ☐ Draws a picture to demonstrate the situation.

---

3. a. Draw a network that is traversable. Identify a path through this network.

   b. Draw a network that is *not* traversable. Explain how you know there is no path through this network.

Objective B

- ☐ Is able to analyze networks.
- ☐ Draws an appropriate traversable network.
- ☐ Identifies a path through the chosen network.
- ☐ Draws an appropriate nontraversable network.
- ☐ Gives a logical explanation why no path exists.

4. Describe an equation of the line that might be the one graphed on the axes at the right.

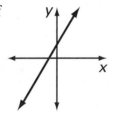

Objective L

- ☐ Is able to graph points and lines in the coordinate plane.
- ☐ Gives an appropriate description of the equation, such as: An equation is $y = 1.5x + 2$.

---

5. Explain how the following calculation is related to distance on a number line.

$$|18 - 42| = |\text{-}24| = 24$$

Write a real-world problem about distance that can be solved using this calculation. Then give the solution of your problem.

Objectives I, K

- ☐ Is able to determine distance on a number line.
- ☐ Is able to apply the definition of distance to real situations.
- ☐ Gives a logical interpretation, such as: The distance between 18 and 42 is 24.
- ☐ Writes an appropriate problem.
- ☐ Gives a correct solution to the problem.

6. Make a perspective drawing of a three-dimensional object or scene of your choice. Identify the vanishing point(s) in your drawing.

Objective C

- ☐ Is able to make and analyze perspective drawings.
- ☐ Draws an appropriate object or scene.
- ☐ Correctly identifies the vanishing point(s).

Teacher Notes

Objectives A, B, F, J, L

Concepts and Skills This activity requires students to:
- read information from text and graphics.
- analyze situations and determine whether they are representative of discrete geometry, synthetic geometry, coordinate geometry, or graph theory.
- draw figures composed of discrete lines.
- draw figures composed of lines on the coordinate plane.
- make and analyze networks.
- analyze and summarize results in a written report.

Guiding Questions
- What do the letters represent in drawing I? What is the meaning of "pen down" and "pen up"?
- In the code for drawing II, what is the meaning of the number 0? the number 1?
- In the method used in drawing III, how can you determine an equation for a horizontal line? a vertical line? an oblique line?
- In each method, how can you draw a letter that has curved paths?

Answers
a. I. graph theory   II. discrete geometry
III. coordinate geometry
Explanations will vary.

b. Answers will vary. Samples:
I. (Given the figure shown at right) (pen down) F-C-D-E
(pen up) -F-A (pen down) -B-C
II. (On a 7-column, 8-row grid)
1: 1-1-1-1-1-1-1-1;   2: 1-0-0-0-0-0-0-0;
3: 1-0-0-0-0-0-0-0;   4: 1-0-0-0-0-0-0-0;
5: 1-1-1-1-1-1-0-0;   6: 1-0-0-0-0-0-0-0;
7: 1-0-0-0-0-0-0-0;   8: 1-1-1-1-1-1-1-1
III. $y = 8$; $y = 3$; $y = 0$; $x = 0$

c,d. Answers will vary. Check students' work.

Extension
It is likely that, in their responses to Part **d**, different students will recommend different methods. Have students who favor the same method work in groups to create an entire alphabet using that method. If time permits, they might create drawings and codes for capital letters, lowercase letters, and numerals.

Evaluation

Level	Standard to be achieved for performance at specified level
5	The student demonstrates an in-depth understanding of the types of geometries and their application to the given situation. All drawings and codes are accurate and complete. The report is neat and thorough, and it may be presented imaginatively. The student offers an articulate analysis of the methods and makes sound recommendations for improvement.
4	The student demonstrates a clear understanding of the types of geometries. The concepts are applied correctly to the given situation, but the drawings and codes may contain minor errors. The report is neat and easy to read, offering a clear rationale for all judgments and at least one recommendation for improving the methods, but it may lack in some detail.
3	The student demonstrates a fundamental understanding of the types of geometries and their application to the given situation. However, the student may make a major error or omit a critical step in creating the drawings and their codes. The student prepares a report, but it may be somewhat disorganized, and the reasoning behind some judgments or suggested improvements may be flawed.
2	The student demonstrates some understanding of the types of geometries, but needs help in applying them to the given situation. Even with assistance, the student may make several major errors or omit critical steps in creating the drawings and their codes. The student attempts to prepare a report containing judgments and recommendations, but the reasoning and presentation are jumbled and incomplete.
1	The student demonstrates little if any understanding of the types of geometries and is unable to apply them to the given situation. The student may attempt to create some drawings and codes, but they are superfluous or irrelevant. There is no attempt to prepare an original report. The student may simply copy or restate the given information.

1. Write a conditional about a real-world situation. Is your conditional true or false? Write the converse of your conditional. Is the converse true or false?

Objectives E, G, H, K
- ☐ Is able to write a conditional and its converse.
- ☐ Is able to evaluate conditionals.
- ☐ Is able to apply conditionals to real situations.
- ☐ Writes an appropriate conditional.
- ☐ Correctly writes the converse.
- ☐ Correctly evaluates the truth of the conditional and its converse.

2. Draw a figure that illustrates this statement:

$$\triangle BET \cap \triangle TEN = \overline{ET}$$

Now, using the figure that you drew, list the segments of $\triangle BET \cup \triangle TEN$.

Objective I
- ☐ Is able to determine the union and intersection of sets.
- ☐ Draws an appropriate figure. See example at the right.
- ☐ Correctly lists the sets in the union: $\overline{BE}, \overline{EN}, \overline{NT}, \overline{TB}, \overline{ET}$.

3. When asked to give a definition of a diagonal, a student wrote the following:

$\overline{AZ}$ is a diagonal of a polygon. $\Rightarrow$ A and Z are vertices of a polygon.

Do you think this response is correct? Explain your reasoning. If you think it is not correct, show how to correct it.

Objectives C, F, G
- ☐ Is able to use the symbols $\Rightarrow$ and $\Leftrightarrow$.
- ☐ Is able to write conditionals and biconditionals.
- ☐ Is able to apply the properties of a good definition.
- ☐ Recognizes that the response is incorrect.
- ☐ Gives a logical explanation, such as: A definition must be written as a biconditional, using the symbol $\Leftrightarrow$; if A and Z are consecutive vertices, then $\overline{AZ}$ is a side, not a diagonal.
- ☐ Gives a correct definition, such as: $\overline{AZ}$ is a diagonal of a polygon $\Leftrightarrow$ A and Z are nonconsecutive vertices of the polygon.

4. Mia, Tran, and Jennifer used an odometer to calculate the distances between their houses. Their results were as follows.

Mia's house to Jennifer's house: 1.9 miles

Mia's house to Tran's house: 4.8 miles

Jennifer's house to Tran's house: 2.7 miles

Explain how you know that at least one of these distances is incorrect.

Objective M
- ☐ Is able to apply the Triangle Inequality Postulate in real situations.
- ☐ Gives a logical explanation, such as: The distances must be incorrect because the three houses can be thought of as the vertices of a triangle. The sum of the lengths of any two sides of a triangle must be greater than the length of the third side. Given these distances, however, $1.9 + 2.7 \not> 4.8$.

5. Separate the figures at the right into two sets. List the figures that are in each set and describe what geometric property you used to decide in which set you would place each figure. Then separate the figures into two sets using a different geometric property. Again, list the figures in each set and name the property.

Objectives A, B
- ☐ Is able to identify polygons by their number of sides.
- ☐ Is able to distinguish between polygons and polygonal regions.
- ☐ Is able to distinguish between convex and nonconvex figures.
- ☐ Correctly separates the figures into two sets, such as: The set of polygons = {A, C, E}. The set of polygonal regions = {B, D, G}.
- ☐ Correctly identifies a different grouping of the figures.

figure A · figure B · figure C · figure D · figure E · figure F · figure G

Teacher Notes

Objectives C, E, F, G, H

Concepts and Skills This activity requires students to:
• write and evaluate conditionals and biconditionals.
• write the converse of a conditional.
• use and interpret the symbols $\Rightarrow$ and $\Leftrightarrow$.
• use the properties of a good definition to write and analyze definitions.
• summarize ideas in an original essay or short story.

Guiding Questions
• What are the properties of a good definition?
• Is each characteristic you identified in your definition of a term important to a person's understanding of the term?
• Is there some other object that might have all the characteristics that you used in defining the term?
• What might be some of the consequences if each of two people has a different understanding of a word?

Answers
a. Answers will vary. Sample: The word *place* is too broad. For example, the United States is a place where human beings live, but it is not a house.
b–d. Answers will vary. Sample responses are given for the word *airplane*.
b. An airplane is a vehicle that has wings and is used for flight.
c. If a vehicle is an airplane, then it has wings and is used for flight (*term* $\Rightarrow$ *characteristics*). If a vehicle has wings and is used for flight, then it is an airplane (*characteristics* $\Rightarrow$ *term*).
d. Both conditionals given in Part **c** are true. A vehicle is an airplane if and only if it has wings and is used for flight.
e. Answers will vary. See Parts **b–d** above for a sample response.
f. Answers will vary. Check students' work.

Extension
Have students create a list of words that have two meanings. (Samples: bat, fan, fork, foot, light, meter, mine, patient, pen, table, yard) Using a dictionary as a reference if necessary, have them write two definitions for each term—one for each meaning—then write each definition as a biconditional.

Evaluation

Level	Standard to be achieved for performance at specified level
5	The student demonstrates an in-depth understanding of conditionals, converses, and their application to the given situation. All definitions are concise and complete. The article makes a convincing argument about the need for good definitions, and it may be presented imaginatively.
4	The student demonstrates a clear understanding of conditionals, converses, and their application to the given situation. The student creates reasonable definitions, but may tend to overlook some minor details. The article is well-organized and easy to read, buy may lack in some detail.
3	The student demonstrates a fundamental understanding of conditionals, converses, and their application to the given situation. The student generally recognizes what constitutes a "bad" definition, but may need assistance in creating original definitions that avoid these pitfalls. The student prepares an article that presents original ideas, but it may be somewhat disorganized, and some of the reasoning may be flawed.
2	The student demonstrates some understanding of definitions, conditionals, converses, and their application to the given situation, but needs considerable assistance in distinguishing "good" definitions from "bad." Even with help, the student may overlook several key ideas when creating definitions. The student prepares an original article, but the reasoning is jumbled, and the presentation is incomplete.
1	The student demonstrates little if any understanding of conditionals and converses and is unable to apply them to the given situation. The student may attempt to write some definitions, but the words are superfluous or irrelevant. There is no attempt to generate an original article; the student may simply copy or restate given information.

1. State as many facts as you can about the lines and angles in the figure at the right.

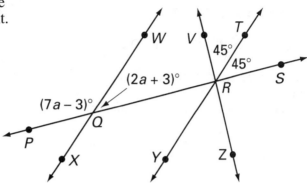

Objectives A, B, C

- ☐ Is able to analyze drawings of angles.
- ☐ Is able to determine measures of angles formed by parallel lines, perpendicular lines, and transversals.
- ☐ Can use algebra to find measures of angles.
- ☐ States several significant facts, such as: $\overleftrightarrow{YZ} \perp \overleftrightarrow{PS}$; $\overrightarrow{RT}$ bisects $\angle VRS$ and $\angle PRZ$; $m\angle SRZ = m\angle VRP = 90$; $m\angle WQS = m\angle PQX = 43$; $m\angle WQP = m\angle XQS = 137$; $m\angle VRT = m\angle TRS = m\angle ZRY = m\angle YRP = 45$.

---

2. Write a brief paragraph to describe the situation that is represented by this picture. In your paragraph, make an estimate of the value of x.

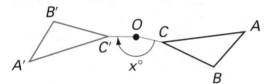

Objective E

- ☐ Demonstrates an understanding of rotations and rotation images.
- ☐ Makes a reasonable estimate of the value of x, such as: about -170.
- ☐ Writes an appropriate paragraph of explanation, such as: The picture shows $\triangle ABC$ rotated $x°$ about point O, the center of rotation. The rotation image is $\triangle A'B'C'$. The amount of rotation is about 170°. You write this as -170° to indicate a rotation in the clockwise direction.

---

3. The figure at the right shows a circular track for running. The small circle is the inner lane of the track; the large circle is the outer lane. How is the trip from A to B on the track similar to the trip from X to Y? How is it different?

Objectives F, I

- ☐ Is able to find measures of central angles and degree measures of arcs.
- ☐ Is able to apply angle and arc measures in real situations.
- ☐ States at least one significant similarity, such as: Both trips span a 148° arc.
- ☐ States at least one significant difference, such as: The trip from X to Y covers a greater distance than the trip from A to B.

---

4. State one property of equality or inequality that was reviewed in this chapter. Then draw a picture of a geometric situation in which you can use this property to make a conclusion. State the given information and the conclusion.

Objective G

- ☐ Is able to recognize and use the postulates of equality and inequality.
- ☐ Gives a correct statement of one property of equality or inequality.
- ☐ Draws an appropriate geometric situation.
- ☐ States a justifiable conclusion.

---

5. **a.** Give equations of two lines that are parallel. Explain how you know that these lines are parallel.

   b. Give equations of two lines that are perpendicular. Explain how you know that these lines are perpendicular.

Objectives K, L

- ☐ Is able to determine the slope of a line from its equation.
- ☐ Is able to determine the slope of a line parallel or perpendicular to a given line.
- ☐ Gives correct equations for parallel lines.
- ☐ Gives correct equations for perpendicular lines.
- ☐ Gives an appropriate explanation.

Teacher Notes

Objectives A, C, D, F, I, J

Concepts and Skills This activity requires students to:
- analyze a drawing involving angles, lines, and circles.
- determine measures of angles formed by parallel lines, perpendicular lines, and transversals.
- find the degree measures of arcs.
- apply parallel lines, perpendicular lines, angle measures, and arc measures in real situations.
- plan and make a precise drawing involving circles, parallel lines, perpendicular lines, and transversals.

Materials
- drawing tools (compass, straightedge, protractor) or an automatic drawer

Guiding Questions
- What assumptions do you think can be made about the geometric figures in the map? (Samples: Angles that appear to be right angles are right angles. Roads are spaced equally around circles.)
- What additional lines might you draw to help you answer the question? (Extend all roads to meet at the centers of the circles.)

Answers
a. State, Maine, Vermont, New Hampshire, Massachusetts
b. Lake, Erie, Huron, Superior
c. 270
d. 60; Explanations will vary. Sample: When the roads around Presidents' Circle are extended to the center of the circle, they form 6 congruent angles of 60° each. Since Maine and State are parallel, the 60° angle between Jefferson and the extension of Maine and the smaller angle formed at the intersection of Jefferson and State are alternate interior angles. Therefore, the angles are equal in measure.
e. Answers will vary. Check students' drawings.

Extension
Have students bring in maps of the city or town in which your school is located or of some cities or towns they have visited, such as Washington, D.C. Have them list ways in which the layout of the streets on the map relates to the geometry they studied in Chapter 3.

Evaluation

Level	Standard to be achieved for performance at specified level
5	The student demonstrates an in-depth understanding of angles, lines, and their application to the given situation. All questions are answered correctly and completely. The proposed street layout reflects careful thought, and the map is drawn neatly and accurately. The student may offer additional insights, such as designating certain streets as one-way to avoid potential traffic hazards.
4	The student demonstrates a clear understanding of angles, lines, and their application to the given situation. All questions are answered thoughtfully, but some calculations may contain minor errors. The proposed street layout is appropriate, but the rendering of the map may lack in some detail.
3	The student demonstrates a fundamental understanding of angles, lines, and their application to the given situation. All questions are answered, but the responses may contain one or more errors. The student proposes a reasonable street layout; however, the map may be somewhat disorganized, and the construction of critical elements may be flawed.
2	The student demonstrates some understanding of angles and lines, but needs assistance in applying the relevant concepts to the given situation. Even with help, the student may make major errors in responding to the questions posed. The student attempts to plan a street layout and prepare a map, but some aspects of the plan may be inappropriate, and the student may make one or more errors or omit critical steps in rendering the map.
1	The student demonstrates little if any understanding of angles and lines, and is totally unable to apply the relevant concepts to the given situation. Any answers to the questions posed are superfluous or irrelevant. There is no significant attempt to plan an appropriate street layout or prepare a map; the student may simply copy the given drawing.

1. In the figure at the right, is △*XYZ* the reflection image of △*ABC* over line *m*? If you think it is, write a convincing argument to support your answer. If you think it is not, first justify your answer; then locate the correct reflection image.

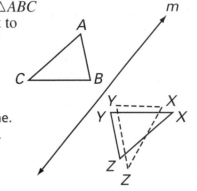

Objectives A, B, E

- ☐ Understands the definition of reflection image.
- ☐ Is able to draw reflection images of polygons over a given line.
- ☐ Is able to apply properties of reflections to make conclusions.
- ☐ Recognizes that △*XYZ* is not the reflection image of △*ABC* over line *m*.
- ☐ Gives a logical explanation.
- ☐ Draws the correct reflection image, as shown at the right.

---

2. Suppose you are asked to make the following a true statement by filling in the blank with the name of one transformation.

     A __?__ is a composite of reflections over lines.

Explain why you cannot complete the statement without being given more information. Make a drawing to illustrate your answer.

Objectives D, G

- ☐ Is able to draw images of figures under composites of two reflections.
- ☐ Is able to apply the Two-Reflection Theorems for Translations and for Rotations.
- ☐ Gives a logical explanation, such as: The statement does not specify whether the lines are parallel or intersecting, nor does it specify the number of lines. A composite of reflections over two lines may be a translation or a rotation. A composite of reflections over three lines may be a reflection or a glide reflection.
- ☐ Makes an appropriate drawing.

3. On the coordinate axes below, draw a translation image of △*RST*. Then give the ordered-pair description of the vector that represents your translation.

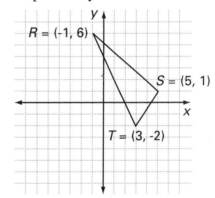

Objectives C, K

- ☐ Is able to draw a translation image of a figure.
- ☐ Is able to find coordinates of translation images.
- ☐ Draws a correct translation image of △*RST*.
- ☐ Gives a correct vector for the translation.

---

4. The figure at the right shows a game table and one student's planned path for getting ball *B* into hole *H*. Is this path possible? Explain why or why not?

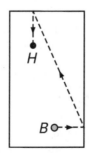

Objective I

- ☐ Is able to use reflections to find a path from an object to a particular point.
- ☐ Recognizes that the path shown is not possible.
- ☐ Gives a logical explanation.

5. Identify a real-world situation that illustrates congruence. Give a brief explanation of how the situation you chose shows congruence.

Objective J

- ☐ Demonstrates an ability to use congruence in real situations.
- ☐ Identifies an appropriate situation, such as: photocopying a document at 100%.
- ☐ Gives a logical explanation of the congruence, such as: All angle measures and distances in the image on a 100% photocopy are equal to the corresponding angle measures and distances in the image on the original.

Teacher Notes

Objectives B, D, E, I

Concepts and Skills This activity requires students to:

- read information from text and a graphic.
- draw images of points under reflection over a given line.
- draw images of points under composites of two reflections.
- apply properties of reflections to make conclusions.
- use reflections in mirrors to find the path of light from an object to a particular point.
- make decisions based on given information.
- summarize results.
- write a coherent explanation.

Guiding Questions

- Which parts of the manufacturing area are clearly visible to the guard? Which parts are most likely visible? Which parts are least likely visible?
- How is the path of light reflected in a mirror similar to the path of a ball reflected off the wall of a game table?

Answers

a. Answers will vary. Sample: If the mirror is on the back wall, for the guard to see activity near P, light from P would have to follow the path indicated by the arrows. However, the side wall obstructs that path, so the guard cannot see any activity at point P. This is also true of other points in both branches of the "U."

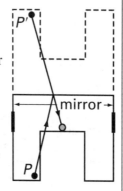

b. Answers will vary.

Extension

Discuss with students the way in which mirrors often are placed at intersections of high-traffic corridors so that a person walking in one corridor can see others approaching from the adjoining corridor. Have them consider where they might place such mirrors in the manufacturing area shown. After they have chosen a placement, have them determine what a person approaching the mirrors will be able to see.

Evaluation

Level	Standard to be achieved for performance at specified level
5	The student demonstrates an in-depth understanding of reflections and their application to the given situation. The explanation concerning the inappropriateness of the given plan is accurate and articulate, and the student may offer additional insights. (For example, the student may identify the entire range of points that are not visible to the guard.) The revised plan and report show evidence of careful thought, and may be rendered imaginatively.
4	The student demonstrates a clear understanding of reflections and their application to the situation. The student presents a valid argument as to why the given plan is inappropriate, but it may contain minor errors. The revised plan is appropriate, and the accompanying report is well-organized and easy to read, but one or both may lack in some detail.
3	The student demonstrates a fundamental understanding of reflections and their application to the situation. The student recognizes that the given plan is inappropriate, but may make a major error in justifying that conclusion. The student prepares a revised plan that is appropriate in concept, but the rendering of the plan and the report may be inaccurate.
2	The student demonstrates some understanding of reflections, but needs assistance in applying the concepts and properties to the given situation. Even with help, the student may make major errors in analyzing the given plan. The student attempts to create a revised plan and prepare a report, but one or both may be jumbled and incomplete.
1	The student demonstrates little if any understanding of reflections and is unable to apply them to the given situation. The student may attempt to analyze the given plan, but any observations are superfluous or irrelevant. There is no attempt to create a revised plan or prepare a report. The student may simply copy or restate the given information.

1. Draw and label two triangles that are congruent. Use symbols to state the congruence between the figures. Then list all pairs of congruent corresponding parts of the two figures.

Objective E

☐ Is able to make and justify conclusions about congruent triangles.
☐ Draws two congruent figures and labels them appropriately.
☐ Correctly states the congruence.
☐ Correctly lists all pairs of congruent corresponding parts.

2. Explain the Perpendicular Bisector Theorem in your own words. Then give an example of a real-world situation that illustrates this theorem.

Objectives C, I

☐ Demonstrates an understanding of the Perpendicular Bisector Theorem.
☐ Demonstrates an ability to use the Perpendicular Bisector Theorem in real situations.
☐ Gives an appropriate description of the Perpendicular Bisector Theorem.
☐ Describes an appropriate real-world application of the Perpendicular Bisector Theorem, such as: Guy wires holding up a newly planted tree.

3. Explain how you can tell that the figure at the right is labeled incorrectly. Suppose you were asked to correct the error by making just one change. What would you suggest? Justify your answer.

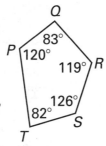

Objective D

☐ Demonstrates an understanding of the Polygon-Sum Theorem.
☐ Gives a logical explanation, such as: The figure is a convex pentagon. By the Polygon-Sum Theorem, the sum of the measures of the angles of a convex pentagon is 540. However, the sum of the labeled angle measures is 530. Therefore, the figure must be labeled incorrectly.
☐ Gives an appropriate suggestion for correcting the figure, such as: The measure of ∠Q is labeled as 83, but ∠Q appears to be an obtuse angle. Change the measure of ∠Q to 93.

4. In the figure at the right, m // n. State one fact about the figure that you can prove by using the Transitive Property of Congruence. Then write an argument to prove that fact.

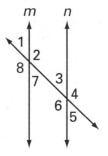

Objective F

☐ Is able to write proofs using the Transitive Property of Congruence.
☐ States an appropriate fact, such as: ∠1 ≅ ∠5.
☐ Writes a correct proof argument. Sample for the fact stated above: ∠1 ≅ ∠7 by the Vertical Angles Theorem; ∠5 ≅ ∠7 by the Corresponding Angles Postulate; ∠1 ≅ ∠5 by the Transitive Property of Congruence.

5. At the end of the school year, Sari found the construction at the right in her geometry notebook. However, she had not identified it, and she could not remember what she had constructed. Identify the construction for Sari. Then write a description of the steps that were taken to perform the construction.

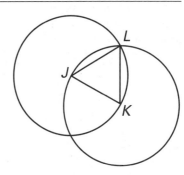

Objective B

☐ Recognizes that the figure shows the construction of an equilateral triangle with one side segment JK.
☐ Writes an appropriate set of steps to describe the construction.

Teacher Notes

Objectives A, B

Concepts and Skills This activity requires students to:

- read information from text and graphics.
- explore ways to analyze figures and determine if they are congruent.
- apply properties of parallel lines.
- perform compass-and-straightedge constructions.
- create a design involving congruent figures.
- analyze and summarize results.

Materials

- paper for tracing
- compass and straightedge

Guiding Questions

- What are congruent figures?
- How can you determine if two figures are congruent? (Trace the first figure onto a sheet of paper, then try to position the tracing so that it fits exactly over the second figure.)

Answers

a. Check students' work. They should notice: $\triangle AED \cong \triangle CEB$ and $\triangle AEB \cong \triangle CED$.

b. $\angle DAE \cong \angle BCE$, $\angle ADE \cong \angle CBE$, $\angle BAE \cong \angle DCE$, $\angle ABE \cong \angle CDE$

c. Check student's work. Students may show congruence by tracing and fitting triangles exactly over one another.

d. Check students' work. Students should construct an equilateral triangle with side length equal to MN, bisect each side to locate its midpoint, then connect the midpoints.

e. Answers will vary.

Extension

Suppose the design can only be made using a six-by-six grid of squares. Find as many different ways as possible to use the grid lines to divide the grid into four congruent regions. Samples are given below.

Evaluation

Level	Standard to be achieved for performance at specified level
5	The student demonstrates an in-depth understanding of congruence and its application to the given situation. The student answers all questions accurately and completely, and its able to provide sound justifications for all responses. The original design is appropriate, and it may be rendered imaginatively. The report presents an accurate description of the design.
4	The student demonstrates a clear understanding of congruence. The concept is applied correctly to the given situation, but there may be minor flaws in the student's responses to the questions posed. The original design is appropriate, but the accompanying report may lack in some detail.
3	The student demonstrates a fundamental understanding of congruence and its application to the given situation. However, the student may make a major error in responding to the questions posed, or may omit a critical step of the required construction. The student prepares an original design, but the rendering is inaccurate. The accompanying report may be somewhat disorganized.
2	The student demonstrates some understanding of congruence, but needs assistance in applying the concept to the given situation. Even with help, the student may make several major errors in responding to the questions posed or in performing the required construction. The student attempts to devise an original design, but it may be flawed. The accompanying report is jumbled and incomplete.
1	The student demonstrates little if any understanding of congruence, and is unable to apply the concept to the given situation. The student may attempt to answer some of the questions posed, but the responses are superfluous or irrelevant. There is no attempt to create an original design. The student may simply copy one of the given designs.

1. When asked to illustrate a trapezoid, Hoa and Jen drew these figures.

Hoa's drawing   Jen's drawing

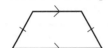

Is either drawing appropriate? Is it possible that both are appropriate? Justify your answer. If you think that neither drawing is appropriate, make an appropriate drawing.

Objectives B, G

☐ Is able to draw polygons satisfying various conditions.

☐ Understands the properties of the seven special types of quadrilaterals.

☐ Recognizes that Hoa's drawing is a trapezoid, but is best called an isosceles trapezoid.

☐ Recognizes that Jen's drawing is a trapezoid, but is best called a parallelogram.

☐ Makes a more appropriate drawing. See sample at right.

2. In the figure at the right, *MNOPQR* is a regular hexagon. State as many additional facts as you can about the figure.

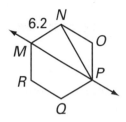

Objectives C, D, F

☐ Is able to apply theorems about isosceles triangles, quadrilaterals, and regular polygons to find angle measures and segment lengths.

☐ Understands properties of the various types of triangles and regular polygons.

☐ States several significant facts about the figure, such as:
m∠ONP = m∠OPN = 30;
m∠RMP = m∠QPM = m∠NMP = m∠OPM = 60;
m∠MNP = m∠QPN = 90;
m∠RMN = m∠MNO = m∠NOP = m∠OPQ = m∠PQR = m∠QRM = 120;
NO = OP = PQ = QR = RM = 6.2;
$\overleftrightarrow{MP}$ is a symmetry line of *MNOPQR*;
△NOP is an isosceles triangle;
PQRM and *MNOP* are isosceles trapezoids.

3. The word *asymmetric* means "not symmetric." Draw a quadrilateral that you think is asymmetric. Then explain why you believe it is asymmetric.

Objective A

☐ Understands the meaning of symmetry lines and centers of symmetry of geometric figures.

☐ Draws an appropriate quadrilateral, such as the one at the right.

☐ Gives a logical explanation why the figure is asymmetric.

4. Taneesha was sick and missed a day of math class. On the day before she was absent, the class was studying regular polygons. When she returned, she wondered why the class was discussing round-robin tournaments. How would you explain this to Taneesha?

Objective J

☐ Demonstrates an ability to make a schedule for a round-robin tournament.

☐ Gives a logical explanation of how regular polygons are related to round-robin tournaments.

5. Luis's little sister spilled grape juice on his homework. He was supposed to do the proof at the right, but now he doesn't know what the given information was. What do you think it might have been? Show how Luis can use your "given" to prove that *JKLM* is a kite.

Objective H

☐ Is able to write proofs using properties of triangles and quadrilaterals.

☐ Identifies an appropriate set of "given" information. See sample.

☐ Writes an appropriate proof. See sample.

Given: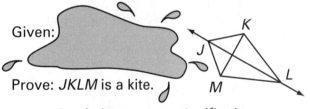

Prove: *JKLM* is a kite.

Conclusions	Justifications
0. △MJK is isos. with base $\overline{MK}$; △KLM is isos. with base $\overline{MK}$.	Given
1. $\overline{MJ} \cong \overline{KJ}$; $\overline{ML} \cong \overline{KL}$	def. of isos. △
2. *JKLM* is a kite.	def. of kite

EVALUATION GUIDES

Teacher Notes

Objectives A, C, D, F, I

Concepts and Skills This activity requires students to:
- identify symmetries of geometric figures.
- apply theorems about isosceles triangles, quadrilaterals, and regular polygons to find angle measures.
- explore the concept of tiling a plane region.
- create and analyze an original real-world design involving polygons.

Guiding Questions
- How many degrees are in a complete rotation? How is this related to the measures of the angles with a common vertex? [The sum of the measures of the angles with a common vertex must be 360.]
- In designing your own blocks, what relationships should there be among angles and sides? [There should be several ways for the angle measures to total 360; many sides should have equal length.]

Answers
a. equilateral triangle, square, regular hexagon, isosceles trapezoid, two rhombuses
b. equilateral triangle: each angle measures 60; square: each angle measures 90; regular hexagon: each angle measures 120; isosceles trapezoid and larger rhombus: two angles measure 120 and two measure 60; small rhombus: two angles measure 30 and two measure 150.
c. The design has a horizontal symmetry line and a vertical symmetry line that each pass through the center of the regular hexagon. The pattern also has 4-fold rotation symmetry.
d. isosceles triangle with base angles that each measure 30 and vertex angle that measures 120; kite with angles at the ends that measure 30 and 90 and two other angles that each each measure 120
e. Answers will vary. Check students' work.

Extension
Use the traditional pattern blocks to explore several questions such as: Is it possible to create a design with no symmetry lines? no rotational symmetry? [yes] exactly three symmetry lines? 3-fold rotational symmetry? [yes] exactly five symmetry lines? 5-fold rotational symmetry? [no, unless gaps are allowed between blocks]

Evaluation

Level	Standard to be achieved for performance at specified level
5	The student demonstrates an in-depth understanding of symmetry and polygons. All calculations involved in answering the questions are accurate and complete, and descriptions are articulate. The original set of blocks reflects careful consideration. The report is accurate and easy to read and includes one or more carefully-executed designs.
4	The student demonstrates a clear understanding of symmetry and polygons. All questions are answered thoughtfully, and articulate descriptions are provided, but the student may make minor errors in calculation. The original set of blocks is appropriate, and the student provides one or more attractive designs, but the report may lack in some detail.
3	The student demonstrates a fundamental understanding of symmetry and polygons. The student recognizes which properties are appropriate to the situation, but has some difficulty in applying them. The student creates an original set of blocks, but some choices may not be carefully considered. The report may contain one or more major errors, and the design may be executed carelessly.
2	The student demonstrates some understanding of symmetry and polygons, but needs assistance in applying the properties to the situation. Even with help, the student may make major errors in answering the questions. The student attempts to create an original set of blocks and write a report, but the presentation is jumbled. The report includes an original design, but it is poorly executed.
1	The student demonstrates little if any understanding of symmetry and polygons, and cannot apply the concepts to the situation. The student may attempt some calculations, but they are superfluous or irrelevant. There is no attempt to create or describe a set of blocks or to make an original design. The student may simply copy the given blocks and design.

1. Sketch a triangle and label it △*ABC*. Then label three measures of your triangle in such a way that any other triangle with those same measures would be congruent to △*ABC*. Explain how you know that any such triangle would be congruent.

2. Based on the theorems that you studied in this chapter, state as many facts as you can about the figure at the right.

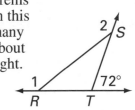

Objective A

☐ Is able to determine whether all triangles satisfying a certain set of conditions are congruent.

☐ Sketches a triangle and labels it appropriately.

☐ Gives a logical explanation why all such triangles would be congruent.

Objectives B, H

☐ Is able to determine measure of angles in polygons using exterior angles.

☐ Is able to determine which sides or angles of triangles are smallest or largest.

☐ States two or more appropriate facts, such as: m∠*SRT* + m∠*RST* = 72; m∠*RTS* = 108; *RS* is the longest side of △*RST*.

---

3. a. The only geometric tool that Clark has is a ruler. How could he use it to determine whether *JKLM* is a parallelogram?

b. The only geometric tool Lois has is a protractor. How could she use it to determine whether *JKLM* is a parallelogram?

4. a. Name one regular polygon that tessellates the plane. Make a sketch of the tessellation.

b. Name one regular polygon that does *not* tessellate the plane. Justify your answer.

Objective J

☐ Is able to draw tessellations.

☐ Identifies a regular polygon that tessellates the plane, such as: equilateral triangle, square, or regular hexagon.

☐ Makes an appropriate sketch of a tessellation involving one of the regular polygons.

☐ Identifies a regular polygon that does not tessellate the plane, such as: regular octagon.

☐ Gives a logical explanation why the chosen regular polygon does not tessellate the plane, such as: [for a regular octagon] The measure of each angle of a regular octagon is 135. Since 360 is not divisible by 135, it is not possible to fit several angles from regular octagons around a point without a gap or an overlap.

Objective G

☐ Is able to determine whether conditions are sufficient for a parallelogram.

☐ Describes an appropriate method for Clark to determine whether *JKLM* is a parallelogram, such as: Determine that *JK* = *ML* and *MJ* = *LK*.

☐ Describes an appropriate method for Lois to determine whether *JKLM* is a parallelogram, such as: Determine that m∠*LMJ* = m∠*JKL* and m∠*MJK* = m∠*KLM*.

---

5. Suppose you were asked to write a proof argument for each of the two situations shown at the right. Describe how your two proof arguments would be alike and how they would be different.

Given: $\overline{AB} \cong \overline{CB}$; $\overline{AD} \cong \overline{CD}$.

To prove: △*ABD* ≅ △*CBD*.

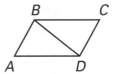

Objectives D, E

☐ Is able to write proofs that triangles are congruent.

☐ Is able to write proofs that segments or angles are congruent using the CPCF Thm.

☐ States one or more appropriate likenesses.

☐ States one or more appropriate differences.

Given: $\overline{AB} \cong \overline{CD}$; $\overline{AD} \cong \overline{CB}$.

To prove: ∠*A* ≅ ∠*C*.

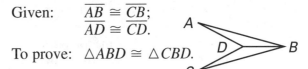

Teacher Notes

Objectives A, C, D, E, I

Concepts and Skills This activity requires students to:

- read information from text and diagrams.
- determine whether triangles are congruent from given information and whether all triangles satisfying certain conditions are congruent.
- write proofs that triangles are congruent.
- apply the triangle congruence and CPCF theorems to prove that segments or angles are congruent.
- apply triangle congruence theorems to a real-world situation.
- summarize results.

Guiding Questions

- How do you determine that a length is reasonable? [Use lengths suitable for roofs and bridges, consider the Triangle Inequality Postulate, and so on.]
- How do you determine that an angle measure is reasonable? [Use angle measures that give appropriate slopes for roofs, consider the Linear Pair Theorem, and so on.]

Answers

a. $\triangle ACD \cong \triangle ECB$

b. Answers will vary. Samples: **i.** This does not specify the location for B or D. **ii.** $\overline{EB} \perp \overline{AC}$ and $\overline{AD} \perp \overline{EC}$ **iii.** AAS Congruence Theorem

c. It has been shown that $\triangle ACD \cong \triangle ECB$, so $\angle A \cong \angle E$ and $\overline{CD} \cong \overline{CB}$ by the CPCF Theorem. By the Addition Property of Equality, $20 - CD = 20 - CB$, so it follows that $\overline{BA} \cong \overline{DE}$. By the Vertical Angles Theorem, $\angle BFA \cong \angle DFE$. So, $\triangle BFA \cong \triangle DFE$ by the AAS Congruence Theorem.

d. Answers will vary. Sample: If the triangles are not congruent, the structure will not be symmetric and will appear unattractive.

e. Check students' work.

Extension

Have students create specifications for *models* of the different types of trusses, then use their specifications to build the models. (Models can be made from straws connected by paper fasteners or gumdrops.)

Evaluation

Level	Standard to be achieved for performance at specified level
5	The student demonstrates an in-depth understanding of triangle congruence and how it relates to the situation. Answers to all questions about the scissors truss are accurate and complete. The student correctly analyzes one of the other designs and prepares a concise set of workable specifications. The student may ask probing questions or offer additional insights.
4	The student demonstrates a clear understanding of triangle congruence and how it relates to the given situation. The student answers all questions about the scissors truss, but the responses may contain minor errors. The analysis of one of the other designs is essentially complete, but it may lack in some detail.
3	The student demonstrates an understanding of triangle congruence and how it relates to the situation. However, the student may make a major error in answering the questions about the scissors truss, or may omit a critical step of the proof argument. The student analyzes one of the other designs and prepares a set of specifications, but the reasoning that justifies a congruence may be flawed, and some measures may be unreasonable.
2	The student demonstrates some understanding of triangle congruence, but needs help in applying the concept to the given situation. Even with help, the student may make several major errors in answering the questions about the scissors truss, or may omit critical steps of the proof argument. The student tries to analyze one of the other designs, but the reasoning is flawed, and the specifications are incomplete.
1	The student demonstrates little if any understanding of triangle congruence, and is unable to relate the concept to the situation. The student may attempt to answer some questions about the scissors truss, but the responses are superfluous or irrelevant. There is no attempt to analyze the other designs. The student may simply copy one or more of the diagrams.

1. Explain why this statement is not true.

If two kites have the same perimeter, then they are congruent.

Make a true statement by replacing "kite" with the name of a different quadrilateral.

Objective A

☐ Is able to calculate perimeters of kites and parallelograms.

☐ Gives a logical explanation.

☐ Recognizes that the statement is true if "kite" is replaced by "square."

2. Sketch a triangle that is equal in area to parallelogram *QRST* at the right.

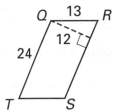

Objective C

☐ Is able to calculate areas of parallelograms and triangles.

☐ Recognizes that the area of *QRST* is 288 units².

☐ Sketches an appropriate triangle, such as the sample at the right.

---

3. State as many facts as you can about quadrilateral *ABCD* below.

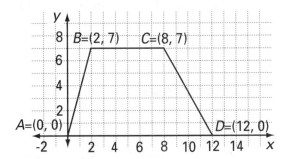

Objectives D, K

☐ Is able to determine the area of polygons on a coordinate plane.

☐ Is able to apply the Pythagorean Theorem to calculate lengths and/or areas.

☐ States several appropriate facts, such as: $AB \approx 7.3$ units; $BC = 6$ units; $CD \approx 8.1$ units; $AD = 12$ units, $\overline{AD} // \overline{BC}$. The area of *ABCD* is 63 units². The perimeter of *ABCD* is ≈ 33.4 units.

4. The sketch below shows three circular disks cut from a rectangular sheet of metal. Explain how you can tell that the sketch is labeled incorrectly. How do you think the sketch should be labeled? Using your labels, calculate the amount of metal that is wasted.

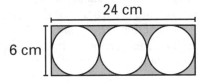

Objectives G, J

☐ Is able to relate various formulas for area.

☐ Is able to apply the formula for the area of a circle to a real-world situation.

☐ Gives a logical explanation why the labels are incorrect, such as: The length of the rectangle must be three times the diameter of one circle.

☐ Gives correct labels, such as: 6 cm and 18 cm.

☐ Correctly calculates the amount of waste, such as: for 6 cm and 18 cm, $108 - 27\pi \approx 23.2$ cm².

---

5. Joel wants to dig a rectangular garden and enclose it entirely with a low fence. He has 30 feet of fencing, and he wants to use it all. Give the dimensions of two different rectangles he could enclose with it. Which of these rectangles has the greater area?

Objectives H, I

☐ Is able to apply the perimeter and area formulas for a rectangle to a real-world situation.

☐ Gives two appropriate sets of dimensions, such as: 6 ft wide, 9 ft long; 7 ft wide, 8 ft long.

☐ Correctly identifies the greater area. For the samples above, the second area is greater.

6. Explain the difference between the Pythagorean Theorem and the Pythagorean Converse Theorem. Give an example of how you might use each theorem.

Objectives D, E

☐ Is able to apply the Pythagorean Theorem.

☐ Is able to apply the Pythagorean Converse Theorem.

☐ Gives a logical explanation of the difference between the theorems.

☐ Describes an appropriate use of the Pythagorean Theorem.

☐ Describes an appropriate use of the Pythagorean Converse Theorem.

Teacher Notes

Objectives B, G, H, I, J

Concepts and Skills This activity requires students to:
- read information from text, a table, and a diagram.
- apply the Pythagorean Theorem to real-world situations.
- apply formulas for perimeter and circumference to real-world situations.
- apply area formulas to real-world situations.
- find the area of an irregularly shaped region.
- create an original landscape plan.
- summarize results.

Materials
- ruler

Guiding Questions
- What does it mean to landscape a park?
- How do you find the lengths of the sides of the plot of land that are not labeled?
- What method can you use to find the area of Hobson Pond?

Answers
a. i. 544 ft **ii.** $2823.36
b. i. 155 ft **ii.** ≈ $3529 (Allow students to consider the walkway as a rectangular region 155 feet long and 3 feet wide.)
c. i. 72 ft **ii.** ≈ $11,197
d. Answers will vary. Sample (using a grid of squares 8 feet on a side): ≈ 1312 sq ft
e. Answers will vary. Check students' work.

Extension
Work with students to identify an open field or an abandoned lot in your city or town that might be converted into a public park. Provide a map of the area so that students can determine the shape and dimensions of the field or lot. Then have students create a plan for landscaping it. After they have completed their plan, have them contact one or more local landscapers to obtain information about current landscaping costs in your vicinity. They should then use this information to estimate the cost of their plan.

Evaluation

Level	Standard to be achieved for performance at specified level
5	The student demonstrates an in-depth understanding of perimeters and areas. Calculations are accurate and complete. The original landscape plan is carefully considered, and it may be rendered imaginatively. The accompanying report is neat and articulate.
4	The student demonstrates a clear understanding of perimeters and areas. The student utilizes appropriate formulas and methods, but some calculations may contain minor errors. The original landscape plan is appropriate, and the report is neat and easy to read, but one or both may lack in some detail.
3	The student demonstrates a fundamental understanding of perimeters and areas. The student recognizes which formulas and methods are appropriate to each situation, but may make a major error in applying them, or may omit critical steps. The student devises an original landscape plan, but some choices may not be carefully considered, and several calculations may be inaccurate. The accompanying report may be somewhat disorganized.
2	The student demonstrates some understanding of perimeters and areas, but needs assistance in applying the formulas and methods to the given situation. Even with help, the student may make several major errors or may omit several major steps of a procedure. The student attempts to devise an original landscape plan and prepare a report, but one or more choices are inappropriate, and the presentation is incomplete.
1	The student demonstrates little if any understanding of perimeters and areas, and is unable to apply the formulas and methods of the chapter to the given situation. The student may attempt some calculations, but they are superfluous or irrelevant. There is no effort to devise an original landscape plan or to prepare a report. The student may simply copy the given table or diagram.

1. In this chapter, you studied ways that two planes can be related to each other. How are these relationships similar to the relationships that can exist between two lines? How are they different?

Objective F

☐ Demonstrates an understanding of the properties of planes.

☐ Identifies at least one similarity, such as: Parallel *lines* are two lines in a plane that are identical or do not intersect. Parallel *planes* are two planes in space that are identical or do not intersect.

☐ Identifies at least one difference, such as: If two distinct *lines* intersect, their intersection is a point. If two distinct *planes* intersect, their intersection is a line.

2. Explain the difference between a *cylindric solid* and a *cylindric surface*. Give a real-world example of each.

Objective H

☐ Recognizes 3-dimensional figures in the real world.

☐ Gives a logical explanation of the difference, such as: A cylindric solid is the set of all points between a region and its translation image. A cylindric surface consists of just the bases and the lateral surfaces of a cylindric solid.

☐ Gives an appropriate real-world example of a cylindric solid, such as: a brick.

☐ Gives an appropriate real-world example of a cylindric surface, such as: an empty cereal box.

---

3. Draw a 3-dimensional figure of your choice. Then do the following

   a. Identify the number of symmetry planes.

   b. Give the top, front, and right-side views of the figure.

   c. Draw a net for the surface of the figure.

Objectives A, C, G, J

☐ Correctly draws a common 3-dimensional shape.

☐ Correctly determines the number of symmetry planes of the chosen figure.

☐ Gives correct top, side, and front views of the chosen figure.

☐ Makes an appropriate net for the surface.

4. Maps A, B, and C below each consist of four congruent L-shaped regions. Does this mean that the same number of colors is required to color each map? Explain your reasoning.

Objective I

☐ Is able to apply the Four-Color Theorem to maps.

☐ Gives a logical explanation, such as: The number of colors required depends not on the size and shape of the regions, but rather on their relative positions. For example, Maps A and B require 2 colors since 2 pairs of regions share only a corner; Map C requires 3 colors since no regions share only a corner.

---

5. The figure at the right is a right square pyramid. If $TU = 24$ and $PS = 20$, give as many additional measures as you can.

Objective D

☐ Is able to calculate lengths and areas in 3-dimensional figures.

☐ Gives several significant measures, such as:
$PQ = QR = RS = 20$ units;
$SV = RV = UV = 10$ units;
$TV = 26$ units = slant height;
area of base = 400 units^2;
area of each lateral face = 260 units^2

6. Why is it useful to give three views of a 3-dimensional figure rather than only one or two views? Make a sketch to illustrate your answer.

Objective E

☐ Demonstrates an ability to determine a 3-dimensional figure from 2-dimensional views.

☐ Gives a logical answer, such as: It is possible for two different 3-dimensional figures to be identical in two views, but to differ in the third.

☐ Makes an appropriate sketch. For instance, the views at the right could be front and side views of either a regular square prism or a cylinder.

front   side

Teacher Notes

Objectives C, E, H

Concepts and Skills This activity requires students to:
- read information from text and graphics.
- draw top, front, and side views of a figure.
- identify a 3-dimensional figure given 2-dimensional views.
- recognize 3-dimensional figures in the real world.

Materials
- ruler

Guiding Questions
- How can you envision the east side of the store? [Imagine how it would appear if you were standing with your back to the west side.]
- What shapes might you consider for "attention-grabber" display racks and merchandise bins? [Samples: cylinders, pyramids]

Answers
a.

b.

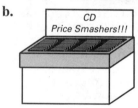

c. Answers will vary. Check students' work. The floor plan of the store should show the placement of all display racks and merchandise bins and identify which type of merchandise will be in each location. Remind students to consider issues such as: sensible placement of merchandise, adequate room for customers to move easily, and clear and easily identified paths to the exits.

Extension
Have students extend their plans to include the adjoining store, a reflection image of the music store. The additional space will house musical instruments, parts, accessories, sheet music, and a repair shop.

Evaluation

Level	Standard to be achieved for performance at specified level
5	The student demonstrates an in-depth understanding of the relationship between 2-dimensional views and 3-dimensional figures. All drawings are neat, accurate, and complete. The student makes creative suggestions for the elevation and merchandise bin, and the presentation may be imaginative.
4	The student demonstrates a clear understanding of the relationship between 2-dimensional views and 3-dimensional figures. All drawings are rendered neatly and with careful consideration, but they may contain minor errors. The student makes sound suggestions for the elevation and merchandise bin, but the presentation may lack in some detail.
3	The student demonstrates a fundamental understanding of the relationship between 2-dimensional views and 3-dimensional figures. The student gives evidence of recognizing which shapes and views are appropriate, but may make a major error in rendering them. The student suggests a suitable elevation and merchandise bin, but the presentation may be somewhat messy and disorganized.
2	The student demonstrates some understanding of the relationship between 2-dimensional views and 3-dimensional figures, but needs assistance in recognizing the shape and views that are appropriate to the given situation. Even with help, the student may make several major errors in rendering them. The student attempts to suggest an elevation and design a merchandise bin, but the presentation is jumbled and incomplete.
1	The student demonstrates little if any understanding of the relationship between 2-dimensional views and 3-dimensional figures, and is unable to recognize them in the given situation. The student may attempt some drawings, but they are superfluous or irrelevant. There is no attempt to create an original elevation or design a merchandise bin.

1. Draw and label a right square prism whose volume is equal to the volume of the right cone shown at the right. Give the exact volume of the figure you drew. Then compare the surface areas of the two figures.

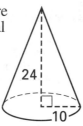

Objectives A, B

☐ Is able to calculate the volume and surface area of a cone and of a prism.

☐ Draws and labels an appropriate prism. See sample at the right.

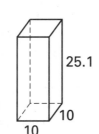

☐ Gives the correct volume of the prism. For the prism at right, $V = 2510$ units³.

☐ Correctly compares the surface areas, such as: The surface area of the prism is ≈ 73 units² greater than the surface area of the cone.

2. Looking at the cubes at the right, Janine said that cube B is twice as big as cube A. Lamar said that cube B is four times as big as cube A. Chris said that cube B is eight times as big as cube A. With whom do you agree? Explain your reasoning.

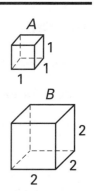

Objective E

☐ Is able to determine what happens to the surface area and volume of a figure when the dimensions are multiplied by a given number.

☐ Recognizes that each of the three students could be correct depending upon the meaning of "big."

☐ Makes a choice and gives a logical explanation, such as: Each linear dimension of cube B is twice as big, its surface area is four times as big, and its volume is eight times as big.

3. The general formula for the lateral area of a right cylindric surface is L.A. $= ph$. What does each variable in this formula represent? Give a formula for a more specific figure that you can derive from this formula. Identify the specific figure and show how the two formulas are related.

Objective F

☐ Is able to develop formulas for specific figures from more general formulas.

☐ Recognizes that L.A. represents the lateral area of a right prism or a right cylinder, p the perimeter of its base, and h its height.

☐ Correctly gives a more specific related formula, such as: For a right cylinder, L.A. $= 2\pi rh$.

☐ Describes how the two formulas are related.

4. Explain what is represented by the picture at the right.

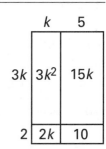

Objective J

☐ Is able to represent products of expressions as areas of rectangles, and vice versa.

☐ Gives an appropriate explanation, such as: The picture represents the multiplication $(3k + 2)(k + 5) = 3k^2 + 15k + 2k + 10 = 3k^2 + 17k + 10$.

5. Write a real-world problem that you could solve by using the formula S.A. $= 4\pi r^2$. Then show how to solve your problem.

Objectives D, H

☐ Is able to calculate the surface area of a sphere.

☐ Is able to apply formulas for surface area to real-world situations.

☐ Writes an appropriate problem.

☐ Shows a correct solution to the problem.

6. Make a sketch that illustrates Cavalieri's Principle. Write a brief paragraph to explain your sketch.

Objective G

☐ Knows the conditions under which Cavalieri's Principle can be applied.

☐ Makes an appropriate sketch. Sample is at the right.

Volume I $=$ Volume II

☐ Gives a logical explanation.

Teacher Notes

Objectives A, H, I

Concepts and Skills This activity requires students to:
- read information from text and diagrams.
- calculate surface areas and volumes of prisms and cylinders.
- apply formulas for lateral area, surface area, and volume to real-world situations.
- make decisions based on given information.
- summarize results.

Materials
- calculator

Guiding Questions
- What is the shape of the brownies in the pan? of each individual brownie? [right rectangular prism]
- Which faces of each brownie will be frosted? [all lateral faces and one base]

Answers
a. 58.5 in^3

b. i. $2\frac{1}{4}$ in. long, $2\frac{1}{6}$ in. wide, $\frac{1}{2}$ in. high **ii.** 9.3 in^2

iii. $2\frac{1}{2}$ in. long, $2\frac{5}{12}$ in. wide, $\frac{5}{8}$ in. high

c. The friend's reasoning is flawed. Explanations will vary. Sample: You also must take into account the linear dimensions of the brownies. Given the dimensions as calculated in Part **b**, there is no practical way to position 24 brownies in the box so that brownies are not damaged and the arrangement is appealing to a customer.

d. i. ≈ 14.4 in^3 **ii.** Answers may vary. Sample: It might increase the height by about .1 in.

e. Answers will vary. Check students' work.

Extension
Have students build off their work in the test to create a plan for several types of brownie products. Encourage them to use their imagination. (Samples: Consider "brownie pies" that are baked in standard round pans 8 inches or 9 inches in diameter; or consider other, unusual shapes of pans that are custom-made.) Have students describe the dimensions of each product they will offer, the dimensions of the box that will be needed to package it, and the amount of cardboard that will be needed to make the box.

Evaluation

Level	Standard to be achieved for performance at specified level
5	The student demonstrates an in-depth understanding of surface areas and volumes and their application to the given situations. All calculations are accurate and complete, and explanations are reasoned and articulate. The report contains a carefully considered plan for baking and packaging one or more types of brownies, and may be presented imaginatively.
4	The student demonstrates a clear understanding of surface areas and volumes. Appropriate formulas are chosen and applied correctly to the given situations, though the student's calculations may contain minor errors. The student prepares a suitable plan for baking and packaging at least one type of brownie, but the report may lack in some detail.
3	The student demonstrates a fundamental understanding of surface areas and volumes. The student recognizes which formulas are appropriate to the given situations, but may make a major error in applying them, or may omit critical steps. The student prepares a plan for baking and packaging a type of brownie, but the reasoning behind the choices may be flawed, and the report may be disorganized.
2	The student demonstrates some understanding of surface areas and volumes, but needs assistance in choosing correct formulas and applying them to the given situations. Even with help, the student may make several major errors or may omit critical steps. The student attempts to devise a plan for baking and packaging a type of brownie, but the reasoning is jumbled, and the report is incomplete.
1	The student demonstrates little if any understanding of surface areas and volumes, and is unable to apply the concepts to the given situations. The student may attempt some calculations, but they are superfluous or irrelevant. There is no reasonable attempt to make a plan for baking and packaging a type of brownie. The student may simply copy one of the given diagrams.

1. In $\triangle ABC$ at the right, X is the midpoint of $\overline{AB}$ and Y is the midpoint of $\overline{BC}$. State as many other facts as you can about the figure.

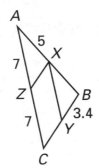

2. On the coordinate axes below, draw two circles that each have the same radius, but have different center points. Give an equation for each circle that you drew.

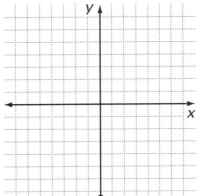

Objective B

☐ Is able to apply the Midpoint Connector Theorem.

☐ States several significant facts about the figure, such as:
Z is the midpoint of $\overline{AC}$;
$BX = 5$; $AB = 10$
$CY = ZX = 3.4$; $BC = 6.8$
$XY = 7$; $AC = 14$
$\overline{XZ} \parallel \overline{BC}$; $\overline{XY} \parallel \overline{AC}$

Objective J

☐ Is able to graph and write an equation for a circle.

☐ Draws two appropriate circles.

☐ Gives correct equations for the circles drawn.

3. How is finding the distance between two points in a three-dimensional coordinate system similar to finding the distance between two points on the coordinate plane? How is it different? Give examples to illustrate your answer.

Objectives A, C

☐ Is able to determine the length of a segment in the coordinate plane.

☐ Is able to find distances between points in 3-dimensional space.

☐ States at least one significant similarity.

☐ States at least one significant difference.

☐ Gives appropriate examples.

4. State two laws of logic that you studied in this chapter. Then give an example of how each law might be applied to a real-world situation.

Objectives D, H

☐ Is able to follow the basic laws of logic to make conclusions.

☐ Is able to apply the laws of logic in real-world situations.

☐ Correctly states two laws that were studied in the chapter.

☐ Gives an appropriate example of each law chosen.

5. When studying for a test, Mari came across this torn page in her notebook. She knows the diagram concerns a proof, but she can't remember what she was trying to prove or how to prove it. Can you help her?

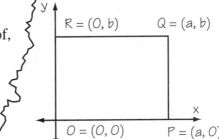

Objectives F, H

☐ Is able to write indirect proofs.

☐ Is able to use coordinate geometry in proofs.

☐ Recognizes that the figure and text show that the diagonals of a rectangle are not perpendicular.

Teacher Notes

Objectives F, G

Concepts and Skills This activity requires students to:
• demonstrate an understanding of the basic concepts of proof.
• write proofs using a variety of methods.
• summarize and analyze results.

Guiding Questions
• How is the idea of a *type* of proof (like direct proof, indirect proof, and coordinate proof) different from the idea of a *style* of proof (like paragraph form and two-column form)?

Answers
a. Answers will vary. Sample: To prove a statement false, you need only provide a counterexample to it. To prove a statement true, you must provide a set of justified conclusions.

b. Answers will vary. Sample: In direct reasoning, you begin with given information and reason from that information to a conclusion. In indirect reasoning, you try to rule out all the possibilities other than the one thought to be true.

c. Answers will vary. Sample: It is a style of proof in which conclusions are numbered and written in the left column, while justifications are numbered correspondingly and written in the right column.

d. Check students' work.

e, f. Answers will vary. Check students' work.

Extension
Introduce students to the *flow proof* form of writing proofs by presenting an example like this.

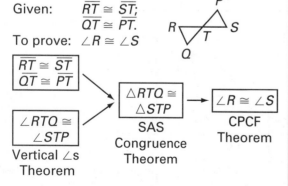

Given: $\overline{RT} \cong \overline{ST}$;
            $\overline{QT} \cong \overline{PT}$.

To prove: $\angle R \cong \angle S$

Have them discuss when they might use this style and write additional examples for their study guides.

Evaluation

Level	Standard to be achieved for performance at specified level
5	The student demonstrates an in-depth understanding of types of proof. All responses to the questions are reasoned, accurate, and articulate. The study guide is thorough and well-organized, and it may be presented imaginatively. The student may ask probing questions or offer additional insights.
4	The student demonstrates a clear understanding of types of proof. All answers to the questions are reasoned and articulate, but they may contain minor inaccuracies. The study guide is complete and easy to read, but it may lack in some detail.
3	The student demonstrates a fundamental understanding of types of proof. Answers are provided for all the questions posed, but the responses may contain a major error or inaccuracy. The student prepares a study guide, but there may be several inaccuracies or a major omission, and it is somewhat disorganized.
2	The student demonstrates some understanding of types of proof, but needs considerable assistance in preparing responses to the questions posed. Even with help, the student may make several major misstatements. The student attempts to create a study guide, but the descriptions and examples are jumbled, and there are major omissions and inaccuracies.
1	The student demonstrates little if any understanding of types of proof, and provides no coherent responses to the questions posed. Attempts to communicate are superfluous or irrelevant. There is no attempt to prepare an original study guide. The student may simply copy or restate the given examples.

1. In the space at the right, draw any size transformation image of $\triangle ABC$. Then answer the following questions about your transformation.

   a. Where is the center?

   b. What is the magnitude?

   c. Is the transformation an expansion or a contraction?

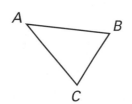

Objectives A, C

☐ Is able to draw size transformation images of figures.
☐ Is able to recognize and apply properties of size transformations.
☐ Correctly draws a size transformation image of the given figure.
☐ Correctly identifies the center and magnitude of the transformation.
☐ Correctly identifies the transformation as an expansion or a contraction.

---

2. In the coordinate plane, the endpoints of $\overline{CD}$ are $C = (x, y)$ and $D = (m, n)$. $\overline{C'D'}$ is the image of $\overline{CD}$ under the transformation S_k. State as many relationships as you can between $\overline{CD}$ and $\overline{C'D'}$.

Objective G

☐ Is able to analyze size transformations on figures in the coordinate plane.
☐ States two or more significant facts, such as: $\overline{CD} \parallel \overline{C'D'}$; $C'D' = kCD$; $C' = (kx, ky)$ and $D' = (km, kn)$

3. Your little cousin has a new doll house that is labeled "$\frac{1}{12}$ actual size." In a toy store, your cousin found a teapot that is $1\frac{3}{4}$ inches tall. Explain why this teapot is not appropriate for your cousin's doll house.

Objective E

☐ Is able to identify and determine proportional lengths in real situations.
☐ Gives an appropriate explanation, such as: Every item in the doll house should be $\frac{1}{12}$ actual size. However, if a teapot $1\frac{3}{4}$ inches high is $\frac{1}{12}$ actual size, the actual height of the teapot would be 21 in. That is an unreasonable height.

---

4. In the trapezoids at the right, explain how you can tell that $SHIP \sim BOAT$ is a false statement. Then show how you can make it true by changing just one of the labeled measures.

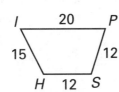

Objective B

☐ Is able to use proportions to find missing parts in similar figures.
☐ Recognizes that corresponding lengths are not proportional in the figures as labeled.
☐ Correctly changes one measure, such as: $IP = 22\frac{1}{2}$.

5. At the right is shown a standard-size box of corn flakes. The manufacturer plans to make a jumbo-size box that is similar to it, but is 15 inches high. Use the Fundamental Theorem of Similarity to describe the important characteristics of the jumbo-size box.

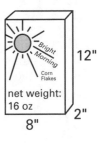

Objective F

☐ Is able to apply the Fundamental Theorem of Similarity in real situations.
☐ Gives several important characteristics, such as: The base would be 2.5 in. wide and 10 in. long. The net weight would be 31.25 oz.

Teacher Notes

Objectives D, F

Concepts and Skills This activity requires students to:
- read information from text and a graphic.
- make decisions based on given information.
- analyze figures to determine whether they are similar.
- use the Fundamental Theorem of Similarity to analyze lengths, areas, and volumes in similar figures, and apply it to a real-world situation.
- analyze and summarize results.

Guiding Questions
- What does the director mean by the "footprint" of the building? [the shape and size of its base]
- How are office space and retail space measured? [by the number of square feet of floor space]
- What features of a building and its structure do you associate with length? with area? with volume?

Answers
a. Yes. Explanations will vary. Sample: Both the old and new footprints are rectangles, so all corresponding angles are congruent. The length and width of the original rectangle are each doubled, so corresponding lengths are proportional, with the ratio of similitude being 2.

b. Explanations will vary. Sample: By the Fundamental Theorem of Similarity, the ratio of the area of the new footprint to the area of the old is 2^2, or 4. So the amount of retail space on the first floor will be quadrupled. Each floor above is congruent to the first, so the area of each floor above also is quadrupled.

c. The conclusion is essentially correct. That is, if there still is only one floor of retail space desired, then the amount of office space when the height is doubled is double the proposed amount plus one additional floor. Students' explanations will vary.

d. Answers will vary. Check students' work.

Extension
Have students determine the dimensions of a building that is similar to the given building and that *does* have twice the floor space. [≈ 93.4 ft × 63.6 ft × 140 ft] Have them determine the ratio of lengths, areas, and volumes in this building to the corresponding measures in the building shown. [$\sqrt{2}$, 2, 2]

Evaluation

Level	Standard to be achieved for performance at specified level
5	The student demonstrates an in-depth understanding of similarity and its application to the given situation. Responses to the questions posed are accurate and complete. The report is articulate and well-organized, containing several sound predictions, and it may be presented imaginatively. The student may ask probing questions or offer additional insights.
4	The student demonstrates a clear understanding of similarity. The concept is applied correctly to the given situation, but the student's responses to the questions posed may contain minor errors. The report is well-organized and easy to read, and the student has made several appropriate predictions, but the report may lack in some detail.
3	The student demonstrates a fundamental understanding of similarity. The student recognizes how the concept relates to the given situation, but may make a major error in responding to the questions posed, or may omit a critical step. The student prepares a report in which some predictions are made, but the reasoning behind them may be flawed, and the report is disorganized.
2	The student demonstrates some understanding of similarity, but needs assistance in applying the concept to the given situation. Even with help, the student may make several major errors in responding to the questions posed, or may omit critical steps. The student attempts to make predictions and prepare a report, but the reasoning is jumbled, and the presentation is incomplete.
1	The student demonstrates little if any understanding of similarity, and is unable to apply the concept to the given situation. The student may write some responses to the questions posed, but they are superfluous or irrelevant. There is no attempt to make predictions or to prepare an original report. The student may simply copy or restate the given information.

1. In $\triangle RST$ at the right, $\overline{MN} \parallel \overline{RT}$ and $w \ne x \ne y \ne z$. Give a possible set of values for w, x, y, and z. Explain how you decided on those values.

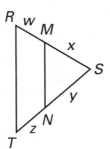

Objective A

☐ Is able to find lengths in figures by applying the Side-Splitting Theorem.

☐ Gives appropriate values for w, x, y, and z, such as: $w = 6$, $x = 9$, $y = 11$, and $z = 7$.

☐ Gives a logical explanation.

2. Describe at least one way in which the figure at the right illustrates the term *geometric mean*.

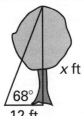

Objective B

☐ Understands the Right Triangle Altitude Theorem.

☐ Gives a logical explanation. (Samples: *MN* is the geometric mean of *LN* and *KN* because $\frac{LN}{MN} = \frac{MN}{KN}$; *KM* is the geometric mean of *KN* and *KL* because $\frac{KN}{KM} = \frac{KM}{KL}$; *LM* is the geometric mean of *LN* and *KL* because $\frac{LN}{LM} = \frac{LM}{KL}$.)

3. The formula for the area A of a triangle is $A = \frac{1}{2}ab$, where b is the length of the base and a is the altitude to that base. Sally says you cannot find the area of the triangle at the right because there is not enough information given. Do you agree? Explain your reasoning.

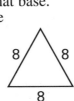

Objective C

☐ Is able to calculate lengths of sides in 30-60-90 triangles.

☐ Recognizes that Sally's statement is incorrect.

☐ Gives a logical explanation, such as: The triangle is equilateral, so the measure of each angle is 60. If an altitude is drawn, it forms two 30-60-90 triangles and is the longer leg of each. Using the 30-60-90 Triangle Theorem, you can find that the altitude is $4\sqrt{3}$ units. So the length of the base of the given triangle is 8 units, the altitude to the base is $4\sqrt{3}$ units, and the area is $16\sqrt{3}$ units^2, or about 27.7 units^2.

4. Marco performed these calculations to find the height of the tree shown at the right.

$$\cos 68° = \frac{x}{12}$$

$$x = \frac{\cos 68°}{12} \approx .03$$

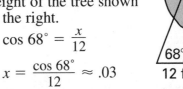

x ft

68°

12 ft

How can Marco tell that he made an error? What error(s) did he make? Correct the error(s) and calculate the height of the tree.

Objectives E, G, I

☐ Is able to estimate values of trigonometric ratios.

☐ Knows the definitions of sine, cosine, and tangent.

☐ Is able to use sines, cosines, and tangents to determine unknown lengths in real situations.

☐ Recognizes that .03 ft is an unreasonable height.

☐ Recognizes that Marco should use the tangent.

☐ Recognizes that, in the second equation, Marco should multiply by 12 rather than divide by 12.

☐ Finds the correct height, ≈ 29.7 ft.

5. State one of the three triangle similarity theorems that you studied in this chapter. Draw and label two triangles that you can prove to be similar as a result of the theorem you chose.

Objective F

☐ Is able to determine whether or not triangles are similar using the AA, SAS, or SSS Similarity Theorem.

☐ Correctly states one of the theorems.

☐ Draws and labels two appropriate triangles.

6. Write a real-world problem that you can solve by finding the magnitude and direction of vector *OA* at the right. Then show how to solve your problem.

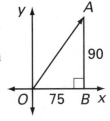

Objective J

☐ Is able to determine components of vectors in real situations.

☐ Writes an appropriate problem.

☐ Gives a correct solution to the problem.

Teacher Notes

Objectives C, E, G, I

Concepts and Skills This activity requires students to:
• read information from text and diagrams.
• calculate lengths of sides in special right triangles.
• estimate values of the trigonometric ratios.
• use sines, cosines, and tangents to determine unknown lengths in real situations.
• create and describe an original design.

Materials
• calculator

Guiding Questions
• How can you find angle measures and lengths by using symmetry lines? auxiliary lines?
• When can you use complements and supplements to help you find unknown angle measures?
• How can your knowledge of regular polygons help you find unknown angle measures and lengths?

Answers
a. i. isosceles right triangle **ii.** 4″, 4″, ≈ 5.66″
b. triangle I: 20, 70, 90, 4″, ≈ 1.46″, ≈ 4.26″; triangle II: 45, 45, 90, ≈ 2.54″, ≈ 2.54″, ≈ 3.59″; triangle III: 50, 65, 65, ≈ 3.59″, ≈ 4.26″, ≈ 4.26″
c. blossom—triangle I: 45, 67.5, 67.5, ≈ 3.31″, ≈ 4.33″, ≈ 4.33″; triangle II: 45, 45, 90, ≈ 2.34″, ≈ 2.34″, ≈ 3.31″
starburst—triangle I: 22.5, 67.5, 90, ≈ 1.66″, 4″, ≈ 4.33″; triangle II: 22.5, 45, 112.5, ≈ 2.34″, ≈ 4.33″, ≈ 5.66″
eight-pointed star: triangle I: 45, 45, 90, ≈ 1.03″, ≈ 1.03″, ≈ 1.46″; triangle II: 30, 60, 90, ≈ 1.03″, ≈ 1.78″, ≈ 2.06″; triangle III: 45, 45, 90, ≈ 3.56″, ≈ 3.56″, ≈ 5.03″; triangle IV: 45, 45, 90, ≈ .73″, ≈ .73″, ≈ 1.03″; square I: ≈ 1.46″ on each side; square II: ≈ .73″ on each side; rhombus: 60, 120, 60, 120, ≈ 2.06″ on each side
d. Answers will vary. Check students' work.

Extension
Have students choose a size for an entire quilt and determine how many blocks are needed to make it. Suppose a sewing machine is set at ten stitches per inch. Have students estimate the number of stitches that will be needed to sew the entire patchwork layer.

Evaluation

Level	Standard to be achieved for performance at specified level
5	The student demonstrates an in-depth understanding of special right triangles and trigonometry and their application to the given situations. All calculations are accurate and complete. The quilt design is appropriate, and it may be rendered imaginatively. The description of the design is thorough and articulate, and the student may use it as a vehicle for offering additional insights.
4	The student demonstrates a clear understanding of special right triangles and trigonometry. The concepts and definitions are applied correctly to the given situations, though the student's calculations may contain minor errors. The quilt design is appropriate and neatly rendered, but the description may lack in some detail.
3	The student demonstrates a fundamental understanding of special right triangles and trigonometry. The student recognizes which concepts and definitions are appropriate to the given situations, but may make a major error in applying them, or may omit a critical step. The student creates a quilt design, but the rendering may be somewhat haphazard, and the description may contain inaccuracies.
2	The student demonstrates some understanding of special right triangles and trigonometry, but needs assistance in applying the concepts and definitions to the given situations. Even with help, the student may make several major errors or may omit critical steps. The student attempts to create a quilt design and prepare a description, but the rendering is messy, and the description is incomplete.
1	The student demonstrates little if any understanding of special right triangles and trigonometry, and is unable to apply them to the given situations. The student may attempt some calculations, but they are superfluous or irrelevant. There is no attempt to create an original quilt design. The student may simply copy one of the given designs.

1. At the right are three figures, labeled I, II, and III. Assume that you are given the measures of all labeled arcs. For each figure, describe the procedure you could follow to find m∠CAB. How are your procedures alike? How are they different?

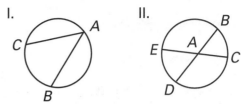

Objectives B, C

□ Is able to calculate measures of inscribed angles from measures of intercepted arcs.

□ Is able to calculate measures of angles between chords and secants from measures of intercepted arcs.

□ States at least one significant likeness, such as: You work with the measure(s) of the arc(s) intercepted by the sides of ∠CAB.

□ States at least one significant difference, such as: In Figure I, you take half the measure of just one arc. In Figure II, you take half the sum of the intercepted arcs. In Figure III, you take half the difference.

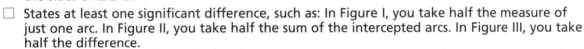

2. In the figure at the right, PQRS is a rectangle inscribed in ⊙O, m∠QPR = 60, and PR = 18. State as many additional facts about the figure as you can.

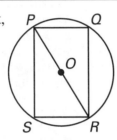

Objective A

□ Is able to calculate lengths of chords and arcs.

□ States several significant facts, such as:
PQ = SR = 9 units;
PS = QR = 9√3 units ≈ 15.6 units;
m$\widehat{QR}$ = m$\widehat{PS}$ = 120°; m$\widehat{PQ}$ = m$\widehat{RS}$ = 60°;
length of $\widehat{QR}$ and $\widehat{PS}$ ≈ 18.8 units;
length of $\widehat{PQ}$ and $\widehat{RS}$ ≈ 9.4 units

3. Give a set of possible values for the lengths labeled a, b, c, d, and e in the figure at the right. Explain how you decided on the values that you chose.

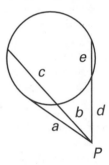

Objective E

□ Is able to apply the Secant Length Theorem.

□ Gives an appropriate set of values, such as: a = 24, b = 16, c = 20, d = 18, and e = 14.

□ Gives a logical explanation.

4. Jameel tried to find the center of a circle by the right angle method. His work is at the right. Clearly, the point he labeled O is not the center. Describe the error(s) he made. Then show how to correct the error(s).

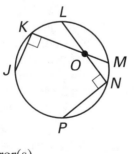

Objective D

□ Is able to locate the center of a circle given sufficient information.

□ Recognizes that Jameel should have drawn $\overline{JM}$ and $\overline{LP}$ and located their point of intersection.

□ Completes the construction correctly.

5. Write a real-world problem that you can solve by applying one of the Isoperimetric Inequalities. Then show how to solve your problem.

Objective K

□ Is able to apply the Isoperimetric Inequalities in real situations.

□ Writes an appropriate problem.

□ Gives a correct solution to the problem.

Teacher Notes

Objectives A, B, C

Concepts and Skills This activity requires students to:
- read information from text and diagrams.
- calculate lengths of chords.
- calculate measures of inscribed angles and angles between chords.
- create and analyze an original design involving angles and segments in circles.

Materials
- calculator
- drawing tools

Guiding Questions
- What auxiliary figures do you need to draw in order to find the length of one segment of each design? [center of the circle and two radii]
- What is the definition of the sine ratio? cosine? tangent? How do these ratios help you find lengths in the designs?

Answers
a. $36°$
b. Figure I: the measure of each angle is 108; Figure II: the measure of each angle is 72; Figure III: the measure of each angle is 36
c. Figure I: $240 \cdot \sin 36° \approx 141.1$ in.; Figure II: $240 \cdot \sin 54° \approx 194.2$ in.; Figure III: $240 \cdot \sin 72° \approx 228.3$ in.
d. i. 144 **ii.** $24 \cdot \sin 18° \approx 7.42$ in.

iii. $\dfrac{12 \cdot \sin 18°}{\sin 72°} \approx 3.90$ in.

iv. $24 \cdot \sin 36° - \dfrac{24 \cdot \sin 18°}{\sin 72°} \approx 6.31$ in.

e. Answers will vary. Check students' work.

Extension
Have students experiment with the results when a different point serves as the "center" of the circle, as shown below.

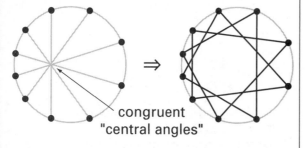
congruent "central angles"

Evaluation

Level	Standard to be achieved for performance at specified level
5	The student demonstrates an in-depth understanding of lengths and angle measures associated with circles, and is able to apply them with ease to the given situations. All calculations are accurate and complete. The original design is appropriate and carefully drawn, and the report describes it accurately. The student may present several additional insights.
4	The student demonstrates a clear understanding of lengths and angle measures associated with circles. Appropriate methods are applied to the given situations, though the calculations may contain minor errors. The original design is appropriate and neatly drawn, but the accompanying report may lack in some detail.
3	The student demonstrates a fundamental understanding of lengths and angle measures associated with circles. The student recognizes which methods are appropriate to the given situations, but may make a major error in applying them, or may omit critical steps. The student prepares an original design, but the accompanying report is disorganized and may contain a major error or misstatement.
2	The student demonstrates some understanding of lengths and angle measures associated with circles, but needs assistance in applying the methods to the given situations. Even with help, the student may make several major errors or may omit critical steps. The student attempts to create an original design and prepare a report, but the drawing is messy, and the report is inaccurate and incomplete.
1	The student demonstrates little if any understanding of lengths and angle measures associated with circles, and is unable to apply appropriate methods to the given situations. The student may attempt some calculations, but they are superfluous or irrelevant. There is no original design or report. The student may simply copy or restate given information.